Primal Sources:
Essays on H. P. Lovecraft

S. T. Joshi

Primal Sources:
Essays on H. P. Lovecraft

S. T. Joshi

Hippocampus Press

New York

TO LESLIE
now and forever

Copyright © 2003 by S.T. Joshi

Published by Hippocampus Press
P.O. Box 641, New York, NY 10156.
http://www.hippocampuspress.com

Cover illustration "Antarktos" by Robert H. Knox.
Cover design by Barbara Briggs Silbert.
Hippocampus Press logo designed by Anastasia Damianakos.

First Edition
1 3 5 7 9 8 6 4 2

ISBN 0-9721644-0-5

Contents

Introduction

I have been involved in the study of H. P. Lovecraft for more than a quarter-century. Right from the beginning—say, around 1975–76, when I first came in touch with such leading figures in the field as Dirk W. Mosig, R. Alain Everts, J. Vernon Shea, and David E. Schultz—I felt that it was vital to achieve two pressing objectives if Lovecraft were to be accorded his true place in weird literature and in American literature in general: the basic facts of his life, work, and thought must be established, and—once that had occurred—an *integration* of that life, work, and thought must take place. It was to fulfil the first of these objectives that I undertook such works as my anthology of criticism, *H. P. Lovecraft: Four Decades of Criticism* (1980); my listing of Lovecraft's library (1980); my bibliography (1981); my corrected editions of Lovecraft's tales (1984–89); my study of Lovecraft's philosophy, *H. P. Lovecraft: The Decline of the West* (1990); and, as a culmination, my full-scale biography, *H. P. Lovecraft: A Life* (1996). In order to fulfil the second objective, I wrote a succession of essays in which I sought to fuse the biographical, critical, and philosophical approaches and so to demonstrate the unity of Lovecraft's life and mind. A representative sampling of those essays, some of them substantially revised, comprises this book.

Most of these essays appeared in *Lovecraft Studies* or *Crypt of Cthulhu* (a few served as introductions to compilations of material by or about Lovecraft published by Necronomicon Press), and were written chiefly in the late 1970s, the 1980s, and the early 1990s, when the study of Lovecraft was advancing dynamically through the pioneering work of Mosig, Schultz, Donald R. Burleson, Steven J. Mariconda, Will Murray, Peter Cannon, Barton L. St Armand, and a number of other scholars. If that period of dynamism seems to have come to an end, it may only be because the basic facts—and also certain basic principles of interpretation—of Lovecraft's life, work, and thought appear to be well-established, so that we may perhaps legitimately expect only further refinements in the future. My own work on Lovecraft, since my biography, has been relatively meagre, not only because I have chosen to focus on other writers, but because I feel that I have largely said what I have to say on this writer and would like to leave the field open to other points of view. My chief interests now are the preparation of annotated editions of Lovecraft's works—whose notes and commentary are drawn chiefly from the basic research that I and others have performed—and in the dissemination of Lovecraft's letters, a body of his work still too little appreciated. In order to foster such appreciation, I reprint my essay "A Look at Lovecraft's Letters" from my earlier collection, *Selected Papers on Lovecraft* (1989).

In order to reduce the number of footnotes, I refer to Lovecraft's works in the text using the following abbreviations:

AHT   Arkham House transcripts of Lovecraft's letters
D   *Dagon and Other Macabre Tales* (Arkham House, 1986)
DH   *The Dunwich Horror and Others* (Arkham House, 1984)
HM   *The Horror in the Museum and Other Revisions* (Arkham House, 1989)
JHL   John Hay Library, Brown University
MM   *At the Mountains of Madness and Other Novels* (Arkham House, 1985)
MW   *Miscellaneous Writings* (Arkham House, 1995)
SL   *Selected Letters* (Arkham House, 1965–76; 5 vols.)

Works by other authors are generally listed in a "Works Cited" section at the end of each essay.

Some of the essays in this book may seem to dwell on excessively minute aspects of Lovecraft's work. As Voltaire stated, after a certain point research is only for curiosity. But with a writer as consumingly interesting as Lovecraft, perhaps no detail is too trivial to pass over. At any rate, it seems to me that most of the essays in this book deal with vital and central aspects of Lovecraft's work and thought, an understanding of which seems essential if we are to unlock the mysteries of his complex temperament.

—S. T. JOSHI

1. LOVECRAFT THE MAN

Lovecraft and the Munsey Magazines

ovecraft's relations with the Munsey magazines have always been fraught with confusion, largely because the exact number and content of his letters to the various magazines were never precisely known; but now that the biographical and bibliographical conundrums surrounding this matter have been solved, we are in a better position to clarify a significant chapter in Lovecraft's early life.

When we read, in his letter to the *All-Story* for 7 March 1914 that Lovecraft had "read every number of your magazine since its beginning in January, 1905," we are taken aback both by the voluminous amount of early pulp fiction he must already have absorbed and by the fact that in later years he would actually conceal this absorption. As early as 1916 he was prevaricating in a letter: "In 1913 I had formed the reprehensible habit of picking up cheap magazines like *The Argosy* to divert my mind from the tedium of reality" (*SL* 1.41). This is one of the few instances where Lovecraft actually lies about himself; no doubt he was already embarrassed at this literary slumming, given that he was then attempting to establish himself as a classicist of the purest sort.

What is more remarkable, the *Argosy* and *All-Story* were by no means the only magazines of this kind that Lovecraft was reading. *The Rhode Island Journal of Astronomy* for 27 September 1903 cites an article in the October *Munsey's Magazine*, so he must have read at least some issues of that journal. In later years other admissions begin to filter through, almost in spite of himself: he read Street & Smith's *Popular Magazine* around 1905–10;[1] he read the entirety of the *Railroad Man's Magazine* (1906–13);[2] he began reading the *Black Cat* around 1904.[3]

What, exactly, was the fascination of these magazines? In 1905 Lovecraft had already gained most of the interests that would persist throughout his life: antiquarianism; chemistry; astronomy; classical literature;

---

1. Lovecraft to Richard F. Searight, 26 September 1935; *Letters to Richard F. Searight* (West Warwick, RI: Necronomicon Press, 1992), p. 64.

2. Lovecraft to Richard F. Searight, 16 April 1935; *Letters to Richard F. Searight*, p. 54.

3. Lovecraft to R. H. Barlow, 14 April 1932 (ms., JHL).

Augustan poetry; and, of course, weird fiction. But he had by no means read all the standard weird fiction that had been written up to that time, and would be surprisingly late in discovering some of the great weird writers of the later nineteenth and early twentieth centuries. Of course, his discovery of Poe at the age of eight (as well as his concurrent reading of dime and nickel novels) had turned his creative energies definitively toward weird fiction; but he would discover Ambrose Bierce and Lord Dunsany only in 1919, Arthur Machen in 1923, Algernon Blackwood and M. R. James in 1924, and Robert W. Chambers in 1927. Accordingly, Lovecraft had little access to *recent* weird writing, and it was this void that the Munsey magazines filled: "In general . . . the Munsey publications did more to publish weird fiction than any other magazine enterprise of the early 20th century."[4] So Lovecraft put up with the vast array of mediocrity in these magazines for the few weird nuggets they contained.

The convoluted history of the various Munsey magazines can be encapsulated briefly here. The *Argosy* began as the *Golden Argosy* in 1882, changing to the *Argosy* in 1888; it had started out as a weekly, became a monthly in 1894, and reverted to a weekly on 6 October 1917. It continued publication until 1948. The *All-Story* began as a monthly in 1905, became the *All-Story Weekly* on 7 March 1914, merged with the *Cavalier* to become the *All-Story Cavalier Weekly* on 16 May 1914, reverted to the *All-Story Weekly* on 15 May 1915, and merged with the *Argosy* to become the *Argosy All-Story Weekly* on 24 July 1920. The editor of the *All-Story* during its entire run was Robert H. Davis. The *Argosy*'s editor during the period of Lovecraft's letters was Matthew White, Jr, although Lovecraft in letters mentions a T. N. Metcalf, who was perhaps a sub-editor or editor of the letter column, entitled "The Log-Book."

Lovecraft's first published letter to the Munsey magazines—discovered only recently—appeared in the *Argosy* for November 1911 (it is identified as by "H. P. L. of Providence, Rhode Island"). "The Log-Book" had only been established in February 1911, and letters were slow to appear; but by the end of the year many readers from around the country had begun to write in, being initially identified only by initials and city of residence. Lovecraft's letter in the September 1913 issue speaks of having "been guilty of an inch or two in the Log-Book," and the letter of November 1911—praising, of all people, Albert Payson Terhune, the future creator of Lassie—is the only one prior to 1913 that can be attributed to him. It may also have been at this time that Lovecraft wrote an effusive poem, "To Mr. Terhune, on His Historical Fiction," which, although specifically addressed to the editor of the *Argosy*, was not published there.

---

4. Lovecraft to R. H. Barlow, 31 March 1932 (ms., JHL).

His next published letter, appearing in the 8 February 1913 issue of the *All-Story Cavalier,* is a praiseworthy comment on Irvin S. Cobb's magnificent tale of a half-man, half-fish hybrid, "Fishhead." It is my feeling that this powerful tale lodged in Lovecraft's mind and would form a significant influence on "The Shadow over Innsmouth" (1931), which similarly treats of the union of fish and human beings. In the fall of that year Lovecraft's letter-writing campaign shifts to the *Argosy;* but at the moment I wish to return to the letter of 1914 that I have already quoted, a letter of close to 2000 words, taking up nearly two full printed pages. It is a sort of grand summation of everything he liked in the magazine and an encapsulation of what he thought the magazine stood for. Scorning the plea of one G. W. F. of Dundee, Scotland, for more "probable" stories, Lovecraft declaims:

> If, in fact, man is unable to create living beings out of inorganic matter, to hypnotise beasts of the forest to do his will, to swing from tree to tree with the apes of the African jungle, to restore to life the mummified corpses of the Pharaohs and the Incas, or to explore the atmosphere of Venus and the deserts of Mars, permit us, at least, in fancy, to witness these miracles, and to satisfy that craving for the unknown, the weird, and the impossible which exists in every active human brain.

That last statement is certainly a little sanguine: if everyone had a craving for the unknown, then weird fiction would not be as unrecognised a literary mode as it is. But the catalogue presented above is not only a series of synopses of some of the celebrated tales published in the *All-Story* but, in several instances, a selection of plot-elements that Lovecraft himself would use in his own later work.

There follow paeans to many of the *All-Story*'s most popular writers. Who is first to be named? "At or near the head of your list of writers Edgar Rice Burroughs undoubtedly stands." Lovecraft goes on to single out *Tarzan of the Apes* (October 1912), *The Gods of Mars* (January–May 1913), and *Warlord of Mars* (December 1913–March 1914), although it is typical that while praising these stories he takes care to point out astronomical and other errors in the works. Later in life Lovecraft seemed embarrassed at his juvenile (or not so juvenile: he was twenty-three when he wrote this letter) fondness for Burroughs, and he sought to distance himself from the creator of Tarzan. In 1929, when urging a correspondent not to yield to the temptations of the market and write hackwork, he lumps Burroughs with Edgar A. Guest and Harold Bell Wright as examples of the fact that "the veriest idiot and ignoramus can sometimes bring down fame on a luck-shot" (*SL* 2.325). Not long thereafter, in saying that "I shall sooner or later get around to the interplanetary field myself," he adds explicitly: "you may depend upon it that I shall not choose Edmond

Hamilton, Ray Cummings, or Edgar Rice Burroughs as my model!" (*SL* 3.88). This gives no indication of how much he had enjoyed the John Carter Martian novels fifteen years before.

In his letter Lovecraft goes on to praise many other writers, few of whom are of any note—William Patterson White, Lee Robinet, William Tillinghast Eldridge, William Loren Curtiss, Donald Francis McGrew, and others. A later letter (published in the *All-Story Cavalier Weekly* for 15 August 1914) praises George Allan England, Albert Payson Terhune, and Zane Grey. What is remarkable is that most of these writers did not even write weird fiction: Zane Grey, of course, was the legendary Western writer; Terhune became famous for dog stories; McGrew was an adventure writer whose "red-blooded" stories met with Lovecraft's thunderous approval; and he even liked the many humorous tales in the magazine. This means that Lovecraft read each issue—sometimes 192 pages, sometimes 240 pages—from cover to cover, month after month or even (when it changed to a weekly) week after week. This is an appalling amount of popular fiction for anyone to read, and in fact it contravened the purpose of the magazines, which was that each member of the family would read only those stories or those types of stories that were of interest to him or her.[5] One begins to develop the impression that Lovecraft was compulsive in whatever he did: his discovery of classical antiquity led him to write paraphrases of the *Odyssey*, *Iliad*, and other works; his discovery of chemistry led him to launch a *daily* scientific paper; his discovery of astronomy led him to publish a weekly paper for years; and now his discovery of pulp fiction caused him to be a voracious reader of both the good and the bad, both the work that appealed to his special tastes and the work that did not.

It is possible that the *All-Story* published this long letter in its issue of 7 March 1914 because Lovecraft himself had become, after a fashion, a celebrity in the entire Munsey chain. This had come about in a very odd way. Lovecraft, reading everything the *Argosy* put in front of him, found some material less appealing to his fastidious taste than others. It is, then, no surprise that a popular *Argosy* writer named Fred Jackson would be blasted by Lovecraft in the issue for September 1913. Jackson had become an *Argosy* staple, and two of his short novels had appeared complete in recent issues, "The First Law" in April 1913 and "The Third Act" in June 1913. This really was an unprecedented amount of space to give to a single author, and the subject-matter of these works was not of a kind to sit well

---

5. See Will Murray, "Lovecraft and the Pulp Magazine Tradition," in *An Epicure in the Terrible*, ed. David E. Schultz and S. T. Joshi (Rutherford, NJ: Fairleigh Dickinson University Press, 1991), p. 103.

with Lovecraft. "The First Law" is an unbelievably sappy, melodramatic, and verbose story of an opera singer; here is a sample:

> She struggled against him fiercely, her whole being outraged, but he was by far the stronger. He held her fast, and his lips touched her ear, her throat, her chin, and eyes, and at last crushed her mouth until she gasped for breath.
>
> Then he drew back and she lay passive in his arms, trembling, terrified at the madness that possessed her. It was as though he had awakened some sleeping demon—a creature unknown to her, a creature thirsty for his kisses, aching for his embrace.

Jackson would probably have made a good Harlequin romance writer today.

What is frequently overlooked is that Lovecraft's tirade was not inspired merely by the unwonted dominance of Jackson in the pages of *Argosy* but by a letter purportedly attacking him in the July 1913 issue. This letter—by one F. V. Bennett of Hanover, Illinois—is, however, so illiterate that Lovecraft believed it to be a sort of self-parody designed indirectly to praise Jackson. Lovecraft's own letter in the September 1913 issue could hardly be taken as a self-parody. He expresses the opinion that Bennett's letter "is in reality a sly attempt at augmenting the fame of your contributor, Fred Jackson," and continues:

> To the eye of a disinterested observer it appears as though an effort were being made forcibly to obtrude Mr. Jackson upon the reading public by an unexampled campaign of advertising, and by the selection for publication in the Log-Book of those letters wherein he receives the greatest amount of adulation.

There is something to be said for this, too: the Log-Book of the previous several issues had been filled with praise for Jackson, many of them from men, curiously enough. Of course, Lovecraft overlooks the possibility that Jackson really was popular with *Argosy* readers; or, rather, overlooks the undoubted fact that most of the magazine's readers had very lax literary standards and were only interested in cheap entertainment. Lovecraft, indeed, does not claim that Jackson's novels "are wholly wanting in merit," noting a little dryly that "There is a numerous set of people whose chief literary delight is obtained in the following of imaginary nymphs and swains through the labyrinthine paths of amorous adventure"; but he strenuously objects to the dominance of such work in the *Argosy*. And it is a fact, maintains Lovecraft, that Jackson is simply a bad writer.

The response to this letter is not likely to have been predicted either by Lovecraft or by Matthew White, Jr. The November 1913 issue contained several more letters on Jackson: one by the redoubtable F. V. Bennett, just as illiterate as its predecessor and evidently unaware that Lovecraft had ranked him as a Jackson supporter; one, by "E. F. W. C." of Paris, Kentucky, attacking Jackson but not alluding to Lovecraft; and two others specifically supporting Jackson and attacking Lovecraft and Bennett. One of these, by T. P. Crean of Syracuse, New York, claims:

> I am still puzzling over H. P. Lovecraft's letter. I can understand how the brilliant F. V. Bennett cannot go Jackson's stories. But Mr. Lovecraft, from his letter, should be able to tell a good story when he reads one. I am personally of the opinion that this letter was merely to display to THE ARGOSY world his vocabulary . . .

This is a refrain that would frequently be rung in the entire controversy.

The affair, however, might not have taken the peculiar turn it did had not the other letter, by John Russell of Tampa, Florida, been written *in verse*. Lovecraft describes it as "a piece of tetrameter verse . . . which had in it so much native wit, that I resolved to answer it" (*SL* 1.41). Sure enough, he responded in the January 1914 issue with a verse epistle of his own in what he fancied was the manner of Pope's *Dunciad*. In fact, it is a very clever poem, and reveals that penchant for stinging satire which would be one of the few virtues of his poetic output. The manuscript of the poem is headed "Ad Criticos" ("To [my] critics") (with the subtitle "Liber Primus," probably inserted at a later date as Lovecraft continued to add to the cycle). He praises Russell for his cleverness and wit, and then proceeds to take his other enemies to task. He concludes the poem by comparing the present time to "Charles the Second's vulgar age," when "Gross Wycherley and Dryden soil'd the stage."

But before Lovecraft's verse letter was printed, he was ferociously assailed in the December 1913 issue. Some of the titles which the editor affixed to the letters give some idea of the outrage Lovecraft had provoked: "Challenge to Lovecraft"; "Virginia *vs.* Providence"; "Elmira *vs.* Providence"; "Bomb for Lovecraft." Two letters did take Lovecraft's side, however; they were each headed "Agrees with Lovecraft."

In a "Liber Secundus" published in the February 1914 *Argosy* Lovecraft takes potshots at these new opponents. The tone of this poem is much sharper than that of its predecessor. Lovecraft was, of course, in a position of overwhelming intellectual superiority to most of his victims, and sometimes it seems as if he is shooting fish in a barrel; but the satire is nonetheless withering for all that. In this issue he begins to gather both friends and enemies—mostly the latter. One of the staunchest of the former is no other than F. V. Bennett, who had unwittingly begun the controversy. Now becoming literate (or having his letter corrected of spelling mistakes and of erroneous or absent punctuation), he writes, "well, shake,

H.P.L.," and claims that "we started the ball that called a halt to the rush of Jackson soft stuff." This remark seems to be confirmed by an editor's note in the issue: "I can promise that you won't get too much Jackson in 1914." This does not mean, of course, that readers would get *no* Jackson: another short novel, "Ambushed" (a mystery story with a romance element), had already appeared in the October 1913 issue, and "Winged Feet" was published in February 1914; but after this there was nothing until "The Marriage Auction" in January 1915. Thereafter, however, Jackson returns with a vengeance: "Red Robin" appeared in July 1915, "The Diamond Necklace" in October and November 1915, "Where's the Woman?" from 6 October to 3 November 1917, and "A Woman's Prey" in 24 November 1917; "Young Blood" appeared serially in *Munsey's* beginning in October 1917. In this sense it could hardly be said that Lovecraft and his supporters had helped to effect any sort of change in the *Argosy's* editorial policy; the fact is that, as various editor's notes make clear, Jackson finally ceased to appear in the Munsey magazines because he decided to take up the writing of plays, and in fact gained considerable success at this new career.

Lovecraft continued to be raked over the coals in succeeding issues, himself adding only a "Correction" of a printing error in his first "Ad Criticos" poem. But something strange now happens: no more replies by Lovecraft himself are published in the *Argosy* until October 1914. There are two further books of "Ad Criticos": did he not submit them for publication? or were they not accepted? The latter seems unlikely, since an editorial note at the end of "Correction for Lovecraft" declares: "You are always welcome in the Log-Book."

By summer the controversy had begun to die down. An editorial note in the May 1914 issue declares that "The same old warfare over Jackson is going on, in prose and verse," and this issue does indeed contain a number of poems attacking Lovecraft. But with Lovecraft himself not replying (or, at least, with his replies not being printed), the debate had little to feed itself upon. The unpublished "Liber Quartus" of "Ad Criticos" does take up some of these attacks, but of course it did not see the dignity of print at the time.

The controversy came to an end in the October 1914 issue. An entire section of "The Log-Book" bears the heading "Fred Jackson, Pro and Con"; inevitably, the "Jackson Boosters" outnumber the "Jackson Knockers." None of the former addresses Lovecraft specifically, but of the latter the loyal F. V. Bennett stands up for his mentor. But the most interesting item is a poem headed "The Critics' Farewell" and bearing both Lovecraft's and Russell's names. They did not actually collaborate on the poem; rather, Lovecraft wrote the first part (headed "The End of the Jackson War") and Russell wrote the second (headed "Our Apology to E. M. W."); Lovecraft's, naturally, is in heroic couplets, and Russell's is in very racy and irregular anapaests. Lovecraft notes that this truce was made at the insistence of T. N. Metcalf, who "intimated that the poet's war must soon end, since correspondents were complaining of the prominence of our verses in their beloved magazine" (*SL* 1.42).

We now come to the two most curious items in this entire matter. A letter by one "Augustus T. Swift" of Providence, Rhode Island, appeared in the *Argosy* for 15 November 1919, and another by the same author in the issue for 22 May 1920. Augustus T. Swift has been assumed to be a pseudonym of Lovecraft's; the letters were first attributed to him in the early fan magazine *Golden Atom*, whose editor Larry Farsaci reprinted these letters (along with the one in the *All-Story Cavalier* for 15 August 1914) in the issue for December 1940. By what authority did Farsaci make this attribution? It seems as if he did so purely by conjecture—in other words, by the mere fact that the letters were written from Providence. But was Lovecraft the only reader of *Argosy* (or the only one who wrote letters to the editor) in the city of Providence? A simple examination of the Providence city directory for 1919–20 establishes that there was a real individual named Augustus T. Swift living at 122 Rochambeau Avenue in Providence. It is manifestly clear that these two letters are not by Lovecraft at all.

It should have occurred to Farsaci, or to many later scholars who have blithely attributed these letters to Lovecraft, that there are some very bizarre features to them. In the first there occur such utterly non-Lovecraftian usages as "snappy," "a bang-up good story," and (in reference to Francis Stevens' *Citadel of Fear*) the comment that it "would make *one amazing moving-picture drama.*" Would Lovecraft really have said such a thing? But the second letter is even more odd; it concludes with the remarkable assertion (concerning a short story about whaling): "Being a native of New Bedford, Massachusetts, and having heard whale-ship talk from infancy, I followed the detailed descriptions of polar scenes with unusual interest." This sentence alone should have raised suspicions, but it does not appear to have done so.

All that remains here is to ascertain the exact chain of events which led to the attribution of these letters to Lovecraft. As I have stated, Farsaci seems to be the culprit here. R. H. Barlow, in his article on "Pseudonyms of Lovecraft" (*Acolyte*, Summer 1943), makes no mention of the Augustus T. Swift "pseudonym"; but it is picked up by Ray H. Zorn in the *Lovecraft Collector* for January 1949 (surely on the basis of the reprinting of the letters in *Golden Atom*), and subsequently in the bibliographies of Wetzel (1955), Chalker (1966), and, it must be admitted, Joshi (1981). As in so many other instances, a massive house of cards has been built up on evidence that could have been demolished in a moment. That demolition has now occurred, and these works should be definitively banished from the Lovecraft corpus.

Some further consequences follow upon the spuriousness of these letters. Although Lovecraft admits to reading A. Merritt's "The Moon Pool" in the *All-Story* for 22 June 1918, there is now no evidence that he read the *Argosy* at all after 1914, or that he read and enjoyed the work of Francis Stevens (which is praised in the Augustus T. Swift letters), although it is conceivable that he might have. Stevens' novels *The Citadel of Fear* and *Claimed* have been reprinted in paperback, with blurbs from Augustus T. Swift attributed to Lovecraft! One hopes this sort of thing will not occur again.

It is worth reflecting on what the whole *Argosy/All-Story* battle over Fred Jackson meant to Lovecraft. In a sense we owe thanks to Mr Jackson (or perhaps F. V. Bennett) for making the rest of Lovecraft's career possible, for there is no telling how long he would have continued to vegetate in the increasingly hothouse atmosphere of 598 Angell Street, where he had lived alone with his mother since 1904 and where he dwelt in hermitry after a "nervous breakdown" that cut short his high school career and prevented his attending college. Lovecraft had no job, was only toying with chemistry and astronomy, was living with a mother who was steadily losing her mental stability, was writing random undistinguished bits of verse about his native region, and was devouring the Munsey magazines but had no thought of contributing any fiction to them or to any other market. But Jackson's work so irritated him that he emerged from his cloister at least to the extent of bombarding letters to the magazines in question. While it was John Russell who initiated the practice of writing in verse, Lovecraft found it a golden opportunity to adapt his beloved Augustan satire against a very modern target.

Lovecraft seems to have responded reasonably well to the abuse with which he was bombarded, although it is evident that at least a few items—especially by Russell—irritated and perhaps even wounded him. Possibly he ceased to submit his work to the *Argosy* after the first few items because he felt the cause was hopeless: it was obvious that he was not changing very many people's minds, and was only irritating many loyal readers. Some of the responses to Lovecraft are surprisingly bitter and hostile, suggesting—whimsically, one hopes—that physical violence be done to the opponent of the beloved Fred Jackson.

The curious thing about the responses to Lovecraft is that many readers took offence at his mere voicing of criticism of Jackson, as if such a thing were in itself somehow off-limits. Some of these comments were on target—those that maintain that the *Argosy* was not published exclusively for one reader's benefit, or that no one is under the obligation to read the magazine—but many readers expressed indignation at the mere levelling of criticism of any kind. The slang terms used to designate this adverse criticism—to "knock" or "kick"—are inherently pejorative, and were interpreted as a sort of personal failing, as if Lovecraft were a misanthrope who could not say anything good about anyone.

One also wonders whether Lovecraft would have engendered the response that he did had he attacked any other writer but Fred Jackson. It certainly appears as if Jackson had a very loyal following both in the *Cavalier* and in the *Argosy;* and I repeat my amazement at the number of men who seemed genuinely to enjoy his love stories. Here again some of the personal attacks are interesting: Lovecraft as the crusty bachelor, as one who has been jilted and is therefore hostile to any expressions of tender emotion, as a cynic who scorns the romantic element in life. Some of these accusations are, indeed, on the mark, but they are irrelevant to the issue of the actual merits of Jackson as a writer; and here Lovecraft is surely correct in declaring Jackson to be sentimental, stylistically careless, and catering rather calculatingly to the expectations of his audience. But Jackson's defenders were on the whole so pathetically ill-educated that they could not even begin to make the fundamental critical distinction between a story that they happened to like and a story that had genuine literary substance. Of course, Jackson's attackers were by and large not much better in this regard.

The ramifications of this entire episode, for Lovecraft, go far beyond the exchange of abuse on a mediocre and insignificant writer. It was, perhaps, the first occasion when he encountered opinions radically different from his own, and coming from a group of people very different (and, quite honestly, quite inferior) in education, culture, and socioeconomic status from his. Although he does not seem to have had much respect for many of his opponents—except, again, Russell—and indeed seems to have had a fairly easy time dynamiting their positions, he would later find such differences of opinion among his friends, colleagues, and correspondents invaluable in shaking him out of his certitudes and broadening his perspective.

What is one to make of Lovecraft's voluminous reading of the Munsey magazines at all? They were certainly not the high literature that he customarily read, and he slogged through an enormous quantity of rubbish to unearth the few flawed gems that he found imaginatively stimulating. But Lovecraft clearly had such a thirst for the weird that he would go to any lengths to come upon it; we can see this same phenomenon in his later reading of *Weird Tales, Amazing Stories,* and the other pulps that emerged in the 1920s and 1930s for a shorter or longer period. Most of them he would drop after an issue or two, realising that they were hopelessly conventional and formulaic; but *Weird Tales* he read to the end, commenting charitably on those few tales (mostly by his own colleagues) that marginally elevated themselves from the general standard of mediocrity. At the same time, however, Lovecraft was under no illusions as to the literary status of the pulp magazines; he knew that they were meant to serve a generally ill-educated public, and the fact that he refused to mention any of this material in *Supernatural Horror in Literature* is one of many telltale signs of the low esteem in which he regarded this literary underworld. While Lovecraft never compromised his own literary standards to cater to popular formula, it becomes somewhat pitiable that he continued to hope against hope that he would encounter truly meritorious work in the pulps.

But the principal immediate result of the *Argosy* experience was, of course, his discovery of—or, rather, by—the world of amateur journalism. Edward F. Daas, then Official Editor of the United Amateur Press Association, noticed the poetic battle between Lovecraft and Russell and invited both to join the organisation. Both did so, Lovecraft officially enrolling on 6 April 1914. In a few years he would be transformed both as a writer and as a human being, eventually resuming the writing of that weird fiction which would ultimately bring him a small modicum of fame as a towering figure in this small realm. That we owe Lovecraft's later career even in part to the unreadable Fred Jackson and the illiterate F. V. Bennett must surely be one of the great ironies of literature.

Lovecraft and Weird Tales

In the days of Senf's covers, monthly Jules de Grandins, Henry S. White-head and Dunwich Horrors, into Rankin's era with his clouded, evil, misty illustrations, bursting into Howard's pulsating epics, Depression days and bi-monthly issues—terrible time of famine—and so on into the present day. *Per ardua ad astra!"* So one reader (Reginald A. Pryke in the October 1937 issue) saw the development of *Weird Tales* and its minor if distinctive place in American civilisation. In spite of the reams of drivel and hackwork that cluttered every issue, in spite of its rejecting the best tales of Lovecraft, Whitehead, Moore, and other serious fantaisistes, in spite of the shaky financial foundations on which it managed to run for an astonishing thirty years, the "unique magazine" has remained exactly that to its current followers (whose number is now far greater than its original readership), and in spite of all shall always have a small place in the study of history and letters; for among its achievements can be named two in particular: its enlivening the confused third and fourth decades of this century with its familiar red covers, thereby becoming an authentic element of American popular culture; and its publishing many of the important works of Howard Phillips Lovecraft, now universally acknowledged as the twentieth century's premier fantaisiste and a figure of growing importance in world literature.

But it would be an error to say that these blessings are unmixed, as it would be presumptuous to assume that Lovecraft would never have reached his present status in weird fiction had he never appeared in *Weird Tales*. Second-guessing history is a tricky proposition for the historian or critic, but in this case some hypotheses can be made on certain effects that *Weird Tales* had on Lovecraft's writing—effects that, had he never submitted there, might not have occurred.

Lovecraft was the first to admit that his habit of writing specifically for *Weird Tales* resulted in a corrupting of his style so that it became more explicit, less suggestive, and more "pulpish." Despite his statements that he never wrote with a particular audience in mind, we have other remarks that attest to his desire to cater to the readership of the magazine—or, at any rate, to gain some needed revenue by placing tales there.[1] By the time Lovecraft realised the results of this cheapening effect, it was too late. It is clear that such tales as "The Horror at Red Hook," with its hackneyed use

---

1. "I shall [soon] devote myself to the composition of more stories to submit to *Weird Tales"* (*SL* 2.37).

of traditional occultism, and "The Dunwich Horror," with its naive confrontation of good vs. evil (Armitage vs. Whateley), were written with *Weird Tales* in mind. Whether Lovecraft could have retained the subtlety of "The Music of Erich Zann" or the delicate prose-poetry of "The Quest of Iranon" in his later years is open to question, since regardless of *Weird Tales* he seemed to be moving toward the cosmic horror of *At the Mountains of Madness* in the course of his development as a weird writer. If it is true, as H. Warner Munn remarked in the magazine's letter column, "The Eyrie" (March 1925), that *Weird Tales* "discovered" Lovecraft, then it must be noted (as Lovecraft often did) that in its discovery it produced a writer significant different from the one who, from 1917 to 1923, was writing solely for "self-expression" and publishing solely in amateur journals.

But *Weird Tales* affected Lovecraft's writing in another way, through its repeated and capricious rejections of his best tales. Ever sensitive to criticism, Lovecraft could not fail to be bothered when his tales were rejected, not on lack of merit, but on their failure to conform to the artificial and hackneyed standards of *Weird Tales* and other pulps. It is ironic, however, that some of his rejected stories were, when later accepted and published, praised more highly than those that editor Farnsworth Wright considered more in tune with *Weird Tales'* audience. Wright knew that Lovecraft was a powerfully original writer, but he made the mistake of underestimating the intelligence and tastes of his readership: like the Valetudinarian of Addison (*Spectator* 25, 29 March 1711) who was so concerned about his health that he became the more ill, Wright was so hesitant to inflict his public with work that departed from the conventional ghost story or "scientifiction" tale (or, as Lovecraft more aptly termed it, "boys' wild west stuff given an interplanetary setting, with handsome young space-pilots instead of cowboys and sheriffs, and 'Martians' and 'moon-men' instead of Indians and outlaws" [*SL* 5.302–3]) that he dared not publish such tales as "The Call of Cthulhu" or "Through the Gates of the Silver Key" without first rejecting them. It is chilling to read Lovecraft's remark that the rejection of *At the Mountains of Madness* by Wright "did more than anything else to end my effective fictional career" (*SL* 5.224).

Wright, however, was not the only one who underestimated his readership: it must be admitted that Lovecraft may have done so as well. When he called the *Weird Tales* audience a "herd of crude and unimaginative illiterates" (*SL* 4.53) he seemed not to consider the numerous readers who, in "The Eyrie," praised Lovecraft's own tales and analysed the sources of their horror quite ably. Indeed, as time passed his views became more and more jaundiced, to such a degree that in 1935 he felt obliged to let loose this jeremiad:

[Pulp magazine editors] aim to please the very lowest grade of readers—probably because these constitute a large numerical majority. When you glance at the advertisements in these cheap magazines (& they wouldn't continue to be inserted if they weren't answered) you can see what a hopelessly vulgar & stupid rabble comprise the bulk of the clientele. These yaps & nitwits probably can't grasp anything even remotely approaching subtlety. *Suggestion*—the most artistic way to present any marvellous event—means absolutely nothing to them. One has to draw a full diagram & drive the idea into their heads with a hammer before they "get" it.[2]

While it cannot be denied that many readers were puerile and had undeveloped tastes in weird fiction (the inane praises of such hacks as E. Hoffmann Price, Edmond Hamilton, Seabury Quinn, and others prove it), there were a good many others whose levels of appreciation were somewhat higher. Lovecraft himself had an inkling of this when he tried to plead with Wright that the "Eyrie-bombarding proletariat" (*SL* 4.322) was not representative of the total readership of the magazine; but this had little effect on Wright, who told Lovecraft "that his index to popular whim is, almost exclusively, the flood of semi-illiterate Eyrie mail which pours in upon him" (*SL* 3.194). A number of current critics have deemed Farnsworth Wright a capable editor; but to hold such an opinion is to ignore his treatment of the writer who, aside from being the most important contributor to the magazine, is now largely responsible for the continuing consideration of the magazine at all. Wright, it is true, managed to keep *Weird Tales* on its feet through the Depression; but it was at the expense of rejecting the best work of its best writers and publishing torrents of pulpish hackwork whose permanent inhumation can only be a blessing to weird fiction.

Who read *Weird Tales* and why? It is an interesting social commentary that a number of them turned to the "unique magazine" simply to escape the "mass of literary farce that we are treated to in the other magazines" ("The Eyrie," August 1929). Lovecraft too recognised that the material published in what H. Warner Munn ("The Eyrie," March 1925) called the "ultraconservative" magazines was becoming "increasingly lifeless, sterile, mannered, preoccupied with form, and obviously linked with obsolescent attitudes and interests and perspectives" (*SL* 5.399). Both *Weird Tales* and the "ultraconservatives" represented two sides of the cultural havoc of American (and European) civilisation between the two World Wars: the latter opted for a blind return to conventionalism, while the former chose imaginative (or sometimes not so imaginative) escape from the hideous realities of Al Capone and the Great Depression. *Weird Tales* was still serving

---

2. Lovecraft to Duane W. Rimel, 16 April 1935 (ms., JHL).

this function in the late 1930s, as a comment in "The Eyrie" of June 1937 (which almost anticipates the decade of the 1950s and Joe McCarthy) shows: "In these days of stark realism of wars and rumors of wars, of cracked politics and politicians, of 200% Americans and enemies that bore from within, it was more than relief to turn to a Lovecraft story."

Here is only one reader of many who identified Lovecraft with *Weird Tales*. Donald A. Wollheim (October 1937) did the same when he said that Lovecraft's myth-cycle (particularly such elements as the *Necronomicon*) "was one of the factors contributing to the making of WT's vivid and unique personality." It is a delicate question whether Lovecraft or such other writers as Seabury Quinn or Edmond Hamilton were actually the most "popular" contributors to the magazine. To be sure, these latter writers, experienced and businesslike pulpsters that they were, contributed far more voluminously to *Weird Tales* than Lovecraft; but readers were constantly clamouring for the latter's work (especially in the 1930s, when the relative sparsity of his original fiction, as well as his reluctance to submit to the magazine and risk additional rejections, caused Wright to appease readers with the feeble expedient of reprinting earlier tales by Lovecraft), and I think it can safely be said that even the magazine's cruder readers recognised that Lovecraft was on a higher plane than Quinn or Hamilton.

Nor was it the case (as with other such accidentally popular geniuses as Beethoven, Virgil, and Shakespeare) that readers failed to appreciate Lovecraft's true merits and enjoyed him for some coincidentally appealing feature of his work. In several letters to "The Eyrie" (many from Lovecraft's own correspondents) we note a vague and confused awareness of the philosophical bases of his work; a few of the letters, indeed, may represent some of the more astute early vignettes of Lovecraft criticism. Robert E. Howard, even before he began corresponding with the Providence writer, grasped that his "range is cosmic" (May 1928); and while we may smile at his remark that Lovecraft "touches peaks in his tales which no modern or ancient writer has ever hinted," we nonetheless must be impressed at Howard's perception of the central doctrine of Lovecraft's work (expressed by Lovecraft himself in his letter to Farnsworth Wright of 5 July 1927, published in the February 1928 issue of *Weird Tales*). A good number of readers were captivated by Lovecraft's polished, erudite, and slightly archaic style, and Ray Cummings expressed the feelings of many when he said, "Never have I encountered any purer, more beautiful diction. [His tales] sing; the true poetry of prose" (June 1926). Harold Farnese maintained that Lovecraft's "weird and eldritch atmosphere has yet to be equalled by other writers" (August 1931), while a comment by E. Hoffmann Price hints at a major philosophical concept in Lovecraft's later work:

In his utter unreality and impossibility, he is like a non-Euclidean geom-
eter who, though working on physically impossible axioms, reasons truly
from them and produces theorems, and subsequent Q.E.D.'s, which are
as true as if they actually were true; or as one who reasons of the incon-
ceivable fourth dimension and by self-consistent hypotheses and logic
deals logically with impossibility. (April 1926)

The "self-consistency" that Price notes is equivalent, more or less, to what
Lovecraft felt must now be the basis for true fantasy: "The time has come
when the normal revolt against time, space, and matter must assume a
form not overtly incompatible with what is known of reality—when it
must be gratified by images forming *supplements* rather than *contradictions* to
the visible and mensurable universe" (*SL* 3.295–96).

Not all of Lovecraft's fans in "The Eyrie," however, were so astute.
Several writers (despite their assertions that they had read Shakespeare and
other such writers) confirmed Lovecraft's opinion of their "semi-
illiteracy"—or, at any rate, their lack of judgment—by proclaiming him and
Weird Tales among the best works in world literature. We know through
Lovecraft's letters that he censured many of his younger correspondents
(R. H. Barlow, J. Vernon Shea, Willis Conover) for holding such views as
"*Weird Tales* is the best magazine ever published" (October 1926) or that
"Lovecraft is as great a writer as ever lived" (June 1929) or that "The Outsider" is "the greatest weird story ever written" (September 1931). And we
can only laugh at the puerility of J. Wasso (February 1930), who wished to
form an H. P. Lovecraft fan club. These opinions reflect the difference between true critical appreciation and that immature adulation which regrettably casts a dubious shadow on the author himself. Indeed, it may have
been precisely such remarks that caused Edmund Wilson, in 1945, to condemn "the Lovecraft cult" as "on even a more infantile level than the
Baker Street irregulars and the cult of Sherlock Holmes" (Wilson 49).
Lovecraft has had to wait too long to escape the pathetic talons of fandom.

Not only was Lovecraft praised to the skies in *Weird Tales,* but many
championed his poorer stories—"The Hound," "The Lurking Fear," "The
Horror at Red Hook." The phenomenal response to "The Dunwich Horror" is a virtual index to its (unconscious) conformity to pulp standards. Still
more amusing are those fans who were so taken with Lovecraft that they
(unconsciously?) imitated his erudite writing style when writing their letters:

"The Dunwich Horror" transported me, upon the wings of imagination, to
the uttermost depths of vast caverns in the bowels of the earth—caverns
which are swept by foul, moaning winds laden with the breath of the grave
and which contain cosmic cesspools wherein the corruption, filth and evil
of millions of centuries have accumulated; from there I traveled, in an in-

stant, to far-off worlds or places where only a brief glimpse of unnamable horrors and formless, space-filling alien entities send me scurrying and screaming (mentally) with terror back to my warm fireside. (April 1930)

Then there were the truly eccentric readers whose minds were somehow ignited by Lovecraft's tales: one tells us that "The Outsider" is a true story founded on an incident in Germany; another notes some mysterious essays on Shakespeare written by Lovecraft during his involvement with amateur journalism; yet another, quoting Ibsen in the process, wishes the *Necronomicon* to be serialised in *Weird Tales*.

This brings up one of the more amusing aspects of Lovecraft's popularity in *Weird Tales:* the remarkably widespread belief that the *Necronomicon* was an actual book, and that his myth-cycle of Cthulhu and Yog-Sothoth had an actual basis in fact or was an authentic cycle of folklore. The hoax was obviously aided by Lovecraft's correspondents, who in their own tales used these very elements as if out of a common pool of esoteric knowledge. Indeed, virtually all of his newer correspondents—Derleth, Conover, Howard, Shea, Rimel, and others—had to be disabused as to the reality of the myth-cycle. The game was of course carried on after Lovecraft's death: in one of the most famous letters in "The Eyrie," one J. H. Stewart, Jr, tells how Manly Wade Wellman nearly stumbled upon a copy of the *Necronomicon* in a bookstore presided over by an ancient crone (July 1952).

What is also interesting is the use of the term "Elder Gods" by readers to describe the gods of Lovecraft's mythos. It was, of course, August Derleth who, after Lovecraft's death (and initially in the story "The Return of Hastur"), launched his own myth-cycle where "Elder Gods" battled the "Great Old Ones" in a puerile struggle of good vs. evil. Derleth, indeed, took every opportunity to foster his myth-cycle and to claim that it represented the development of the mythos as Lovecraft himself would have done had he lived (cf. his letter in the May 1941 issue). The "Elder Gods" have no existence in Lovecraft's tales (certainly not the all-powerful one that Derleth gave them), and even in "The Strange High House in the Mist" there are mentions only of strange, unexplained entities called "Elder Ones." *Weird Tales* readers seem to have confused them with the Great Old Ones (Cthulhu, Nyarlathotep, Yog-Sothoth, et al.), for Bernard Austin Dwyer (June 1930) makes reference to "Other Gods in the Elder World." Another writer, B. M. Reynolds (October 1936), mentions the Elder Gods themselves—this being the earliest mention of them in a quasi-Derlethian sense that I have found. Robert Leonard Russell makes note of "Cthulhu, Azathoth and the other Elder Gods" (August 1937), and Jacques Bergier speaks of Lovecraft's "cycle of the Elder Gods and strange civilisations" (September 1937). It is tempting to wonder whether these mentions in any way

way helped to shape Derleth's perverted conception of Lovecraft's myth-cycle.

The facility with which many readers noticed the Lovecraftian flavour of some of his revisions published in *Weird Tales* is striking. Hazel Heald's tales in particular were called out for mention, one reader soberly inform-ing us that "Even Lovecraft . . . could hardly . . . have surpassed the gro-tesque scene" that served as the climax to "The Horror in the Museum" (May 1934). Aside from Heald, this "female Lovecraft" (June 1935), Wil-liam Lumley's "The Diary of Alonzo Typer" was praised, Paul S. Smith claiming that Lumley had a fair chance of being "a worthy successor to the late master" (August 1938). Lovecraft himself wryly remarked that "some of my revision clients congratulate *themselves* when the readers praise stories (like 'The Last Test', 'The Curse of Yig', 'The Horror in the Museum', 'Winged Death', etc.) that *I* wrote" (*SL* 4.394).

Not all readers expressed favourable views, of course: despite the obvi-ously sensible policy that only letters of praise were allowed, in the main, to appear in "The Eyrie," some dissenting letters emerged; interestingly, these came largely during the editorships of Edwin Baird (1923–24) and Dorothy McIlwraith (1940–54), and their absence during Wright's tenure can only be another sign of his paranoiac insecurity. Toward the latter days of the magazine, when the end was perhaps visible, there flared up a minor debate about Lovecraft's worth as a writer which is interesting not so much for the arguments expressed (being on both sides basically subjective and irrele-vant), but for the fact that a majority of adverse critics have taken precisely the view here adopted by Joseph V. Wilcox, who put forth the claim that Lovecraft's style was "turgid"[3] and not suitable for the weird tale.

The number of Lovecraft's correspondents who wrote letters praising him in "The Eyrie" (many of these letters appearing before their writers even began corresponding with him) is interesting. These included not merely his fellow fantaisistes—Derleth, Munn, Wandrei (although only after Lovecraft's demise), Bloch, Kuttner, Price, Clark Ashton Smith, and others—but associ-ates only marginally involved in weird fiction—James F. Morton, Harold S. Farnese, J. Vernon Shea, Bernard Austin Dwyer, Paul J. Campbell, and the like. Several writers, in fact, became associates of Lovecraft through "The Eyrie" itself—Derleth, Howard, and perhaps Jacques Bergier. On the other hand, it is odd that such colleagues as Frank Belknap Long, Robert H. Bar-low, and others, who were both Lovecraft's close friends and significantly

---

3. This is curiously echoed by the classical scholar and critic Gilbert Highet in his idiosyncratic snipe at Lovecraft in *A Clerk of Oxenford* (New York: Oxford Univer-sity Press, 1954), p. 9.

involved in either *Weird Tales* itself or fantasy fandom, never sent letters to
"The Eyrie"—or, at any rate, never had them published.

Lovecraft's death in March 1937 produced the most overwhelming
tide of letters of comment ever found in "The Eyrie," and far exceeded the
amount for other such deceased writers as Robert E. Howard or Henry S.
Whitehead. A great many of Lovecraft's correspondents, from those who
had known him in the 1920s (Smith) to those who had corresponded with
him only a few months before his death (Robert A. W. Lowndes, Earl
Peirce), sent letters of regret, while other associates (particularly Henry
George Weiss and Kenneth Sterling) extolled him as a great writer, thinker,
and epistolarian. Those who had known Lovecraft only through his work
were as moved by his death as they had been by his stories: "I feel," writes
Robert Leonard Russell, "as will many other readers of *Weird Tales,* that I
have lost a real friend" (August 1937). But Lovecraft's work by no means
stopped appearing upon his demise: many tales previously rejected were
now printed, and when these ran out poems were used to satiate the readers' demands. But, as L. Sprague de Camp (435) has pointed out, Lovecraft's death, so closely following that of Robert E. Howard and the virtual
surcease of Clark Ashton Smith's fictional output, dealt a fatal blow to
Weird Tales, caused it to lose much of its "vivid and unique personality,"
and heralded a death that, though staved off for some seventeen years, was
as inevitable as Lovecraft's own. There were still, under the none too competent guidance of Dorothy McIlwraith, some fine writers appearing in its
pages—Bloch, Bradbury, Wellman, and others—but the lack of any writer
of the stature of a Lovecraft or a Howard, plus the rising competition of
the science fiction magazines and the emergence of the paperback book as
an alternative to the pulp magazine, ensured *Weird Tales'* collapse. In its decline "The Eyrie" too dwindled from the lively readers' column of the
1920s and 1930s to the dry editorial ramblings of the 1940s and 1950s.
From a full 160 pages to a small digest size—such was the ignominious
end of a magazine that had seen in its pages the work of Lovecraft, Whitehead, Smith, Long, Wandrei, Bloch, and so many of the most important
figures in modern weird fiction; but perhaps it could have met no other
fate, for it was very much a product of its time, very much a part of the
Roaring Twenties and Depression Thirties from which it had sprung.

It is needless to say that both Lovecraft and *Weird Tales* would have
been very different without each other; but whether for better or for
worse, their fortuitous joining helped to bring about what is probably the
finest weird fiction that the twentieth century has ever seen. In view of
this, the crudities and absurdities of *Weird Tales* become trivial, just as re-
fulgent gold outshines its dross.

Works Cited

de Camp, L. Sprague. *Lovecraft: A Biography*. Garden City, NY: Doubleday, 1975.

Wilson, Edmund. "Tales of the Marvellous and the Ridiculous" (1945). Rpt. in S. T. Joshi, ed., *H. P. Lovecraft: Four Decades of Criticism*. Athens: Ohio University Press, 1980, pp. 46–49.

A Look at Lovecraft's Letters

The publication of the five volumes of Lovecraft's *Selected Letters* (1965–76) could be said to have singlehandedly initiated a newer, deeper trend in Lovecraft studies; for before the 2000 pages of this series emerged, few were aware of the many different sides of Lovecraft the man and writer, and few had any perception to what degree his correspondence in sheer bulk dwarfs the rest of his work—fiction, poetry, essays, revisions—combined. The 930 letters published in the *Selected Letters* were in almost every case abridged—indeed, in one anomalous instance (#484), only the greeting and the closing were printed, and the body of the letter entirely excised—and only a tiny fraction of the surviving correspondence was published. And yet, the editing of these 930 letters took nearly forty years—August Derleth began collecting letters from correspondents almost upon Lovecraft's death in 1937—and the tireless work of three editors, Derleth, Donald Wandrei, and James Turner. The sheer audacity of Arkham House in publishing the letters—initially planned for one volume, then augmented respectively to three and five volumes[1]—may be lost on some of us now, since Lovecraft's greatness as an epistolarian is taken for granted by all scholars and many enthusiasts; yet it must be remembered that no figure in fantasy or science fiction has been accorded this treatment save Poe, Bierce, John W. Campbell, and Philip K. Dick. Arthur Machen's selected letters only appeared in 1988; Robert E. Howard's appeared in two volumes in 1989–91; an interesting volume of correspondence between Lord Dunsany and Arthur C. Clarke was published in 1998; a selection of Clark Ashton Smith's letters has been published, but their interest stems as much from the fact that they were written to Lovecraft as that they were written by Smith; and probably few others in the field deserve to have their letters published. At a time when T. S. Eliot's and W. B. Yeats's letters have yet to be published in a definitive format, five volumes of Lovecraft's letters is a remarkable achievement.

And yet, how infinitesimal is even this amount when compared to the whole of Lovecraft's surviving correspondence, or—even more unthinkable—his total correspondence, surviving and destroyed. How many letters did Lovecraft write? The exact number has been hotly debated and of

---

1. A supplementary volume of letters and an index were announced in Arkham House catalogues before Derleth's death in 1971, but copyright disputes evidently derailed these plans. I supplied the index in 1980 (Necronomicon Press).

course can never be truly ascertained. The figure of 100,000 arrived at (probably by sheer speculation) by L. Sprague de Camp seems a bit high. Lovecraft variously gave his daily output of letters at anywhere between 5 and 15; if we assume a middle ground of 8 or 10, we reach some 3500 letters a year; over a twenty-five year period (1912–37) we already reach 87,500 at what is probably a conservative estimate. Of these, it is my belief that no more than 10,000 now survive. We know that such correspondents as Alfred Galpin, Samuel Loveman, and—most tragically for us—his wife Sonia Greene destroyed all or many of their letters from Lovecraft, and many other letters have surely been lost or destroyed by time and carelessness. Now if those 930 letters in the *Selected Letters* were published complete (and the abridgements in some instances have been radical—only three paragraphs of a 46-page letter to J. Vernon Shea were published), they could easily have taken up twice the space they now occupy. This means that every 100 letters of Lovecraft would fill an average (400 pp.) volume. The 10,000 surviving letters would then fill 100 volumes!

But let us descend from these vertiginous figures. As R. Alain Everts has recently pointed out,[2] most of Lovecraft's letters were not the treatise-length works that have excited our wonder, but were short, one- or two-page letters written on the front and back of a single sheet of paper. And yet, those long letters are clearly in evidence—30, 40, 50, and evidently in at least one instance (#381 of the *Selected Letters*) 70 handwritten pages long. One can only wonder at the reaction of Lovecraft's correspondents at receiving novel-length letters of this sort. How did they answer them? Did they try to do so? Or did they merely imitate some of Lovecraft's characters and lapse into a merciful fit of fainting?

Lovecraft was, curiously enough, at first a very reluctant letter-writer. In 1931 he testified: "In youth I scarcely did any letter-writing—thanking anybody for a present was so much of an ordeal that I would rather have written a two-hundred-fifty-line pastoral or a twenty-page treatise on the rings of Saturn" (*SL* 3.369–70). He declares that it was his cousin Phillips Gamwell (who died in 1916) whose stimulating correspondence urged Lovecraft into the letter-writing habit, but it was his joining the amateur journalism movement in 1914 that really impelled his voluminousness in this regard. As an official of the United Amateur Press Association (at various times Chairman of the Department of Public Criticism, Vice-President, President, and Official Editor) Lovecraft wrote much official correspondence, some of which we would very much like to have. Each year the UAPA selected several important literary figures to be Laureate Judges to select prize-winning stories, articles, and poems published in that year, and

---

2. Letter to the editor, *Fantasy Commentator* 5, No. 3 (Fall 1985): 217.

at one point Lovecraft notes his intention of writing to the poets Vachel Lindsay and Harriet Monroe to offer them the post.[3] Whether he did so I do not know, but it would have been one of the only times when Lovecraft came into contact with literary figures outside the narrow worlds of amateurdom and fantasy fiction.

That the bulk of his total correspondence was with amateur writers—or, at least, with associates whom he first met in amateurdom—is easy to see from the enormous number of letters surviving to such figures as Rheinhart Kleiner, Maurice W. Moe, Alfred Galpin, James F. Morton, Frank Belknap Long, and many others. The various round-robin correspondence cycles in which Lovecraft participated—the Kleicomolo, the Gallomo, and others—are too well known to require description. It was tragically short-sighted of Derleth and Wandrei to have failed to publish many of these early letters dealing with Lovecraft's complex and multifaceted involvement with amateurdom: interested as they were only in his relations with the fantasy field, Derleth and Wandrei did not realise that amateurdom was a lifelong pursuit of Lovecraft's and one that may well have been more important to him—certainly one that shaped more of his attitudes—than the tiny realm of pulp fiction. If Lovecraft had ever corresponded with some of the contemporary giants of weird fiction—he just missed corresponding with Bierce, and felt too diffident to write to Machen, Blackwood, or Dunsany—this emphasis may have had slightly greater justification; but, in truth, his correspondence with such figures as Seabury Quinn, Henry S. Whitehead, or even Derleth himself is of much less significance than that with Moe, Kleiner, Galpin, and Morton.

And yet, it is this amateur correspondence that either has been largely lost or is still unpublished and even unknown. Only recently has a correspondence cycle from Lovecraft to Arthur Harris (the Welsh amateur who issued Lovecraft's first pamphlet, *The Crime of Crimes,* in 1915) come to light; and his letters to Helm C. Spink and Hyman Bradofsky—important amateurs of the 1930s—have recently surfaced. Lovecraft corresponded with almost all important, and many unimportant, amateurs of his day, and many must surely have kept at least some of these letters. If unearthed and published, they would shed valuable light on a crucial period of Lovecraft's life given short shrift in the *Selected Letters.*

Of course, when Lovecraft began publishing his stories in *Weird Tales,* many fans and writers came into contact with him through that magazine: in this way Lovecraft began to correspond with the nineteen-year-old Donald Wandrei, the nineteen-year-old J. Vernon Shea, the eighteen-year-

---

3. Letter to Rheinhart Kleiner, 5 May 1918; now rpt. in Lovecraft's *Uncollected Letters* (West Warwick, RI: Necronomicon Press, 1986), p. 25.

old August Derleth, the fifteen-year-old Robert Bloch, the thirteen-year-old R. H. Barlow, and more established writers like Henry S. Whitehead, E. Hoffmann Price, and Robert E. Howard. Needless to say, many of these correspondents became very important to Lovecraft: Barlow became, at nineteen, his literary executor (perhaps because Lovecraft saw in him the same incandescent brilliance which, a decade earlier, had impressed him in Alfred Galpin; and in this he may not have been far wrong), Derleth and Wandrei his posthumous editors, and Howard a close associate whose own voluminous replies to Lovecraft's letters would lend themselves ideally to combined publication, as has been done with other figures—notably Alexander Pope and Horace Walpole—where both sides of a correspondence cycle survive. In its own way the Lovecraft-Howard correspondence rivals the Pope-Swift correspondence of the early eighteenth century, and would perhaps be of as much importance to fantasy scholars as the latter is to students of the Augustan age.

As Lovecraft became the fountainhead of the fantasy fandom movement of the 1930s, his correspondents in almost every instance were eager youths—Barlow, Duane Rimel, F. Lee Baldwin, Donald A. Wollheim, Kenneth Sterling, W. F. Anger, Willis Conover, and others—who all looked up to him as a mentor and teacher. Lovecraft naturally slipped into this role, for it finally made real his wistful dream of being a "grandpa" surrounded by excited young children. The Grand Old Man had at last found his respectful audience.

And this raises a matter of utmost importance in considering Lovecraft's letters: the varying tones he adopted when dealing with different correspondents. Far from showing Lovecraft to be insincere or hypocritical, this adaptation of tone and matter to the individual reveals the consideration and courtesy ingrained in his behaviour. Nothing could exemplify this aspect of Lovecraft better than the correspondence to Elizabeth Toldridge, a disabled would-be poet[4] in Washington, D.C., with whom he corresponded faithfully for eight years, until his death. Even the voluminous published correspondence to Toldridge does not tell the whole story: only the unabridged, unpublished letters show how carefully and tactfully Lovecraft answered each point raised by his correspondent, tirelessly gave kind and constructive advice on her insipid poetry (much of which, evidently kept by Lovecraft, survives in manuscript in the John Hay Library), acknowledged the newspaper "cuttings" she sent him, and in general adopted a patient and interested tone in all his correspondence to her.

---

4. Actually, as James Turner has pointed out to me, she published two slim books of poetry in the teens, years before ever encountering Lovecraft; but these were probably published at her own expense.

Hypocrisy? Hardly: Lovecraft was merely trying to bring a few moments' pleasure into an invalid's drab existence; and the fact that the correspondence ceased only with his death testifies that Lovecraft must have been successful in his attempt.

Other correspondence cycles reveal analogous shifts in tone: tongue-in-cheek archaism to Rheinhart Kleiner (himself a polished poet adhering to older standards in prose and poetry); ludicrous slang and colloquialism to James F. Morton; playfully horrific greetings to Clark Ashton Smith; studied—perhaps excessive—politeness to Helen Sully (to the point that eventually she became infuriated that Lovecraft continued to address her as "Miss Sully" instead of as "Helen"); and the like. The correspondence differs, of course, in substance as well, depending on the interests of the correspondent: the letters to Derleth are primarily about weird fiction or regional/historical matters, in accordance with Derleth's mainstream literary work; the letters to E. Hoffmann Price are almost solely about weird fiction (and—rather monotonously—about Lovecraft's resolutely non-commercial stance, something Price, as a "professional" writer, found almost incomprehensible); heavily philosophical is the correspondence to Galpin (in his youth as fervent a Nietzschean as Lovecraft), Moe (an idealist who formed the perfect counterweight to Lovecraft the materialist), Morton (an atheist even more extreme than Lovecraft), and, to a degree, with Robert E. Howard: to no one else could Lovecraft have written the lengthy and stalwart defences of civilisation over barbarism than to the creator of Conan. It is not certain that Lovecraft got the better of this argument. The correspondence to Wandrei is also primarily literary, but not restricted narrowly to horror fiction as it is to Derleth and Price; rather, Wandrei, holding many of the same philosophical and literary attitudes as Lovecraft, elicited from his correspondent some very profound statements of his literary theory, and the recent unabridged publication of their illuminating joint correspondence may be the vanguard of several such volumes now in the planning stages.

Two correspondence cycles perhaps stand apart, and may represent the pinnacle of Lovecraft's epistolary art: the letters to Frank Belknap Long and to Clark Ashton Smith. The letters to Smith, of course, also centre primarily on weird fiction; but do so in such a way as to reveal volumes about Lovecraft's aesthetic theory. Lovecraft confided in Smith much more than he did, say, in Derleth: Smith shared Lovecraft's "cosmic" viewpoint, as Lovecraft knew Derleth (the "self-blinded earth-gazer" [*SL* 3.295]) did not; as a result, Lovecraft had no difficulty communicating his sense of "cosmic outsideness" and "adventurous expectancy" to Smith. But the correspondence to Frank Belknap Long may be the greatest Lovecraft ever wrote: Long and Lovecraft, extremely close friends for fifteen years through many personal meetings, let their hair down completely in their letters, talking about everything from eroticism to cosmicism, amateur affairs to weird fiction, Colonial architecture to aesthetic sincerity to the decline of the West to Greek philosophy to Anglo-Catholicism. The massive letter #466 contains more philosophical substance and rhetorical flourishes than any story or essay he ever wrote, and ought to stand next to "The Colour out of Space" and *At the Mountains of Madness* as one of his towering literary achievements.

It is now, of course, scarcely to be doubted that Lovecraft's letters are great literary works, but Lovecraft was the first to disavow the claim: "Nobody expects anything of a letter, or judges any man's style by one. Even when I write one by hand I pay no attention to rhetorick, but just sail along at a mile-a-minute pace. . . . If you were to analyse the language of this letter you would find it shot all to hell with solecisms and bad rhythms" (*SL* 3.337). This passage tells us many things. When Lovecraft wrote, early in his career, that "my reading of publish'd letters hath largely been confined to those of 18th century British authors" (*SL* 1.88) along with Cicero and Pliny the Younger, he should have added an important qualification: his letters—those written, at any rate, in his prime—are leagues away from the laboured pomposity of Pope's or Johnson's correspondence (the former consciously wrote with the expectation that his letters would one day be published), but resemble instead the easy grace and fluency of Gray or Cowper. And in spite of the "mile-a-minute" rate, there are in fact few solecisms in Lovecraft's letters[5]—and this is one more reason why his letters are one of his greatest accomplishments, for the obvious rapidity with which most of his correspondence was written by no means excludes some dazzling rhetorical strokes: we have the bizarre "stream-of-consciousness" letters (cf., e.g., #454) where Lovecraft free-associates for pages on end; we have devastating destructions of his opponents' arguments, as in the early letter to Moe on the subject that "the Judaeo-Christian mythology is NOT TRUE" (*SL* 1.60f.); unexpected poignancy or eloquence as Lovecraft records important episodes in his life, such as his return to Providence from New York in 1926 ("HOME—UNION STATION— *PROVIDENCE!!!!*"—*SL* 2.47) or the death of Robert E. Howard ("But it is damn hard to realise that there's no longer any REH at Lock Box 313!"—*SL* 5.277). It is certainly not the case that Lovecraft "paid no attention to rhetorick"; rather, that rhetorical instinct—in the best sense of the

---

5. Vernon Shea, however, once piqued Lovecraft by pointing out the doubtful usage "three alternatives" in one letter (*SL* 4.99); and there are other solecisms— found also in the stories—such as the use of "data" in the singular (and this from one who was a Latin scholar) and the continual misspelling of "accommodate" (as "accomodate") and "Portuguese" (as "Portugese").

term, as the ability to express each idea in the language best suited to it—was so imbued in him that it emerged in even the most hastily written epistle.

J. Vernon Shea was one of several who suggested that there were many potential essays buried in the letters (see *SL* 4.351), and such is indeed the case. Lovecraft actually did make some attempts to create essays out of letters, but only sporadically and half-heartedly. As I have pointed out elsewhere,[6] in the 1930s Lovecraft (and/or Barlow) extracted the philosophical portions of the three open letters he had sent through the Transatlantic Circulator in 1921 and assembled them into an independent essay—a somewhat problematical procedure, since much of the "essay" is a polemic directed toward a single opponent whose views cannot always be accurately inferred only from Lovecraft's side of the debate. Posthumously, of course, Lovecraft's letters have been mined for essay-material: "Some Backgrounds of Fairyland" (in *Marginalia*) is part of a letter to Wilfred Talman, as are the two Lovecraft items in *The Occult Lovecraft* (1975); the autobiographical *E'ch-Pi-El Speaks* (1972) is a letter to an unknown correspondent; even the "Observations on Several Parts of America" (1928) began life as a letter to Maurice Moe, but Lovecraft found that his summary of his travels of 1928 would save him the trouble of writing the same thing to many correspondents, so he typed up the letter with few modifications and circulated it as a travelogue. It is, in fact, unfortunate that Lovecraft did not seriously try to market letter-excerpts as essays, for if published in important magazines of the day—*Atlantic, Harper's, Scribner's*—they might have led to his developing a reputation as a man of letters instead of merely as a pulp fictionist.

Conversely, sometimes Lovecraft's lengthy letters were planned out as carefully as any story or essay. For his "last" letter (dated in the *Selected Letters* to 15 March 1937, but obviously begun earlier, perhaps months earlier) we have been given a brief series of notes and topics to be covered in the letter, and Lovecraft confessed that this was a frequent practice of his; an unpublished document in the John Hay Library entitled "Objections to Orthodox Communism" (1936) is nothing more than the outline of a letter on that subject written to C. L. Moore (19 June 1936; #856). And yet, one of the most exciting things about Lovecraft's longer letters is their almost kaleidoscopic shift from one topic to the other, a shift determined only by the course of the argument or the various points raised by the correspondent. In a magnificent letter to Woodburn Harris (prefaced by the sensible caveat: "WARNING! Don't try to read this all at once!"—*SL* 3.58) Lovecraft proceeds from the collapse of American culture to a comparison of

---

6. See my introduction to *In Defence of Dagon* (Necronomicon Press, 1985), pp. 8–9.

the Greek tragedians and Shakespeare to the growth of the machine-culture to the notion of love to styles of discourse in debates to democracy to the nature of the human psyche, with asides about Joseph Wood Krutch and Havelock Ellis (and this is merely the portion of the letter—obviously abridged—published in the *Selected Letters*).

Indeed, one could cull an entire volume of pithy utterances from the letters; here is an example from Volume 1 alone:

Peace is the ideal of a dying nation. (*SL* 1.12)

Our philosophy is all childishly *subjective*. (*SL* 1.24)

Frankly, I cannot conceive how any thoughtful man can really be happy. (*SL* 1.26)

Truth-hunger is a hunger just as real as food-hunger. (*SL* 1.45)

Possibly it is better to be near-sighted and orthodox like Mo[e], trusting all to a Divine Providence, R.I. (*SL* 1.57)

Entity precedes morality. (*SL* 1.63)

Adulthood is hell. (*SL* 1.106)

Success is a relative thing—and the victory of a boy at marbles is equal to the victory of an Octavius at Actium when measured by the scale of cosmic infinity. (*SL* 1.111)

The cosmos is a mindless vortex; a seething ocean of blind forces, in which the greatest joy is unconsciousness and the greatest pain realisation. (*SL* 1.156)

The one sound power in the world is the power of a hairy muscular right arm! (*SL* 1.209)

Honestly, my hatred of the human animal mounts by leaps and bounds the more I see of the miserable vermin. (*SL* 1.211)

A gentleman shouldn't write all his images down for a plebeian rabble to stare at. (*SL* 1.243)

I no longer really desire anything but oblivion. (*SL* 1.302–3)

The aeons and the worlds are my sport, and I watch with calm and amused aloofness the anticks of planets and the mutations of the universes. (*SL* 1.327)

And who can forget the imperishable "What is anything?" (*SL* 3.83 etc.).

We can learn more about Lovecraft's development as a stylist from reading his letters than from reading either his stories or his poems or his essays; for his letters both document and exemplify the gradual modifica-tion—and mastery—of his style in his stories, poems, and essays. We should note that Lovecraft's first published work was a letter to the editor of the *Providence Sunday Journal* (published 3 June 1906) on a point of as-tronomy. This indicates the dominance of science in Lovecraft's literary output in his early years, when he was writing many more scientific treatises than stories or poems. The shift toward literature came around 1911, and shortly thereafter we see Lovecraft don the ill-fitting cloak of eighteenth-century diction in stories, letters, and poems alike. The verse letter *Ad Criti-cos* (composed in four "books," only two of which were evidently pub-lished) initiated a literary controversy in the *Argosy* and other early pulps, and shows Lovecraft to have mastered the rococo externals—but, alas! not the inner fire or living music—of Dryden's and Pope's great satires (*Ad Criticos* clearly looks back to Dryden's *Mac Flecknoe* and Pope's *Dunciad*), and it is not surprising that much of his prose had also adopted the "inef-fably pompous and Johnsonese" style (*SL* 4.360) he was later to condemn in his early story "The Beast in the Cave" (1905). Indeed, throughout much of Lovecraft's early career there is a curious cleavage between his fiction and verse on the one hand, full of eighteenth-century affectations, and his scientific and philosophical works, written in a forceful, direct, uncluttered prose reminiscent of Swift or T. H. Huxley. His early letters mirror the split; in remarking on his literary preferences, he writes in a letter of 1918 (addressed as from "Will's Coffee House/Russell Street, Covent-Garden, London"):

> I like the novels of J. Fenimore Cooper and of N. Hawthorne, and the verse of O. W. Holmes. The critical dissertations of J. R. Lowell likewise gratify my taste. . . . On second perusal, I find Mr. Emerson not altogether wanting in good sense, tho' I much prefer my older friend Mr. Addison. (*SL* 1.73)

Pure eighteenth century! It is all very clever, but one can never be quite certain whether Lovecraft is in fact writing with tongue in cheek or is somehow actually trying—naively and pitifully—to transport himself psy-chologically to the eighteenth century. But a few months *earlier* than the above, in a heated controversy about religion, Lovecraft could write the following:

> What am I? What is the nature of the energy about me, and how does it affect me? So far I have seen nothing which could possibly give me the notion that cosmic force is the manifestation of a mind and will like my own infinitely magnified; a potent and purposeful consciousness which deals individually and directly with the miserable denizens of a wretched little flyspeck on the back door of a microscopic universe, and which sin-

gles this putrid excrescence out as the one spot whereto to send an onlie-
begotten Son, whose mission is to redeem these accursed flyspeck-
inhabiting lice which we call human beings—bah!! Pardon the "bah!" I
feel several "bahs!", but out of courtesy I only say one. But it is all so very
childish. I cannot help taking exception to a philosophy which would
force this rubbish down my throat. 'What have I against religion?' That is
what I have against it! (*SL* 1.63–64)

This passage is actually much more rhetorically elaborate than the previous
one, but it is so in a direct and straightforward manner, with telling colloquialism ("I feel several 'bahs!'"), parody ("onlie-begotten Son"), piquant
compounds ("flyspeck-inhabiting lice"), and rhetorical questions. It is as if
Lovecraft, when spurred into arguments about issues important to him,
sheds his archaism like a cloak and writes with the vigour and force we
know from the later fiction.

As the years progress Lovecraft's letters become longer and more involved, filled with lengthy philosophical, historical, and literary disquis-
itions. But more importantly, the split between his fiction and his essays
narrows and finally disappears, so that in a story like "The Shadow out of
Time" (1934–35) the bulk of the narrative has the same forceful directness
as his letters, except as the climax approaches and Lovecraft gradually begins to modulate the tempo of the story and raise the tone to a higher
pitch, introducing emotion-laden words to prepare the reader for the cataclysmic conclusion.

What is even more remarkable is that the eighteenth-century pretence
is sloughed off even in his later poetry, and it is here that the letters to
Elizabeth Toldridge gain their great importance. She began to correspond
with Lovecraft in late 1928, just at the time when he was beginning to re-
think his entire theory of poetry prior to writing his late triumphs, "The
Ancient Track," "The Outpost," "The East India Brick Row," and *Fungi
from Yuggoth*. It was precisely her adherence to older norms in poetry that
impelled Lovecraft to clarify his own new poetics:

> As for the archaisms and inversions whose elimination I am advising—I
> really do not think you will miss them as much as you imagine. Certainly
> straightforward verse will soon come to 'feel like poetry' to you; since the
> poetic essence is not a superficial thing of outward trappings, but a deeply
> seated type of pattern and symbolic vision whose force is all the greater for
> simple and unbedizened formulation. So much more effective will you find
> this sincere way of writing, that in time it is the artificial and inverted sort
> of thing which you will consider ineffective and unpoetic. (*SL* 3.11–12)

Lovecraft could not more accurately have described what he was trying to do in the *Fungi from Yuggoth,* especially the poignant and autobiographical opening of "Background" (XXX):

> I never can be tied to raw, new things,
> For I first saw the light in an old town,
> Where from my window huddled roofs sloped down
> To a quaint harbour rich with visionings.

It is by now clear that Lovecraft's letters contain a mine of information; and before concluding with some observations on the place of his letters in his work it may be well to adumbrate their manifold importance to Lovecraft studies. Without the letters we would not know of Lovecraft's hand in the overwhelming bulk of his revisions, from C. M. Eddy's "Ashes" to Hazel Heald's "Out of the Aeons"; in recent years it is consultation of unpublished letters that has resulted in the addition of several "new" revisions—"Ashes," Duane Rimel's "The Tree on the Hill" and "The Disinterment," Henry S. Whitehead's "The Trap," R. H. Barlow's "The Night Ocean"—to the Lovecraft corpus. We learn countless details about his writing—dates of stories, poems, and essays; publications of works not otherwise known; sources and origins of works—as well as incalculable details about the particulars of his life. But more important, we learn of Lovecraft's keenness as a thinker—his absorption of ancient philosophy, of the philosophy of Nietzsche and the Social Darwinists, of Spengler's *Decline of the West* and Bertrand Russell's *Our Knowledge of the External World;* his powerful materialist stance—expressed in his letters much more cogently than in essays such as "Idealism and Materialism: A Reflection" (1919)—and the modifications of that stance in the light of Einstein, Planck, and the astrophysicists; his towering condemnations of conventional religion; his aesthetic theory, founded upon Poe and the Decadents and constantly refined into the doctrine of non-commercial "self-expression"; the increasing attention given in his later years to the problems of the world economy and of government, to the point that Lovecraft became a socialist who wished FDR to be yet bolder in his reforms. All these things we would know dimly and perhaps not at all without the letters: the long digressions on the political and economic system of the Old Ones and the Great Race in *At the Mountains of Madness* and "The Shadow out of Time" suddenly make sense, given Lovecraft's later interests; the glancing allusions to Einstein and to "intra-atomic action" in "The Shunned House" and "The Dreams in the Witch House" dimly mirror his reconciliation of materialism with modern indeterminacy; and, more profoundly, the increasingly cosmic scope of his later fiction is an echo of the expansion of his thought from his early absorption in the prettiness of the Queen Anne poets to his later interests in the nature of the world and the universe.

What, then, did Lovecraft's letters mean to him—and what do they mean to us? The first branch of the question is easier to answer than the second, for Lovecraft plainly declared that correspondence was essentially a substitute for conversation. Both early and late in his career he testified to the importance of correspondence to him:

> As to letters, my case is peculiar. I write such things exactly as easily and as rapidly as I would utter the same topics in conversation; indeed, epistolary expression is with me largely replacing conversation, as my condition of nervous prostration becomes more and more acute. I cannot bear to talk much now, and am becoming as silent as the Spectator himself! My loquacity extends itself on paper. (*SL* 1.52)

> As a person of very retired life, I met very few different sorts of people in youth—and was therefore exceedingly narrow and provincial. Later on, when literary activities brought me into touch with widely diverse types by mail—Texans like Robert E. Howard, men in Australia, New Zealand, &c., Westerners, Southerners, Canadians, people in old England, and assorted kinds of folk nearer at hand—I found myself opened up to dozens of points of view which would otherwise never have occurred to me. My understanding and sympathies were enlarged, and many of my social, political, and economic views were modified as a consequence of increased knowledge. Only correspondence could have effected this broadening; for it would have been impossible to have visited all the regions and met all the various types involved, while books can never talk back or discuss. (*SL* 4.389)

Many critics seem to detect, in this use of correspondence as vicarious conversation, one more indication of Lovecraft's eccentricity, as if he could not conduct a personal relationship except on paper. But with whom could he have discussed such philosophical and literary matters among his known acquaintances in Providence? Surely C. M. Eddy was not as stimulating as Clark Ashton Smith or Robert E. Howard, and Lovecraft's New York period—with the heyday of the Kalem Club and its regular meetings full of variegated discussion—belie the picture of him as tight-lipped recluse. Lovecraft's mind simply required the diverse stimulus of correspondence with all manner of associates, each of very different character and interests.

The only disadvantage in all this was that Lovecraft almost never corresponded with his intellectual equal, so that his own arguments and rebuttals—occasionally superficial or fallacious—can appear triumphs of logical reasoning. It was pitifully easy for Lovecraft to destroy Maurice Moe's or his opponent Wickenden's idealism (the latter in the *In Defence of Dagon* essay-letters); only Clark Ashton Smith, Alfred Galpin, possibly Robert E. Howard, and especially the little-known but brilliant amateur Ernest A. Edkins could hold a candle to Lovecraft in both intellectual capacity and argumentative skill; and with Smith he very rarely disputed. One cannot help wishing that Lovecraft could have corresponded with a true authority in some of the fields—philosophy, Colonial history, general literature—on which he held forth with such apparent authority. Certainly, in his later years when most of his correspondents could have been his sons, he had little trouble dispensing with the occultist leanings of Nils H. Frome, the incredibly erroneous views on sex of Woodburn Harris, or the elementary historical errors of Bernard Austin Dwyer. He might have had a little more trouble with T. E. Hulme's mysticism, and Bertrand Russell might not have been quite as sanguine about Lovecraft's modified late materialism (which involved a fundamental misunderstanding of quantum theory) as Lovecraft himself was.

To the charge—made frequently in recent years—that Lovecraft "wasted his time" writing so many letters we must respond more critically. The charge carries the hidden premise that, since Lovecraft is currently best known for his stories, he should have written more of them and fewer letters. This premise is questionable on several grounds. Lovecraft is certainly well known for his fiction now, but who is to say that that situation will persist in the future? The current literary status of Horace Walpole rests not upon *The Castle of Otranto* or his other fictions (now only of historical importance) but to the thousands of letters he wrote in his career— it is those letters that have been lavishly and painstakingly edited in a landmark 43-volume edition by Yale University Press. Thomas Gray is heralded equally as a poet and as an epistolarian, and William Cowper's letters now considerably outshine his conventional poetry in critical esteem. But even if Lovecraft continues to hold the attention of future generations with his stories (as, indeed, is very likely and entirely justified, for there are complexities and profundities in the fiction that scholars are only now reaching), the claim that Lovecraft "wasted his time" in his correspondence implies that we know better than Lovecraft what Lovecraft should have done with his life. But no one has the right to tell Lovecraft what to do: he led his life to suit himself, not us, and it is very clear that correspondence was very important to him; if he had never written any stories but only letters, it would certainly be our loss, but it would have been his prerogative. In any case, it is by no means certain that Lovecraft would have written more stories even had he curtailed his correspondence, for his fiction-writing was always a sporadic thing dependent upon mood, inspiration, and many other temperamental factors.

The world of Lovecraft's letters is almost inassimilably rich; one can re-read the letters indefinitely and find new things each time. The publication of his complete correspondence may be an unrealisable dream, but it is one worth keeping in our minds: the image of hundreds of bound volumes of letters, dwarfing to insignificance the dozen or so volumes of what would be his collected fiction, poetry, and essays, will make us comprehend the full literary and personal achievement of H. P. Lovecraft, the man who lived to write and wrote to live.

Lovecraft and the Films of His Day

H P. Lovecraft's opinion of film was not high. This fact should not be surprising: to one so devoted to the written word, the crude films of Lovecraft's early years could only engender a shudder of disgust. Moreover, his first love in the performing arts was drama, and on the whole he preferred the stage to the cinema. He wrote in 1934:

> I first saw a play at the age of 6. Later, when the cinema appeared as a separate institution (it had been part of the Keith vaudeville since 1898 or 1899), I attended it often with other fellows, but never took it seriously. By the time of the first cinema shows (March 1906, in Providence) I knew too much of literature and drama not to recognise the utter and unrelieved hokum of the moving picture. (*SL* 4.355)

Lovecraft was, however, a little disingenuous here, because his early letters actually testify to a considerable enjoyment of the films of the 1910s and 1920s—not merely horror or fantasy films, which he might be expected to enjoy, but comedies and melodramas as well. In 1915 he actually wrote a poem to Charlie Chaplin ("To Charlie of the Comics"), and in a later letter compares the merits of Chaplin and Douglas Fairbanks (*SL* 1.50–51). At this time he declared himself "a devotee of the motion picture," remarking that "Some modern films are really worth seeing, though when I first knew moving pictures their only value was to destroy time" (*SL* 1.18).

In 1917 occurred a peculiar episode. Lovecraft went to see a film, *The Image-Maker of Thebes*,[1] at Fay's Theatre in Providence. The theatre was offering a prize of $25 for the best review of the film, and Lovecraft decided to participate. He found the film very poor: ". . . a rough-hewn amateurish affair dealing with reincarnation in a pitifully feeble and hackneyed manner, containing not the slightest subtlety or technical skill in plot, directing, or setting" (*SL* 1.42–43). His review was very harsh, and yet it won the prize! Regrettably, the review was never published, and now appears to be lost.[2] It perhaps constitutes the only instance of film criticism by Lovecraft!

---

1. I have had difficulty finding any reliable information on this film. *The Motion Picture Guide, Vol. X: Silent Film 1910–1936* (Chicago: Cinebooks, Inc., 1986) lists no film of this title, although there is a 1917 film entitled *The Image Maker*.

2. Some years ago Marc A. Michaud and I attempted to locate the files of Fay's Theatre in Providence, but were unsuccessful.

By 1919 Lovecraft was professing that "I formerly attended the cinema quite frequently, but it is beginning to bore me" (*SL* 1.89). Nevertheless, he saw D. W. Griffith's *The Birth of a Nation* (1915) both as a stage play[3] and as a film (*SL* 1.89), and also read the book on which they were based, Thomas Dixon's *The Clansman* (1905). It must be admitted that Lovecraft's enjoyment of this film about the Ku Klux Klan in the years following the Civil War may well have stemmed from his agreement with the film's racialist bias.

The Image-Maker of Thebes may not have been the first "weird" or supernatural film Lovecraft saw; he earlier notes seeing the film version (1915) of George du Maurier's novel *Trilby*, although he remarks that "it seemed incomplete to me because I have seen the actual play, and have attached so much importance to the deep, fiendishly insinuating *voice* of Svengali" (*SL* 1.18). A later letter is very harsh concerning some of the great horror films of the day:

> As a thorough soporific I recommend the average popularly "horrible" play or cinema or radio dialogue. They are all the same—flat, hackneyed, synthetic, essentially atmosphereless jumbles of conventional shrieks and mutterings and superficial, mechanical situations. *The Bat* made me drowse back in the early 1920's—and last year an alleged *Frankenstein* on the screen *would* have made me drowse had not a posthumous sympathy for poor Mrs. Shelley made me see red instead. Ugh! And the screen *Dracula* in 1931—I saw the beginning of that in Miami, Fla.—but couldn't bear to watch it drag to its full term of dreariness, hence walked out into the fragrant tropic moonlight! (*SL* 4.154–55)

To those who have come to regard these films as "classics" in their own right, it must be remembered that the film medium was still new and unrecognised in Lovecraft's day, and that it had scarcely begun to show the subtlety and profundity of later works; as an aesthetic medium it was decidedly inferior to literature, and Lovecraft's response is by no means unusual or unexpected. It is from this perspective that we must interpret his comparison of the film version of Gustav Meyrink's *The Golem* with the original novel. Of the book he stated that it was "the most magnificent weird thing I've come across in aeons! The cinema of identical title in 1921 was a mere substitute using the name—with nothing of the novel in it" (*SL* 5.138). And yet, Lovecraft did find praise for the film version of *The Invisible Man* (1933): "Surprisingly good—might easily have been absurd, yet succeeded in being genuinely sinister" (*SL* 4.362). In an unpublished letter to August Derleth, Lovecraft says that he wanted to see the bizarre

---

3. See "In a Major Key," *The Conservative*, July 1915; reprinted in H. P. Lovecraft, *The Conservative*, ed. S. T. Joshi (West Warwick, RI: Necronomicon Press, 1990), p. 9.

Cabinet of Dr. Caligari (1921), but never did so.[4] And let us not forget his enthusiasm at seeing *The Phantom of the Opera* (1925) in New York:

> . . . what a spectacle it was!! It was about a *presence* haunting the great Paris opera house . . . but was developed so slowly that I actually fell asleep several times during the first part. Then the second part began—horror lifted its grisly visage—& I could not have been made drowsy by all the opiates under heaven! Ugh!!! The *face* that was revealed when the mask was pulled off . . . & the nameless legion of *things* that cloudily appeared beside & behind the owner of that face when the mob chased him into the river at last![5]

His diary reports a viewing of *The Lost World* (an adaptation of the Conan Doyle novel) on 6 October 1925, but there is no corresponding letter testifying to his reaction to this remarkable film, a landmark in the use of special effects in its depiction of dinosaurs in South America. One would like to think he would have appreciated the nightmarish futuristic visions of Fritz Lang's *Metropolis,* since they coincide so starkly with Lovecraft's own foreboding prophecies of a future controlled by soulless machines.

Perhaps Lovecraft did not approach films in the proper light, especially films that adapted existing literary works. He seems to have believed that the sole criterion of excellence in such works was the faithfulness of their adaptation of the original text. But a "film adaptation" is very much an adaptation—a transference of moods, images, and effects from one medium to another. Many have asserted that Lovecraft's own tales are "unadaptable" to film or any other medium; and in a sense that is true, if one assumes that such an adaptation will mechanically duplicate the effect of the written word on to the screen. Such an undertaking is futile from the start.

An entirely different type of film that Lovecraft found very stimulating was the historical film, especially those set in his beloved eighteenth century. In 1921 he noted that he had seen both the stage and the cinema version of *David Garrick,* based on a play by T. W. Robertson.[6] Of the cinema version Lovecraft remarks: "This was one of the finest scenic productions I ever saw—the eighteenth century and Dr. Johnson's day mirrored without flaw or anachronism. In matters of scenery the moving picture can of course leave the stage far behind; though this hardly atones for the lack of sound

---

4. "Too bad we both missed 'Dr. Caligari,' for it was by all accounts the best fantastic cinema ever produced." Lovecraft to August Derleth, 16 December 1926 (ms., State Historical Society of Wisconsin).

5. Lovecraft to Lillian D. Clark, 18 September 1925 (ms., JHL).

6. There were several film versions of this play: one in 1912, two in 1913, one in 1916, and one in 1928. Lovecraft could have seen any of the first four. The play dates to 1864.

and colour" (*SL* 1.127). Late in life Lovecraft saw several films of this kind. Interestingly, he enjoyed Cecil B. DeMille's *Cleopatra* (1934), stating that it "had excellent Roman scenes" (*SL* 5.100); evidently the daringly scanty attire worn by Claudette Colbert did not offend his usually prudish sensibilities.

But the historical film that Lovecraft enjoyed above all others was *Berkeley Square* (1933), based on a play by John Balderston. This film is a sort of historical fantasy in which a man of the twentieth century somehow merges his personality with that of his eighteenth-century ancestor. Lovecraft saw the film four times in late 1933 and praised it highly, largely because it echoed some of his deepest sentiments:

> It is the most weirdly perfect embodiment of my own moods and pseudo-memories that I have ever seen—for all my life I have felt as if I might wake up out of this dream of an idiotic Victorian age and insane jazz age into the reality of 1760 or 1770 or 1780 . . . the age of the white steeples and fan-lighted doorways of the ancient hill, and of the long-s'd books of the old dark attic trunk-room at 454 Angell St. God Save the King! (*SL* 4.364)

In a recent article[7] Darrell Schweitzer argues for the possible influence of this film on Lovecraft's own time-travel story, "The Shadow out of Time" (1934–35).

But a much earlier influence of film upon Lovecraft's stories can be cited. In the prose-poem "Nyarlathotep" (1920) the mysterious Egyptian figure of the title presents strange pictures "shadowed on a screen." In a letter describing the dream that inspired the story, Lovecraft remarks that among the exhibitions in Nyarlathotep's presentation was "a horrible—possibly prophetic—cinema reel" (*SL* 1.161). This is certainly the earliest use of explicit film imagery in Lovecraft; and his later stories show many signs of such imagery. The whole issue of Lovecraft and movies has yet to be explored in detail; but in spite of his generally low opinion of the films of his day, it can be argued that film played no insignificant role in his life. May we not, then, expect that someday film makers will repay the favour by producing an adaptation of Lovecraft's work that is worthy of the name?

---

7. "H. P. Lovecraft's Favorite Movie," *Lovecraft Studies* Nos. 19/20 (Fall 1989): 23–25, 27.

Lovecraft's Library

The reasons for studying H. P. Lovecraft's personal library may not be immediately evident to the casual reader. To be sure, there is some intrinsic curiosity value in knowing that he owned a 1567 black-letter edition of Ovid, or a complete file of *Weird Tales, The Fantasy Fan,* and other now fabulously rare journals of fantasy fiction, or several issues of *The Rhode Island Almanac,* by a writer (or, rather, a series of writers) disguised by the classic Augustan pseudonym of Isaac Bickerstaff, a pseudonym once used by Lovecraft himself.[1] And yet, a listing of Lovecraft's library is far more than a farrago of *curiosa;* for Lovecraft, like Samuel Johnson (to mention only one other whose library has been catalogued), was so thoroughly a man of letters that his library—not greatly distinguished from a bibliophilic point of view—was an essential part of his life and thought: it shaped his intellectual growth; it was one of his most prized possessions; it was a storehouse of ideas that found expression in all phases of his literary work. To understand the man, we must first understand his books.

Amidst the glaring and outré covers that adorn the paperbound editions of his stories—now distributed in the millions of copies throughout the world—it is often forgotten that Providence-born Howard Phillips Lovecraft did far more than write the greatest horror fiction since Poe. Poems, essays, and particularly letters would occupy a far greater proportion of his collected writings than his admittedly great fiction; indeed, his letters may perhaps be his greatest achievement, so full as they are of a stupefyingly diverse erudition. If nothing else, he wrote more letters than almost anyone in the twentieth century and, perhaps, in all literary history: an estimated 80,000 letters emerged from his pen, although probably fewer than 10,000 now survive. The letters alone may confirm that Lovecraft, aside from being Rhode Island's greatest native writer, might occupy—or come to occupy—a significant place in modern intellectual history. That he was, intellectually, highly gifted is beyond doubt: from the age of four to his death at forty-six he was an omnivorous reader, thus abundantly making up for the missed opportunity (because of poor health) of attending Brown University. Fittingly for a man who had not the world but the cosmos for his subject of study, his reading tastes were bewilderingly wide, and his li-

---

1. In Lovecraft's debate with the astrologer J. F. Hartmann in the Providence *Evening News,* September–December 1914 (cf. *SL* 1.4–5); now rpt. in *Science vs. Charlatanry,* ed. S. T. Joshi and Scott Connors (Strange Co., 1979).

brary in large measure reflects the *crème de la crème* of his readings—those books that he was satisfied not merely with reading, but with owning.

It is therefore regrettable that a complete listing of Lovecraft's library is not available to us; instead, fewer than 1000 of his 1500 or so volumes have hitherto been located and catalogued. Though it is possible to estimate the nature of the missing portions of the library, and though certain areas have surely been catalogued with comparative thoroughness, there is nonetheless little chance that these lacunae will ever be filled. To begin with, it seems that many of Lovecraft's volumes on science and philosophy are absent from the present list: of the books by Darwin, Haeckel, Huxley, Margaret Murray, and many others to which Lovecraft frequently referred in his letters there is hardly a trace (possibly he consulted many of these only in libraries); nor do we find much by Santayana, Bertrand Russell, Hobbes, Spinoza, and the other thinkers whom Lovecraft admired. Volumes of history—especially modern history—seem, too, in rather short supply.

But on the positive side we are aware of a great many volumes that Lovecraft often proclaimed often to be dear to his heart. In particular we note the profusion of Greek and Latin classics, books on ancient history and civilisation, English poetry and belles lettres (particularly of the eighteenth century), New England history and antiquities, and—most important of all to the literary scholar—his holdings of weird fiction, which may be considered virtually complete thanks to the availability of a list in Lovecraft's own hand—"Weird &c. Items in Library of H. P. Lovecraft"— which he prepared late in life, evidently "for the benefit of distant members of the 'weird fiction gang' [i.e., his literary correspondents] who wish to borrow spectral volumes not obtainable in their home-town bibliothecae" (*SL* 5.243–44).

Lovecraft's poverty precluded extensive campaigns of book-buying, and a good many of the volumes in his library—particularly those of eighteenth- and early nineteenth-century imprint—were holdovers from his family library. This may explain the profusion of works by Dickens, Thackeray (who "induceth drowsiness" [*SL* 1.73] in Lovecraft), Jane Austen, and others (in particular the totally un-Lovecraftian romances of Mrs Mulock) in which he found little interest. Many other volumes—beginning, perhaps, with the presentation of Lang's *Arabian Nights* by his mother in 1898—were gifts, as the inscriptions on the volumes by Donald Wandrei, Walter J. Coates, Samuel Loveman, and others testify. A small number must have been acquired gratis as a consequence of Lovecraft's being a contributor to the volume: thus we find the Christine Campbell Thomson anthologies published by Selwyn & Blount, Hammett's *Creeps by Night,* Harré's *Beware After Dark!,* and others. But a substantial residue was purchased by Lovecraft himself, either upon publication or through used-book stores, where, as he remarked, "one can obtain astonishing bargains" (*SL* 2.287).

In many ways Lovecraft's library was an enviable one. He possessed a remarkable collection of Augustan and early Romantic poetry, encompassing both the great—Keats, Shelley, Coleridge, Thomson, Gray—and the near-great—Shenstone, Beattie, Trumbull, Crabbe. His statement that "I picked up my peculiar style from Addison, Steele, Johnson, and Gibbon" (*SL* 1.11) is confirmed by his significant holdings of these and other eighteenth-century masters of English prose.

Although Lovecraft knew a smattering of many tongues—though not, as Zealia Bishop would have us believe, of African dialects!—he could read only English and Latin fluently; so that what volumes of French, Italian, German, and Greek literature he owned were almost exclusively in translation. (His possession of Baudelaire's *Lettres* in French was the result of a gift.) Moreover, many of his Latin volumes were in translation or in bilingual editions with interlinear translations (a technique upon which Latinists now look with horror). Needless to say, he owned those celebrated translations of the Latin and Greek classics which have in turn themselves become classics—Dryden's *Aeneid*, Pope's *Odyssey* and *Iliad*, Garth's Ovid, Dryden's Plutarch (revised by Clough), Chapman's *Hymns of Homer*, Murphy's Tacitus, and the like. His volumes on ancient history and civilisation were largely high-school or college textbooks, some rather shoddy and most now outdated; but Lovecraft never claimed to be a specialist, and his knowledge in this field, as in so many others, was admirable for a layman.

The few science books in his library of whose existence we know—largely astronomy, biology, and chemistry—are almost without exception textbooks or general, non-technical manuals. Lovecraft's disinclination for mathematics prevented him from penetrating the mysteries of astronomy and physics as deeply as he would have liked; perhaps a fortunate circumstance, else we might have seen competent if dry astronomy volumes from him rather than the brilliant weird fiction by which he is now achieving a tardy if universal fame. It was, in fact, precisely because Lovecraft did not become a specialist in any single field that he could coordinate his multifarious knowledge and distil it into his fiction and essays: without being a geologist he could write such a convincing narrative as *At the Mountains of Madness;* without being a specialist in New England history, he could pen such a tale as *The Case of Charles Dexter Ward*. But had he been a scholar either in one field or the other, we might perhaps never have seen one or the other of these tales. True enough, his knowledge can be picked apart and criticised by any specialist; but could that specialist boast the catholicity of taste, the inveterate curiosity in so many academic fields, and the impressive integration of this knowledge into a single and coherent philosophy such as Lovecraft achieved? Although the concept of the Renaissance man may be becoming increasingly obsolete with the bewildering expansion of knowledge in all fields, it is hard to doubt that Lovecraft was the latest to attempt and, perhaps, to succeed in filling that role.

But there was perhaps one field in which Lovecraft could justifiably claim authority—weird fiction; for it is the belief of many that Lovecraft's essay on *Supernatural Horror in Literature* is the finest study of its kind, providing not only a succinct history of the genre from antiquity to the present, but also guidelines toward its aesthetic bases and a defence of its worth as a literary form. Lovecraft not only read all types of weird literature, from the best to the worst, but sought to establish a collection encompassing his personal favourites in the field. It is not surprising that Dunsany, Machen, Poe, Shiel, Bierce, Hawthorne, Blackwood, and others who significantly influenced Lovecraft's own writings are heavily represented in his library; but these are just the tip of the iceberg of his holdings. Such tantalisingly obscure volumes as Leonard Cline's *The Dark Chamber*, J. Provand Webster's *The Oracle of Baal*, Henri Béraud's *Lazarus*, James De Mille's *A Strange Manuscript Found in a Copper Cylinder*, and others filled his shelves; and their perusal might unearth literary influences hitherto unknown to scholars.

Lovecraft the *littérateur*, then, cannot be separated from his library; it was as integral to his being as the New England landscape he adored. That Lovecraft would "part with all my furniture and squat and sleep on the floor before I'd let go of the 1500 or so books I possess" (*SL* 2.287) is eloquent enough testimony to a man for whom books were, not an evasion from the "real" world, but the essence of that real world itself: reality may comprise not only the prosiness of daily existence, but the thoughts of the great minds that have, perhaps more than the conquests of war or the complexities of political manoeuvring, shaped our civilisation. It is this reality that Lovecraft devoted a lifetime in seeking.

II. Lovecraft the Writer and Thinker

Autobiography in Lovecraft

O n a certain level we can all accept Maurice Lévy's dictum that "in most of Lovecraft's tales, the main character—whether his name be Charles Dexter Ward, Edward Derby, Olney, Malone, or simply 'I'—*is* the author" (Lévy 118). This fact, Lévy contends, allows us to assume that Lovecraft is vicariously attempting to bestow the horror in his tales upon himself. While there are many points of validity in this interpretation, one flaw emerges in the obvious fact that Lovecraft's characters are autobiographical in radically differing degrees. There are some tales where the character or characters are only superficially autobiographical; where they are given various external characteristics that are not central to the tale as a whole. On the other hand, other tales gain some of their poignancy and significance precisely through the central character's sharing important attitudes with his author. An exploration of the relative degrees of autobiography present in Lovecraft's fiction may help us the better to understand his oft-misunderstood theory of characterisation.

In many of Lovecraft's tales one or the other of the characters is given a trait shared by Lovecraft himself. The narrator of "The Shadow over Innsmouth" is essentially a colourless character—since the main emphasis of the tale is not on what he *is* but on what he will *become*—but has certain idiosyncrasies that were Lovecraft's own. He embarks upon a tour of New England for "sightseeing, antiquarian, and genealogical" (*DH* 305) purposes; so, too, did Lovecraft visit many antiquarian (Marblehead, Portsmouth, Salem) and ancestral (Foster and Greene, R.I.) sites in his life. When the narrator, forced to stay in Innsmouth for the night, dines in a restaurant, he declares: "A bowl of vegetable soup with crackers was enough for me" (*DH* 342). Clearly he is reflecting Lovecraft's own parsimonious diet. (He is, indeed, one of the few characters in Lovecraft's fiction who partakes of any food at all. Another is Albert Wilmarth in "The Whisperer in Darkness," whose eating of a meal is similarly crucial to the development of the plot.) A still obscurer reference is the narrator's description of the Order of Dagon Hall with the "black and gold sign on the pediment" (*DH* 318). From a letter we learn that "I never liked any other colour combination so well as *black-and-gold* . . . perhaps because that was the scheme in the front hall of my birthplace, 454 Angell Street" (*SL* 2.165). Whether the mention of "black and gold" is even a conscious reference to his favourite colours can certainly be doubted; it only underscores the relatively insignificant nature of the autobiographical elements in the tale. The narrator is not even important save as a conveyer of data, as the victim of the pursuit by the entities of Innsmouth, and as the subject of the final twist where he himself becomes one with the monsters. The narrative clearly centres upon the horrors at Innsmouth—the result of an unholy inbreeding—and the narrator is merely the vehicle for the exposition of this theme.

Elsewhere the autobiographical element is equally trivial. In one amusing passage in "Herbert West—Reanimator" the narrator tells that West "secretly sneered at my occasional martial enthusiasms and censures of supine neutrality" (*D* 142). Here we see Lovecraft ridiculing the militaristic attitudes he expressed during World War I, exhibited in such essays as "The League," "The Renaissance of Manhood," and "At the Root," and in such poems as "The Peace Advocate." The cause of temperance, which initially found Lovecraft a staunch supporter ("A Remarkable Document," "Liquor and Its Friends," "Temperance Song"), is similarly undermined hilariously in the celebrated drinking song (the manuscript of which bears the title "Gaudeamus" = "Let us delight") in "The Tomb." But neither of these two autobiographical touches is at all central to the two stories in question.

In other tales certain autobiographical elements hold somewhat more importance to the theme of the tale, but cannot be considered significant enough to warrant the conclusion that the tale hinges upon these elements. In "The Tomb" the central character certainly shares Lovecraft's antiquarianism, but this antiquarianism is born only of his unusual fascination with death. To be sure, the narrator is "temperamentally unfitted for the formal studies and social recreations of my acquaintances" (*D* 9), as Lovecraft perhaps was, and spent "my youth and adolescence in ancient and little-known books, and in roaming the fields and groves of the regions near my ancestral home," as Lovecraft certainly did; but the narrator ultimately resembles not Lovecraft but some of Poe's characters, whom Lovecraft described aptly as "melancholy, intellectual, highly sensitive, capricious, introspective, isolated, and sometimes slightly mad" (*D* 379). The whole tale is saturated with Poesque elements—the narrator's remark that he is a "dreamer and visionary" echoes phrases found in Poe's tales, as in "Berenice" where the narrator declares that his "line has been called a race of visionaries"—to the point that Lovecraft's character never achieves true vitality.

The antiquarianism so significant to Lovecraft's personality is utilised with still greater strength and with much less affectation in *The Case of Charles Dexter Ward*. The autobiographical details in the novel—the external elements of Ward's character, the careful descriptions of Providence sites—are almost too numerous to mention: especially striking is Ward's return home to Providence from his three-year trip to Europe, which so parallels Lovecraft's own return to his native city from two years in New York; and the fact that Lovecraft transcribed into the novel, almost verbatim, certain passages from his letters describing Providence[1] clearly shows that he incorporated many details of his personal existence into the tale. But in the final analysis these details remain only details. Ward's antiquarianism is only a device to introduce the machinations of the real central character, Joseph Curwen; Ward becomes only the hapless victim whose death is in the end avenged by Dr Willett. Only in random passages do we sense that Lovecraft is drawing authentic parallels with incidents in his own life and with ideas central to his thought.

Two other ambivalent cases are "Cool Air" and "The Outsider." That the former was, at least in part, inspired by Lovecraft's inability to stand the cold seems undeniable; but from this nucleus he has created a plot which ties in with an important theme in his work: the Faustian theme of questing for knowledge that will conquer death (manifested in wholly different ways in *The Case of Charles Dexter Ward*, "The Thing on the Doorstep," and "Herbert West—Reanimator"). The autobiographical inspiration is entirely dwarfed by this theme, and cannot be said to be of importance to the tale proper; just as this same element has even less importance in *At the Mountains of Madness*, although here again it could have partly served as inspiration. As for "The Outsider," it is certainly tempting to look upon the central character as embodying Lovecraft's view of himself; and an attractive autobiographical interpretation may be derived from the possibility (suggested by Dirk W. Mosig) that the tale was written not long after the death of Lovecraft's mother in May 1921. Unfortunately, no concrete evidence to corroborate this theory has emerged.[2] But the central character's unhappy

---

1. Compare particularly a passage from the letter to the *Providence Sunday Journal* of 5 October 1926 (*SL* 2.75) with the description of South Water Street in Chap. 1, Sec. 2 of *The Case of Charles Dexter Ward* (*MM* 108).

2. The tale must have been written after the writing of "The Quest of Iranon" (28 February 1921; cf. A.Ms., JHL) and before that of "The Other Gods" (14 August 1921; cf. A.Ms., JHL). Lovecraft never hints at the date of writing in any letters seen by me. There may even be slight evidence that the tale was written *before* the death of his mother. On 23 April 1921 he wrote to Rheinhart Kleiner (*SL* 1.128): "I am picking up a new style lately—running to pathos as well as horror. The best thing I have yet done is 'The Quest of Iranon'." Now a "new style" cannot consist of merely one tale; and the only other tale written in this period that can claim both pathos and horror is "The Outsider." It could then have been written between 28 February and 23 April 1921. The fact that Lovecraft does not mention it in the let-

childhood does not at all find an echo in Lovecraft, who always looked back with fondness to his childhood, unusual though it may have been; so that he once declared: "Adulthood is hell" (*SL* 1.106). The narrator's discovery of his own monstrous appearance does seem to relate to the fact that Lovecraft's mother deemed him "ugly" and "hideous"; there seems no denying that he had a severe inferiority complex about his facial appearance, most poignantly embodied in what he once said to his future wife: "How can any woman love a face like mine?"[3] Nevertheless, "The Outsider," like "The Tomb," is so clearly derivative of Poe (as Lovecraft himself admitted[4]) that it may not be possible to draw many authentic parallels with Lovecraft's own life and character. The first four paragraphs of the tale—which seem to contain many autobiographical elements—are almost a paraphrase of the opening paragraphs of "Berenice."

In "The Shadow out of Time" occurs an autobiographical element that, though intriguing, is merely incidental to the tale. Nathaniel Peaslee suffered his "amnesia" from 14 May 1908 to 27 September 1913 (*DH* 370, 374); can we not parallel this with Lovecraft's own hermitry during this time? In 1908 his "health completely gave way" (*SL* 1.40–41), and he did not recover until late 1913, when he began to engage in his celebrated epistolary battles in the *Argosy* and subsequently joined amateur journalism. This coincidence of dates is, as mentioned, not at all central to the tale's theme, but may be seen as an interesting "in-joke" on Lovecraft's part—a joke which none but he and his closest associates could understand.[5]

In many early stories, however (and in some later ones as well), the central characters are imbued with attitudes so central to Lovecraft's thought that these tales read virtually like fictionalised essays. The celebrated and bitter opening of "He," recording Lovecraft's increasing hatred of New York—with its "squalor and alienage, and the noxious elephantiasis of climbing, spreading stone . . . and the throngs of people

---

ter to Kleiner may simply imply that he did not believe it to be as good a tale as "The Quest of Iranon." In any case, it is certainly possible that the stress caused by his mother's hospitalisation may have inspired the tale, as it inspired the bitter poem "Despair," even though her death (as a result of a gall bladder operation) was quite unexpected. For this autobiographical interpretation see Dirk W. Mosig, "The Four Faces of 'The Outsider,'" *Nyctalops* 2, No. 2 (July 1974): 3–10. Mosig, incidentally, ultimately rejects the autobiographical interpretation.

3. *The Private Life of H. P. Lovecraft* (West Warwick, RI: Necronomicon Press, 1985), p. 12.

4. "It represents my literal though unconscious imitation of Poe at its very height" (*SL* 3.379).

5. I owe this observation to Donald R. Burleson.

that seethed through the flume-like streets" (*D* 231)—certainly comes from Lovecraft's heart, and the narrator's fleeing this garish reality for the night and the past certainly reflects his disgust for the metropolis' uncouth modernity. Especially poignant is the narrator's concluding remark that he has now "gone home to the pure New England lanes up which fragrant sea-winds sweep at evening" (*D* 239), when in fact Lovecraft would not return to Providence until nine months after the writing of "He": there can hardly be a clearer expression of a wish-fulfilment fantasy than this. "The Horror at Red Hook," written only a week before "He" in early August 1925, also reflects Lovecraft's loathing of New York, but this time not directly through the central character, Thomas Malone, whose mysticism ("Daily life had for him come to be a phantasmagoria of macabre shadow-studies; now glittering and leering with concealed rottenness as in Beardsley's best manner, now hinting terrors behind the commonest shapes and objects as in the subtler and less obvious work of Gustave Doré" [*D* 242]) Lovecraft certainly did not share. Indeed, although Malone "had the Celt's far vision of weird and hidden things" (*D* 241), Lovecraft makes the following remark in a late letter: "Oddly—for one whose Devonian and Welsh and Cornish lines imply a good proportion of Celtic blood—my weird imagination is not at all Celtic. I not only lack but dislike the Celt's whimsical angle toward the unreal world."[6] One wonders, in fact, whether the character of Malone might not have been based upon the Welshman Arthur Machen, whose work Lovecraft had discovered in 1923. The engulfing of the poetic Malone in the filth and decadence of Brooklyn might be Lovecraft's fictional parallel to Machen's hard years in London (as recorded in his autobiographies) and to the similar experiences of Machen's autobiographical character Lucian Taylor in *The Hill of Dreams*.

In "The Horror at Red Hook" the autobiographical element is manifested only through the setting, for which Lovecraft has drawn upon his own travels and residences. Of this same type are many of the tales set either in Providence ("The Shunned House," "The Call of Cthulhu," *The Case of Charles Dexter Ward*, "The Haunter of the Dark") or in New England ("The Picture in the House," "The Festival," "In the Vault," "Pickman's Model," "The Dunwich Horror," "The Whisperer in Darkness"). It is well known that Lovecraft based "Pickman's Model" upon an actual site in Boston, while of "The Festival" he wrote: "It formed a sincere attempt to capture the feeling that Marblehead gave me when I saw it for the first time—at sunset under the snow, Dec. 17, 1922" (*SL* 4.275). In the present

---

6. Lovecraft to R. H. Barlow, 13 June 1936 (ms., JHL).

study, however, I shall restrict myself to the analysis of the autobiographical element in Lovecraft's fiction as manifested by his characters.

In "Celephaïs" the central character bears important traits found in Lovecraft himself. Not only is King Kuranes "the last of his family," with "his money and lands gone," but "he did not care for the ways of people about him, but preferred to dream and write of his dreams." Moreover, Kuranes "was not modern, and did not think like others who wrote. Whilst they strove to strip from life its embroidered robes of myth, and to shew in naked ugliness the foul thing that is reality, Kuranes sought it in fancy and illusion, and found it on his very doorstep, amid the nebulous memories of childhood tales and dreams" (D 60). Not only is this a faithful recording of Lovecraft's attitudes (at this stage of his life, at any rate), but it is also the nucleus for Randolph Carter's great quest for his "sunset city," told in *The Dream-Quest of Unknown Kadath* and "The Silver Key." Moreover, it is precisely the personality of King Kuranes that engenders the events recorded in "Celephaïs"; so that it can truly be said that the autobiographical element is pivotal to the tale.

"The Thing on the Doorstep" is the tale where Lovecraft perhaps mined the greatest amount of material from his own life. With some oddities which we must consider later, the character of Edward Derby certainly emerges as that of Lovecraft himself:

> Perhaps his private education and coddled seclusion had something to do with his premature flowering. As an only child, he had organic weaknesses which startled his doting parents and caused them to keep him closely chained to their side. He was never allowed but without his nurse, and seldom had a chance to play unconstrainedly with other children. All this doubtless fostered a strange, secretive inner life in the boy, with imagination as his one avenue of freedom. (*DH* 277)[7]

Later on it is written: "Edward's mother died when he was thirty-four, and for months he was incapacitated by some odd psychological malady." Lovecraft's mother died when he was thirty-one; he too was psychologically disturbed for a long period following. "Afterward he seemed to feel a sort of grotesque exhilaration, as if of partial escape from some unseen bondage. He began to mingle in the more 'advanced' college set despite his middle age" (*DH* 279). This last detail may perhaps be paralleled with Lovecraft's frequent trips to New York after his mother's death (his first trip to the metropolis was in April 1922) and his friendship with such sophisticates as Frank Belknap Long, Samuel Loveman, Alfred Galpin, and

---

7. Steven J. Mariconda has suggested to me that even this passage may not be strictly autobiographical, but could be an allusion to Frank Belknap Long.

even—sporadically—Hart Crane. In the character of Asenath Waite we may trace the over-possessive and domineering nature that made up the personalities of both his wife Sonia and his mother. In all this Lovecraft reveals an acute ability at self-psychoanalysis; and his noting of significant connexions between Derby's affection for his mother and for Asenath (hence Lovecraft's mother and Sonia) anticipates the views of many recent critics. Although, as mentioned previously, the theme of the tale involves the unholy prolongation of life through superhuman means, the philosophical message that marriage is not a healthy institution—at least for such a one as Lovecraft or Derby—is clear. It is expressed in a different context in "The Horror at Red Hook."

There remains one group of tales whose autobiographical elements have yet to be examined. These are the so-called Randolph Carter stories. While it may be a truism to say that Carter is Lovecraft, it seems to have gone unnoticed that the personality of Carter differs in every one of the four (or five) tales involving him. The most that can be said is that Carter embodies various aspects of Lovecraft's character in each of the tales. The least significant tale, from the autobiographical context, is "The Statement of Randolph Carter." Since this tale is simply the transcription of a dream, the characters are not at all important; instead, Lovecraft was attempting to capture the images of horror presented by his dream. Carter is given some of Lovecraft's external characteristics—most particularly "frail nerves" (*MM* 286)—only as a plot device and because Lovecraft himself filled the role of Carter in his dream, just as Samuel Loveman filled that of Harley Warren. The autobiographical element is certainly not significant to the tale.[8]

In "The Unnamable" (often inexplicably ignored as one of the Randolph Carter tales) the precisely opposite circumstance holds true. Here no physical characteristics of either character are described, but only their respective attitudes as they debate the merit of the weird tale. The story is actually a significant enough statement of Lovecraft's aesthetic principles, though often the language is couched in a Biercian cynicism and satire which slightly lessen the seriousness of the message through exaggeration. Carter, here the author of weird fiction, is certainly Lovecraft; but who is Joel Manton?[9] It must clearly be Maurice W. Moe. Manton is "prin-

---

8. Similarly, in "The Hound," the character St John is modelled upon Rheinhart Kleiner (whom Lovecraft often referred to as a descendant of Henry St John, Viscount Bolingbroke), but his personality—which is hardly described—is wholly unimportant to the tale, as it seems more intent on displaying Poesque rhetoric than on making any serious parallels with Lovecraft's life or with that of his associate.

9. The name might perhaps have been derived from Bierce, the character of whose "The Middle Toe of the Right Foot" is named Manton; cf. *Supernatural Horror in*

cipal of the East High School" (*D* 196); Moe taught English at West Division High School in Milwaukee. Manton believes that "We know things . . . only through our five senses or our religious intuitions" (*D* 196); Lovecraft frequently engaged in arguments with Moe over religion, once declaring nastily: "Perhaps it is better to be near-sighted and orthodox like Mo[e], trusting all to a Divine Providence, R. I." (*SL* 1.57). "The Unnamable" is not so much a story as a fictionalised essay; and thus resembles such of Poe's works as "The Imp of the Perverse" or "The Premature Burial." It is true, however, that the tale does not fit as well into what has come to be the "Randolph Carter cycle" (never so termed by Lovecraft) as the other four tales involving him; it merely presents certain of his aesthetic attitudes that are more fully developed in the three succeeding tales.

The chronology of the next Randolph Carter tales is somewhat confused, since it appears that "The Silver Key" was written before the writing (or, at any rate, before the completion) of *The Dream-Quest of Unknown Kadath*, although the former records events occurring to Carter subsequent to those in the latter. This can only indicate that Lovecraft certainly had a clear idea of the denouement of the *Dream-Quest*, although August Derleth curiously wrote that he seemed to have "had no very clear plan" for the novel.[10] Certainly, Carter's quest for his "sunset city" and his discovery of it in the memories of his childhood find significant echoes in Lovecraft's thought, although it can hardly be imagined that very many of the episodic, odyssey-like incidents throughout the novel (often told with an unwonted tongue-in-cheek humour) have any autobiographical significance. The more concise and serious (and bitterly cynical) "Silver Key" returns to the central theme of "Celephaïs" and the *Dream-Quest*, but there are of course many details of Carter's life that certainly find no echo in Lovecraft's own: Lovecraft never attempted to find solace in religion (even if to be repelled by it), nor to "taste . . . modern freedoms" (*MM* 388) (unless we see in this a dim allusion to his period of decadent sophistication in the 1920s); instead, Carter's sampling of these various aspects of life are obvious symbols meant to show "how shallow, fickle, and meaningless all human aspirations are" (*MM* 387). "The Silver Key" is still less of a story than "The Unnamable," and is as close to a philosophical allegory as anything in Lovecraft.

Carter completes his metamorphosis from trivial character ("The Statement of Randolph Carter") to mouthpiece for Lovecraft's ideas ("The Unnamable") to pure symbol (*The Dream-Quest of Unknown Kadath*, "The Silver Key") in "Through the Gates of the Silver Key." Being an artificial

---

Literature (*D* 386). There is also a Manton Street in Providence.

10. "H. P. Lovecraft's Novels," in Lovecraft's *At the Mountains of Madness and Other Novels* (Sauk City, WI: Arkham House, 1964), p. x.

collaborative effort forced upon Lovecraft by E. Hoffmann Price, the tale is somewhat lacking in unity and is clumsy in structure, although containing some of the most superbly cosmic writing in all Lovecraft's fiction. Here Carter wavers between a mere device for the conveyance of the central philosophical message and a strikingly animated figure, showing more vigour than almost any other Lovecraft character save perhaps Thomas Malone, the central character of "The Shadow over Innsmouth," and Carter himself in the *Dream-Quest.* In neither of these guises does Carter reveal either a similarity to Lovecraft or to his persona as sketched in other of the Randolph Carter tales. Thus, as we have seen, the statement that "Carter is Lovecraft" must be severely qualified; applicable to the first four Randolph Carter tales in significantly different ways, and evidently applicable to the last tale not at all.

At this point we must consider some curiosities in Lovecraft's descriptions of some of the characters whom we have discussed above. Let us return first to "The Thing on the Doorstep." If we have satisfactorily determined that Edward Derby is Lovecraft, what then are we to make of this remark: "He [Derby] was the most phenomenal child scholar I have known" (*DH* 277)? Would Lovecraft have been so arrogant as to have written such a thing about himself? It hardly seems likely. Yet his early letters reveal a great admiration for the precocity of his associate Alfred Galpin. "He is intellectually *exactly like me* save in degree. In degree he is immensely my superior," Lovecraft wrote in 1921 (*SL* 1.128); and in 1923 he called Galpin "the most brilliant, accurate, steel-cold intellect I have ever encountered" (*SL* 1.256). Galpin was Lovecraft's junior by eleven years, just as Derby is eight years younger than Daniel Upton, the narrator of "The Thing on the Doorstep." Moreover, Galpin was in his youth somewhat susceptible to female charms: Lovecraft's pastoral poems involving the character "Damon" (i.e., Galpin) all tell of Damon's ensnarement at the hands of various beauteous nymphs.[11] The play *Alfredo* (whose central character is obviously Galpin) also concerns this theme, which ties in with Derby's later involvement with Asenath Waite.

Yet this identification of Galpin with certain of Derby's traits raises some further curiosities: Galpin certainly never wrote "verse of a sombre, fantastic, almost morbid cast" (*DH* 277), nor did he publish a volume of verse, *Azathoth and Other Horrors,* at the age of eighteen. But did not Clark Ashton Smith, Lovecraft's associate since 1922, create a stir by the publication of *The Star-Treader and Other Poems* in 1912, when he was nineteen? Moreover, it is mentioned that Derby "was a close correspondent of the

---

11. Cf. Galpin's "Memories of a Friendship" (1959), in *Lovecraft Remembered,* ed. Peter Cannon (Sauk City, WI: Arkham House, 1998), p. 165.

notorious Baudelairean poet Justin Geoffrey, who . . . died in a madhouse in 1926" (*DH* 277). Now Smith was a close associate of George Sterling, who, curiously, died by suicide in 1926. The figure of Justin Geoffrey was, however, the creation of Robert E. Howard, in "The Black Stone" (1931); and the date of his death as given by Lovecraft does seem to tally with that supplied by Howard (who mentions that Geoffrey died five years previously), so it appears to be a fortuitous coincidence that Geoffrey and Sterling died in the same year. Derby, in any event, seems to have been an interesting amalgam of Lovecraft, Galpin, and Smith, and perhaps also Samuel Loveman or Frank Belknap Long, whose extreme sensitivity and shyness is shared by Derby. While Derby's basic personality can be said to be Lovecraft's, he also owns some traits and surface details of Lovecraft's associates.

Turning now to "The Silver Key," we find some equally curious descriptions of Randolph Carter:

> Then he began once more the writing of books, which he had left off when dreams first failed him. But here, too, was there no satisfaction or fulfilment; for the touch of earth was upon his mind, and he could not think of lovely things as he had done of yore. Ironic humour dragged down all the twilight minarets he reared, and the earthy fear of improbability blasted all the delicate and amazing flowers in his faery gardens. The convention of assumed pity spilt mawkishness on his characters, while the myth of an important reality and significant human events and emotions debased all his high fantasy into thin-veiled allegory and cheap social satire. His new novels were successful as his old ones had never been; and because he knew how empty they must be to please an empty herd, he burned them and ceased his writing. They were very graceful novels, in which he urbanely laughed at the dreams he lightly sketched; but he saw that their sophistication had sapped all their life away. (*MM* 389–90)

This certainly does not sound like a description of Lovecraft's own work, since he always claimed that he wrote only for "self-expression" in spite of whatever unconscious corrupting influences were gained through incessant writing for the pulp market. Lovecraft certainly used "ironic humour" very infrequently in his fiction: it appears only in "The Silver Key" itself, "The Strange High House in the Mist" (with similar Juvenalian bitterness), and in a few other tales. But if the description does not apply to Lovecraft, to whom could it apply if it is not meant as only an element in the tale? Note this comment on the work of Lord Dunsany written in 1936:

> Of course Dunsany is uneven, and his later work . . . cannot be compared to his early productions. As he gained in age and sophistication, he lost in freshness and simplicity. He was ashamed to be uncritically naive, and be-

gan to step aside from his tales and visibly smile at them even as they unfolded. Instead of remaining what the true fantaisiste must be—a child in a child's world of dream—he became anxious to shew that he was really an adult good-naturedly pretending to be a child in a child's world. (*SL* 5.353–54)

Dunsany then appears as a very fitting model for this aspect of Carter's personality; indeed, the choice is the more apt since Dunsany's work inspired imitations by Lovecraft, of which *The Dream-Quest of Unknown Kadath* and "The Silver Key" may be said to form the final examples. Here again we encounter in Carter an amalgam of Lovecraft and a figure—Dunsany—who played an important part in his philosophical and literary development.

Another interesting example of autobiography occurs in "The Whisperer in Darkness." Researches by Donald R. Burleson indicate that the character of Henry Akeley was based in part upon Lovecraft's Vermont associate Vrest Orton, although there was a real Vermont rustic named Bert G. Akley whom Lovecraft met in his travels of 1928, and whose character figures indirectly in the portrayal of Akeley; indeed, the whole setting of the tale seems to be a compendium of impressions received in Vermont—in travels with Orton and visits with the poet Arthur Goodenough—during his trips there in 1927 and 1928. (Descriptive passages from the essay "Vermont: A First Impression" [1927] were incorporated directly into the tale, although the element of weirdness in the landscape was heightened.) But Akeley also bears some resemblances to Lovecraft. Aside from delving into scholarship that borders upon the weird, Akeley is as firmly tied to his native soil as Lovecraft was: "It is not easy to give up the place you were born in, and where your family has lived for six generations," Akeley writes to Wilmarth; and again: "[I] suppose I'll be ready for moving in a week or two, though it nearly kills me to think of it" (*DH* 218, 234). Indeed, it is precisely Akeley's reluctance to depart that causes his doom—although this should not allow us to assume that Lovecraft ever regretted his "sense of place"; rather, it is this facet of Akeley's character that explains why he did not flee the horrors long before, and we are meant to regard it as an entirely understandable motivation. Nevertheless, Akeley's personality is not wholly central to the tale (the major emphasis is upon the setting and the machinations of the fungi from Yuggoth—the "phenomena" that Lovecraft recognised as the true "heroes" for a fantastic tale), hence the autobiographical element—such as it is—is of less importance.

One final case does not concern an amalgamation of several real figures in the personality of a fictional character, but a relation between a fictional character and a real figure that has hitherto passed unnoticed. In "The Shadow over Innsmouth" we are presented the following description of Barnabas ("Old Man") Marsh, whose grandfather's dealings in the

South Seas caused the decadence of Innsmouth's race stock: "He had once been a great dandy, and people said he still wore the frock-coated finery of the Edwardian age, curiously adapted to certain deformities" (*DH* 323). Compare Lovecraft's judgment upon Oscar Wilde as written in a letter to August Derleth:

> As a man, however, Wilde admits of absolutely no defence. His character, notwithstanding a daintiness of manners which imposed an exterior shell of decorative decency and decorum, was as thoroughly rotten & contemptible as it is possible for a human character to be. . . . So thorough was his absence of that form of taste which we call a moral sense, that his derelictions comprised not only the greater & grosser offences, but all those petty dishonesties, shiftinesses, pusillanimities, & affected contemptibilities which mark the mere "cad" or "bounder" as well as the actual "villain." It is an ironic circumstance that he who succeeded for a time in being the Prince of Dandies, was never in any basic sense what one likes to call a gentleman. . . . It is hard to feel much charity or affection toward the bloated, dissipated, & diseased old high-liver who virtually rotted to pieces & exploded in "Valdemar" fashion on that grey winter day of 1900.[12]

Of particular note is the use of the word "dandy." Certainly Lovecraft condemns both Old Man Marsh and Oscar Wilde for their unorthodox sexual practices, although of course the nature of those practices was radically different in the two cases.

Thus we emerge with the conclusion that Lovecraft's characters—when they are not absolutely colourless—tend to share some traits not only with their creator but with figures whom that creator encountered either in life or in literature. Let it be noted, however, that in the overwhelming bulk of cases the autobiographical element (as regards the personalities of the fictional characters) is not central to the tales' theme, and in some cases is not even present. We are hard put to find any significant Lovecraftian echoes in the figures who people such tales as *At the Mountains of Madness,* "The Shadow out of Time," "The Colour out of Space," "The Dunwich Horror," "The Call of Cthulhu," and many other important tales, as well as most of the "Dunsanian fantasies." The characters in most of these tales are not significant save as devices for the unfolding of the plot; and in those stories where the characters do hold some intrinsic importance, Lovecraft gives them a semblance of realism by basing them upon his own attitudes or those of his associates. As he wrote to E. Hoffmann Price:

---

12. Lovecraft to August Derleth, 20 January 1927 (ms., State Historical Society of Wisconsin; published in part in *SL* 2.98).

All of us are more or less complex, so that our personalities have more than one side. If we are reasonably clever we can make as many different characters out of ourselves as there are sides to our personalities—taking in each case the isolated essence and filling out the rest of the character with fictitious material as different as possible from anything either in our own lives or in any other characters we may have manufactured from other sides of ourselves. . . . Another mode of deriving varied characters is that of simple and accurate observation. Often we may be neither fertile in imagining alien motives and manners nor apt in personifying different sides of ourselves; yet may be able to record varied characters through our clear perception and faithful memory of the way other people whom we have actually known act and seem to think and feel. When we are of this type it is obligatory for us to possess a wide acquaintance among a great variety of people of all classes, in order that we may have an ample reservoir on which to draw. We are then able to populate a story not only with a character drawn from ourselves (although that will naturally be the strongest and most vivid one, since we can never know anybody else as well as we know ourselves), but with other characters drawn from those whom we have studied. (*SL* 4.117–18)

But it is obvious that characterisation was not important to Lovecraft because it would not serve his fictional goal: the depiction of the vastness of the cosmos and the inconsequence of humanity within it. With such a principle as the basis for his work it would be positively detrimental to have characters who obtrude from the tale by their distinctiveness:

Individuals and their fortunes within natural law move me very little. They are all momentary trifles bound from a common nothingness toward another common nothingness. Only the cosmic framework itself—or such individuals as symbolise principles (or defiances of principles) of the cosmic framework—can gain a deep grip on my imagination and set it to work creating. In other words, the only "heroes" I can write about are *phenomena.* (*SL* 5.19)

Characterisation, then, was decidedly a secondary matter to Lovecraft; and his only care was to make his characters sufficiently realistic as not to be noticeably unconvincing. And the obvious mine for the traits of his characters was himself, "since we can never know anybody else as well as we know ourselves."

"Reality" and Knowledge

SOME NOTES ON LOVECRAFT'S AESTHETIC

One of the more misunderstood aspects of Lovecraft's theory of aesthetics—misunderstood because, perhaps, Lovecraft himself uttered it in a peculiar way—is his concept of "reality" as expressed through his fiction. One of his favourite remarks was that he wrote weird fiction so as to create the image of defying natural law. Taken literally, this idea is quite contradictory and impossible: how is it possible, we might ask, that natural law can be "defied"? Any event that occurs in reality—or that, in fiction, is postulated as occurring in reality, as is the case with the majority of Lovecraft's tales—must perforce be obeying some natural law. There can, in effect, logically be no such thing as a "supernatural" occurrence, since its very occurrence implies its adherence to the laws of nature and entity. Are we to conclude that Lovecraft naively failed to realise this, and that his fiction, aesthetically and philosophically, is an excursion into futility?

Care must be taken in interpreting Lovecraft's remarks. His most forceful statement of his aesthetic of horror is found in "Notes on Writing Weird Fiction," where he states:

> I choose weird stories because they suit my inclination best—one of my strongest and most persistent wishes being to achieve, momentarily, the *illusion* [my italics] of some strange suspension or violation of the galling limitations of time, space, and natural law which forever imprison us and frustrate our curiosity about the infinite cosmic spaces beyond the radius of our sight and analysis. (*MW* 113)

The final section of this credo is the most important. Here we see that Lovecraft understood the notion that natural law is inviolable and that it is simply the limitations of the human mind that prevent us from conceiving "reality" in its ultimate state. When he speaks of the "galling limitations of time, space, and natural law," he is really referring to the galling limitations of our mental and sensory apparatus. Lovecraft knew that time and space "at bottom possess no distinct and definite existence" ("Hypnos" [*D* 166]—he had read his Einstein well—but were themselves "illusions" engendered by a human mind incapable of conceiving reality other than spatially and sequentially. What Lovecraft, then, sought to do in his fiction was to hint of these other realms beyond "reality" as we know it, and thereby to achieve that sense of liberation from the "galling limitations" of the ordinary reality that he failed to find "interesting and satisfying" (*SL* 3.140).

Note that Lovecraft wished to achieve only the "illusion" of defying natural law: he was certainly no mystic, and did not believe in the "reality" of the bizarre realms he depicted. His appreciation of them was aesthetic rather than intellectual.

> My big kick comes from *taking reality just as it is*—accepting all the limitations of the most orthodox science—and then permitting my symbolising faculty to build outward from the existing facts; rearing a structure of *indefinite promise and possibility* whose topless towers are in no cosmos or dimension penetrable by the contradicting-power of the tyrannous and inexorable intellect. But the whole secret of the kick is *that I know damn well it isn't so.*" (*SL* 3.140)

The whole Lovecraftian universe presents "images forming *supplements* rather than *contradictions* of the visible & mensurable universe" (*SL* 3.295–96). Lovecraft's materialistic stance could not allow him to conceive of realms that overtly contradicted reality as known to science: instead, he chose to work in what E. F. Benson called "the strange uncharted places that lie on the confines and borders of science" (Benson 289), borders that the "tyrannous and inexorable intellect" does not yet have the power to refute. When Lovecraft defined "the crux of a weird tale [as] something which *could not possibly happen,*" he meant something that could not be explained by present-day science. "If any unexpected advance of physics, chemistry, or biology were to indicate the *possibility* of any phenomena related by the weird tale, that particular set of phenomena would cease to be *weird* in the ultimate sense" (*SL* 3.434).

"From Beyond" (1920) contains one of the earliest concrete expressions of this whole idea. Here the means for perceiving this "supra-reality" (as I term it) is a mechanical device invented by Crawford Tillinghast. The story is more interesting because it states, through the character Tillinghast, Lovecraft's views on reality and the feebleness of the human mind perhaps more clearly than anywhere in his other fiction or letters:

> "What do we know," he had said, "of the world and the universe about us? Our means of receiving impressions are absurdly few, and our notions of surrounding objects infinitely narrow. We see things only as we are constructed to see them, and can gain no idea of their absolute nature. With five feeble senses we pretend to comprehend the boundlessly complex cosmos, yet other beings with a wider, stronger, or different range of senses might not only see very differently the things we see, but might see and study whole worlds of matter, energy, and life which lie at hand yet can never be detected with the senses we have." (*D* 91)

Another story that reiterates this idea is "Hypnos" (1922), but here the mechanism used to perceive realms beyond reality is drugs, which launch the two characters into "dreams" or, more properly, visions. Lovecraft's use of the word "dream" may be somewhat paradoxical unless we collate fragments from other tales: in "Beyond the Wall of Sleep" it is postulated that certain "dreams" are not the usual "nocturnal visions [that] are perhaps no more than faint and fantastic reflections of our waking experiences" but are in effect "possible minute glimpses into a sphere of mental existence" (*D* 25) not usually exhibited to human beings. Dreams, then, are of two sorts, and it is this second sort—this perception of supra-reality—in which the characters in "Hypnos" engage. It is significant that Lovecraft frequently equates the terms "dream" and "vision" (cf. "Dagon": "I do not know why my dreams were so wild that night; . . . Such visions as I had experienced were too much for me to endure again" [*D* 16])—the latter of which would perhaps better describe these glimpses of supra-reality. "Hypnos," too, enunciates this same conception:

> . . . our studies . . . were of that vaster and more appalling universe of dim entity and consciousness which lies deeper than matter, time, and space [i.e., as we normally conceive them], and whose existence we suspect only in certain forms of sleep—those rare dreams beyond dreams which come never to common men, and but once or twice in the lifetime of imaginative men. The cosmos of our waking knowledge, born from such an universe as a bubble is born from the pipe of a jester, touches it only as such a bubble may touch its sardonic source when sucked back by the jester's whim. (*D* 165)

We need not catalogue the other tales that express this concept; in effect, all Lovecraft's fiction does. The means, however, of perceiving this "reality" beyond reality are quite varied. "Dreams" or visions are often used, as in "Beyond the Wall of Sleep," "The Dreams in the Witch House," and several others (as well as the poem "The Poe-et's Nightmare"). Sometimes the accidental presence of a character in a certain geographical area results in his perception of "reality," or an embodiment of it—i.e., an entity or event not explainable by present scientific knowledge. Tales of this type are "Dagon," "The Call of Cthulhu," "The Whisperer in Darkness," *At the Mountains of Madness,* "The Shadow out of Time," and many others. In effect, Lovecraft's entire myth-cycle of fantastic entities could be interpreted merely as the vast revelation of that level or plane of reality that normal human beings cannot perceive but which certain individuals, usually by chance, stumble upon.

In effecting this "convincing illusion of the thwarting, suspension, or disturbance of . . . basic natural forces" (*SL* 3.436), it was important to

Lovecraft that the characters experiencing visions of supra-reality could not explain them away by recourse to hallucination or (ordinary) dream. Although Lovecraft sought to depict only the "illusion" of a defiance of natural law (since an actual defiance is, as noted, logically impossible), that illusion had to be convincing if it were to give him the aesthetic and imaginative thrill he sought: he required that the illusion be so realistic, so based upon reality as we know it, that it could neither blatantly defy known laws of matter and entity nor be dispensed with as the phantasms of a disordered mind. Thus when, in "The Dreams in the Witch House," Gilman finds in his room the "exotic spiky figure which in his monstrous dream he had broken off the fantastic balustrade" (*MM* 279), he becomes increasingly unable to pass off his visions of hyperspace as mere dreams. Indeed, the title of the story reflects Gilman's frantic wish to deny the reality of his cosmic voyages—voyages that he finds at once fascinating and appalling. But such a wish now becomes difficult as he is faced with this material, objective proof of these voyages. In "The Shadow out of Time," the narrator's witnessing of the manuscript that he must have written millions of years ago forms the proof that his psychic displacement by a member of the Great Race was not a dream, as he would have liked to believe, but a reality. Lovecraft conveniently allows the narrator to lose this manuscript when he returns to his excavation party, but it is made all too clear that the manuscript actually existed, and was not a product of the narrator's imagination. So, too, when Wilmarth, in "The Whisperer in Darkness," sees the face and hands of Henry Wentworth Akeley. In other tales this is made even clearer: Arthur Jermyn sees the hideous contents of a box from Africa; the narrator of "The Shadow over Innsmouth" notes the changing of his features into the Innsmouth look; the narrator of "The Lurking Fear" sees the horde of deformed entities chasing one another; and so on throughout Lovecraft's fiction. Always does he assert the brutal, objective reality of these sights of supra-reality: although in some instances no concrete evidence is available as proof, it is precisely because the narrators cannot pass off their adventures as dreams or hallucinations that their minds are shattered.

Related to this idea of perceiving supra-reality, or fragments of it, is the role of knowledge. It is knowledge that usually permits the characters to break through "normal consciousness and reality" ("Hypnos" [*D* 165]) to perceive this other reality. This applies even in some of the tales where "dreams" are used: in "Beyond the Wall of Sleep," it is the central character's mechanical device—a "cosmic 'radio'" (*D* 32)—that allows him to glimpse a different reality through Joe Slater's brain; in "The Dreams in the Witch House," it is Gilman's formidable knowledge of "Non-Euclidean calculus and quantum physics" (*MM* 263)—and, perhaps, his fortuitous occupancy of the queerly angled room in the Witch House—that permits him to jaunt through hyperspace. Science, then, is one of the major keys to the revelation of reality. This readily harmonises with Lovecraft's strongly positivistic and empirical outlook, forcefully expressed through his letters.

Yet some of Lovecraft's remarks seem to indicate a loathing and hatred of this very science that is leading man to visions beyond his five senses. Do we not read in "Facts Concerning the Late Arthur Jermyn and His Family" (1920) that "Science, already oppressive with its shocking revelations, will perhaps be the ultimate exterminator of our human species" (*D* 73), or in "The Call of Cthulhu" (1926) that although "The sciences . . . have hitherto harmed us little; . . . some day the piecing together of dissociated knowledge will open up . . . terrifying vistas of reality" (*DH* 125)? Moreover, do not many of his characters who pursue this knowledge end disastrously, either in death or madness? Does this not reveal a fear of knowledge and reality?[1]

Such a view can be gleaned only through a careless reading of Lovecraft's work. Surely his letters reveal that he could not have hated knowledge—else, we wonder, why did he so arduously pursue it throughout his life?—nor dreaded "reality." Lovecraft was possessed of an "acute, persistent, unquenchable craving TO KNOW"; this meant an "overpowering desire to know whether I am asleep or awake—whether the environment and laws which affect me are external and permanent, or the transitory products of my own brain." Moreover, "If there be not some virtue in plain TRUTH; then our fair dreams, delusions, and follies are as much to be esteemed as our sober waking hours and the comforts they bring. If TRUTH amounts to nothing, then we must regard the phantasmata of our slumbers just as seriously as the events of our daily lives" (*SL* 1.61–63). Yet do we not here encounter another contradiction? Did not Lovecraft say in "Beyond the Wall of Sleep" that "Sometimes I believe that this less material life [revealed through dreams] is our truer life, and that our vain presence on the terraqueous globe is itself the secondary or merely virtual phenomenon" (*D* 26)? But here he is alluding to that less material and normal life which those apocalyptic visions of supra-reality reveal to us, not our normal dreams, which "are no more than faint and fantastic reflections of our waking experiences"; and it is only logical to believe that supra-reality is "truer" than the illusory reality that we normally perceive through our senses.

---

1. Such a view has actually been adopted by some critics: Colin Wilson believes that Lovecraft "rejected 'reality'" (Wilson 2), while Maurice Lévy feels that Lovecraft "hated reality" (Lévy 25). Barton L. St Armand maintains that Lovecraft thought it "dangerous to know too much" (St Armand 14).

Clearly, then, Lovecraft did not hate either knowledge or reality. One way of interpreting the themes in his stories is to believe that "Lovecraft is not deploring knowledge, but rather, *man's inability to cope with it*" (Mosig 105). This certainly explains the events in certain tales and poems, particularly "Facts Concerning the Late Arthur Jermyn and His Family," "The Poe-et's Nightmare," "The Call of Cthulhu," and others. But an even stronger statement is that Lovecraft, while certainly not deploring knowledge as such, is deploring either the *misuse* of knowledge or the *effects*—often cataclysmic—that knowledge can have.

Observe that in such tales as "From Beyond" and "Hypnos," it is not knowledge itself but the ends to which that knowledge was to have been directed that caused the doom of the central characters. Both Crawford Tillinghast and the unnamed character in "Hypnos" who leads the narrator in their peregrinations through time and space (it is immaterial for our purposes whether he actually existed or was merely a figment of the narrator's imagination) intend to use the knowledge that they have acquired for pernicious ends: Tillinghast shouts, in a burst of pure hubris, "I have harnessed the shades that stride from world to world to sow death and madness. . . . Space belongs to me, do you hear?" (*D* 96). The central character in "Hypnos" "had designs which involved the rulership of the visible universe and more; designs whereby the earth and the stars would move at his command, and the destinies of all living things be his" (*D* 166). Rather than questing for knowledge simply for their own enlightenment, these characters are aiming for goals that are ludicrously and impiously vast; and—perhaps because Lovecraft, believing man so inconsequential in the realms of space and time, felt that the idea of a human being ruling all entity was so grotesquely ridiculous that anyone's thinking such a thing was only indulging in vainglory—the result is not their success, but their fitting doom.

The ancient Greek idea of hubris—"overweening pride"—was a strong one in Lovecraft. But while the Greeks applied it to a man's belief that he was the equal or superior of the gods (who would then castigate him for such a notion), Lovecraft seemed to apply it to a human being's notion that he could subvert or control natural law—and who, in many cases, came very close to doing it. Lovecraft seemed to take a rich satisfaction in condemning such figures in his fiction to utter annihilation.

One of the finest examples of this is *The Case of Charles Dexter Ward*. Some commentators have believed that Ward himself is the quasi-villain of this novel—for does he not aspire to unholy knowledge?—and that Willett is the "hero." But this is a fatal misreading of the tale. Ward is certainly the "tragic hero," but the true villain is of course Joseph Curwen, who has not only used his diabolical knowledge to perpetuate himself far beyond the normal lifespan of a human being, but who aspires for goals that could af-

fect "all civilisation, all natural law, perhaps even the fate of the solar system and the universe"(*MM* 181–82). Ward, on the other hand, is never
deemed "evil"—at least, not when he is still himself, before he is sup-
planted by Curwen—precisely because his searches into the past were done
"for the sake of knowledge" (*MM* 182). This comment is Ward's sole—
and, for Lovecraft, sufficient—justification for all the actions he has undertaken in resurrecting Curwen and relearning his unholy secrets of the res-
urrection of the dead. Ward, like Lovecraft, was simply attempting to
quench his own thirst for knowledge, and Lovecraft never condemns him
for doing so; and if he has "brought to light a monstrous abnormality"
(*MM* 182), then it was not really through his own doing but through the
evil influence of Curwen. Ward certainly perishes, but he ends almost happily, buried in his family plot at the North Burial Ground. It is Curwen, the
villain, who dies hideously, and Lovecraft gains much satisfaction from it;
Willett, in effect, is only the instrument of his death. It is to be observed,
also, that the death of Curwen's associates, Orne and Hutchinson, is
caused by the very things they called up from the dust of centuries; they
thus suffer a doom similar to that of Herbert West in "Herbert West—
Reanimator," who tried to subvert natural law by reanimating the dead.

The same incidents roughly occur in "The Dreams in the Witch
House." Gilman is never blamed or castigated for venturing into hyperspace, since he is venturing there as a student and learner, with no ulterior
aims. Gilman also perishes, and hideously enough, but rather than passing
a moral judgment upon him, Lovecraft only remarks wryly, "Possibly Gilman ought not to have studied so hard" (*MM* 263). The real villains are
Keziah Mason and Brown Jenkin, and they too suffer death—indeed,
partly through Gilman's own actions. Gilman's death is perhaps a necessary effect of the destruction of two such cosmic villains.

An early tale that features the hubris theme in a more purely Greek
fashion—i.e., as an offence to the gods—is "The Other Gods." Barzai,
given the ironic soubriquet of "The Wise," was "a man deeply learned in
the Seven Cryptical Books of Hsan, and familiar with the Pnakotic Manuscripts of distant and frozen Lomar"; but not satisfied with mere knowledge, Barzai, who "knew so much of the gods that . . . he was deemed half
a god himself," determines to see the gods on the peak of Hatheg-Kla. He
declares: "The wisdom of Barzai hath made him greater than earth's gods,
and against his will their spells and barriers are as naught. . . ." But this
outburst of hubris does not go unpunished by the gods, who "suffer no
man to tell that he hath looked upon them": Barzai falls into the sky
through "the *other* gods! The gods of the outer hells that guard the feeble
gods of earth!" (*D* 127–32). The quaintly simple moral of this tale should
not allow us to believe that Lovecraft was abandoning the cosmic and ra-

tionalistic approach of his other narratives: this tale, along with several of his other early fantasies, shows how pervasive was the influence of Lord Dunsany at this time. Lovecraft was captivated by Dunsany's artlessly simple and moralistic tales, which themselves show the strong influence of pagan mythology in their themes of divine retribution and human hubris; and Lovecraft sought to capture this intentionally and ostensibly naive manner of story-telling, reminiscent of folklore, in many of his early tales, notably "The Cats of Ulthar," "The Quest of Iranon," "The Tree" (which of all Lovecraft's tales is the most strongly Grecian in theme and flavour), and others. It is not to be wondered that, as Lovecraft's rationalistic outlook grew, the Dunsanian influenced waned, and that his theme of hubris began to be manifested in a less classically Grecian manner.

Closely related to this notion of the misuse of knowledge by hubristic human beings is the idea that certain revelations of life, matter, and entity as they "really" are could result in disaster, either for human civilisation or for the cosmos at large. Thus in *At the Mountains of Madness* the narrator strives to prevent the exploration of the antarctic because any further study—particularly one involving "a thoroughness far beyond anything our outfit attempted" (*MM* 35)—would surely result, not only in mental perturbation (as with Danforth) at the realisation of the existence of such an entity as a shoggoth, but in the possible loosing of this entity (and however many others may still be lurking) upon the world, with the subsequent destruction of mankind. Lovecraft makes it clear that what is involved here is not merely the threat of madness through revelation—not merely "the inability to cope" with knowledge—but the fate of the world:

> It is absolutely necessary, for the peace and safety of mankind, that some of earth's dark, dead corners and unplumbed depths be let alone; lest sleeping abnormalities wake to resurgent life, and blasphemously surviving nightmares squirm and splash out of their black lairs to newer and wider conquests. (*MM* 105)

This sentiment is expressed, though not as strongly, in "The Shadow out of Time." Here the narrator is urging "a final abandonment of all attempts at unearthing those fragments of unknown, primordial masonry which my expedition set out to investigate" because if further discoveries are made,

> then man must be prepared to accept notions of the cosmos, and of his own place in the seething vortex of time, whose merest mention is paralysing. He must, too, be placed on guard against a specific, lurking peril which, though it will never engulf the whole race, may impose monstrous and unguessable horrors upon certain venturesome members of it. (*DH* 368)

Here again is the notion that we may be unable to cope with the knowledge of our own ludicrously insignificant position in the cosmos and that this knowledge—or rather the actions that may be implemented based upon it— could lead to destruction, if only of "certain venturesome" individuals.

Yet there are undoubtedly other tales where the inability to cope with knowledge—a comment not on the evil of knowledge but on the feebleness of humanity's psychological state—seems to be the main theme. Arthur Jermyn certainly kills himself because of what the knowledge he gleaned from his African explorations implied; and in "The Call of Cthulhu" the narrator discourages the "piecing together of dissociated knowledge" such as he did because it would result only in our going "mad from the revelation or flee[ing] from the deadly light into the peace and safety of a new dark age" (*DH* 125). Here mental, not physical, destruction might result from knowledge. In either case it would lead to the destruction of civilisation as we know it. But unlike *At the Mountains of Madness*, it seems that here the knowledge—or even the acting upon the knowledge—that Cthulhu exists would not directly endanger the physical well-being of mankind. Cthulhu cannot rise, as might a shoggoth, through any direct actions of human beings: he rose in 1925 only because of a freak earthquake that momentarily brought R'lyeh to the surface, but he and his minions will be freed from their underwater prison only when the "stars and the earth might once more be ready for Them" (*DH* 140), and there is no telling how many years or millennia in the future that may be. So, too, in "The Colour out of Space": to be sure, "something terrible" (*DH* 81) still remains after all the events of the tale; and that something will presumably grow and spread regardless of the wishes or knowledge of mankind. In such instances, Lovecraft seems to be saying, where men can have no effect on the suppression or releasing of these cosmic forces, it is best not to know about them; not because the knowledge is in itself an evil, but because with this knowledge, "even the skies of spring and the flowers of summer must ever afterward be poison" ("The Call of Cthulhu" [*DH* 154]). For our own peace of mind, it is better to preserve the illusion of our safety than to face the existence of cosmic forces that may destroy mankind and the universe and against which man can have no deterrent effect in any case.

We can note that this concept of the dire effects of knowledge is manifested in the more "amoral" of Lovecraft's tales, where there is no real "villain" but only forces and entities working in their own interest. It is only logical that the hubris theme could not apply here, since there would be no character through whom it could be expressed. Certainly we cannot regard Cthulhu as the "villain" of "The Call of Cthulhu" who is questing for power beyond his "station": Cthulhu simply exists and is only "evil" in relation to mankind. The hubris theme seems to have been applied only to human beings who tried to exalt themselves to some level of cosmic ruler-ship. It certainly cannot be applied to any characters in the tales of Love-craft's pseudomythology: not to the titanic extra-terrestrial entities such as Yog-Sothoth or Nyarlathotep, who *already* rule the cosmos; not to the other intergalactic races, most of whom (such as the fungi from Yuggoth in "The Whisperer in Darkness," the Old Ones in *At the Mountains of Mad-ness,* and the Great Race in "The Shadow out of Time") are themselves questing scientifically and disinterestedly for knowledge; not even to the human characters who piece together the facts of the case, since they too are working in a scientific spirit. The hubris theme seems to have been generally an early one in Lovecraft—despite its occurrence in "The Dreams in the Witch House" (1932) and perhaps in "The Thing on the Doorstep" (1933), in the figure of Asenath/Ephraim Waite—when he was still strongly under the influence of the heavy classical reading of his youth. Moreover, the hubris theme, with its connotations of morality even in Lovecraft's modified and rationalistic form, may have seemed to him out of place in his "cosmic" narratives, since he readily recognised the aimless-ness and amorality of a blindly impersonal cosmos.

It is clear, then, that Lovecraft the positivistic materialist envisaged realms of reality beyond that revealed by our mental and sensory data; and although he did not believe in the literal reality of these realms—did not believe in the literal existence of a Cthulhu—he nonetheless felt them symbolically true, i.e., felt that such realms might be true if only our senses were keener or our knowledge of the universe greater. But if this supra-reality is in his work almost always horrifying—although on one occasion it is deemed "picturesque" ("The Dreams in the Witch House" [*MM* 285])—then it only underscores Lovecraft's belief in the inconsequentiality of mankind, belittled as it is by cosmic forces that could easily crush it; forces not only beyond humanity's comprehension, but even its imagination.

Works Cited

Benson, E. F. "Mrs. Amworth." In *The Collected Ghost Stories of E. F. Benson.* New York: Carroll & Graf, 1992.

Lévy, Maurice. *Lovecraft: A Study in the Fantastic.* Trans. S. T. Joshi. Detroit: Wayne State University Press, 1988.

Mosig, Dirk W. "H. P. Lovecraft: Myth-Maker" (1976). In S. T. Joshi, ed., *H. P. Lovecraft: Four Decades of Criticism.* Athens: Ohio University Press, 1980.

St Armand, Barton L. "Facts in the Case of H. P. Lovecraft." *Rhode Island His-tory* 31, No. 2 (February 1972): 3–19.

Wilson, Colin. *The Strength to Dream: Literature and the Imagination.* Boston: Houghton Mifflin, 1962.

In Defence of Dagon *and Lovecraft's Philosophy*

The Transatlantic Circulator may still form one of the minor mysteries in the study of H. P. Lovecraft, no less from a biographical than from a bibliographical standpoint. While the affair of the Transatlantic Circulator may not be exactly pivotal in Lovecraft's life and thought, it did represent one of the earliest occasions in which he defined his literary theory and championed his philosophy of mechanistic materialism over idealism or religiosity or uncritical mysticism.

The Transatlantic Circulator was a loose organisation of amateur journalists in England and the United States who exchanged stories and poems in manuscript and criticised them. How long the organisation was in existence before Lovecraft's entrance into it in July 1920 is unknown, but it is certainly not correct, as L. Sprague de Camp has said, that Lovecraft himself "organized . . . the Transatlantic Circulator" (de Camp 115). Indeed, there is nothing to suggest either this or that the organisation collapsed after Lovecraft's exit from it in September 1921, for new members were entering it at precisely the time Lovecraft was withdrawing.

Also in doubt is the matter of who introduced Lovecraft to the Circulator. The choice would perhaps fall on John Ravenor Bullen, a major member of the organisation. Bullen is the only one of the known members of the Circulator with whom Lovecraft continued an acquaintance in later life; but did he know Bullen as early as 1920? There is no especial reason to doubt it. Lovecraft published a poem of Bullen's in the July 1923 issue of the *Conservative,* but this issue appears to have been prepared much earlier; and in 1927 Lovecraft edited and wrote the preface to Bullen's posthumous collection of poems, *White Fire.*

These matters are, however, relatively unimportant; the crux of the affair is Lovecraft's own activities in the Circulator. Being at the time both a critic and a creative writer of poetry and fiction, Lovecraft found the organisation very congenial. In this group, as (more successfully) with his other correspondence cycles, the Kleicomolo and the Gallomo, and later with his literary associates to whom he almost invariably sent manuscripts of his tales for criticism before submitting them to a publisher, he could indulge in literature as a form of "self-expression" without any thought of a preconceived audience. In Lovecraft's mind, the aesthetic enjoyment and satisfaction of literary creation itself—the act of capturing in an artistic manner images, moods, and attitudes that are clamouring to be captured—is the sole reward for that literary creation. This product need reach only the eyes of a few discerning friends and critics; whether it reaches a wider audience is immaterial.

The very fact that Lovecraft felt compelled to write at least four essays defending his literary philosophy (one of them, the first, is non-extant) shows that some members of the Circulator were perhaps not as discerning as Lovecraft would have liked. This is, however, not to say that they were either incompetent or immature literary critics; in some of their remarks we find astute and even prophetic comments on Lovecraft's work. A Dr John Munday recorded: "I suspect that [Lovecraft's] letters are more interesting than his stories"—a view held by at least a few current scholars. In saying that Lovecraft "makes one *think*" and that "Mr Lovecraft does not write for lazy readers," Elsye Tash Sater was a vague and perhaps unintentional precursor of that school of critics—of which T. O. Mabbott is one of the earliest notable examples—who regarded Lovecraft's works as expressions of a distinctive philosophy rather than as fiction intended merely to horrify. John Ravenor Bullen, perhaps the keenest of the Circulator's critics, recognised Lovecraft's "art for art's sake" attitude, and mentions him in the same breath as Wells and Maeterlinck.[1] The conclusion, then, cannot be drawn that the critical abilities of the Circulator in general were inadequate, or that the members failed (again in general) to satisfy Lovecraft's desire for friendly yet perspicacious criticism of his work. The fact that he granted the logic of several remarks on his pieces, and that he even revised slightly one work—"Psychopompos"—on the basis of a suggestion made in the Circulator, shows that Lovecraft did enjoy the intellectual stimulus provided by the Circulator. Only illness and overwork forced him to remove himself from the organisation in September 1921.

It was, however, those particular comments by some members—comments that Lovecraft considered subjective, irrelevant, or simply a different viewpoint from his own—that spurred the three essays now referred to as *In Defence of Dagon*. Important in this regard is a comment of John Munday's on "Dagon": "Do you remember Kipling's little poem with the refrain 'But is it art'? So would I courteously ask: 'Is it wholesome' of Mr Lovecraft's story." Here we see the impetus for the writing of "The Defence Reopens!" Munday later says, "You are . . . giving us food for thought. But, unless I am very greatly mistaken, your 'The White Ship' will be succeeded by cleverer, and (pardon me) healthier, writings." To this Lovecraft brandished Oscar Wilde's dictum that "no artist is ever morbid."

---

1. "In 'The Island of Dr. Moreau' H. G. Wells makes animals into men. In 'Dagon' H. P. Lovecraft makes men into fish and vice versa. In a recent paper Maeterlinck reveals that every animal, fish, and insect since creation is bound up in man to-day. . . ." All comments by members of the Transatlantic Circulator survive in ms. at JHL.

One of Bullen's observations also prompted a response by Lovecraft: ". . . the reader, search and probe as he may, is unable to discover any trace of humour in [the stories]. The essence of a man's whole work (noticeable in these contributions) generally presents itself more or less in the form of a view of the univese. Can a view of the universe which does not take humour into consideration be complete or correct?" And, of course, A. H. Brown's remark that Lovecraft's work should more fully reflect "the thoughts and actions of ordinary people," thereby allowing them "to appeal to a larger class," again caused Lovecraft to unearth the major tenets of his literary aesthetic.

What these comments by the Circulator really allowed Lovecraft to do was, for the first time, to defend his view of weird fiction as a significant art form. In so doing he anticipated many of the remarks he would make in the introduction to *Supernatural Horror in Literature* (1925–27), although by that time Lovecraft's "art for art's sake" stance—inspired by his reading of the critical theory of Poe, Wilde, and the Decadents—had been merged into a broader aesthetic emphasising a need for sincerity and disinterested self-expression. By dividing literature, somewhat unorthodoxly, into three categories—romantic, realistic, and imaginative—he stresses the importance of the last by declaring that it draws upon the best features of both the other two: like romanticism, imaginative fiction bases its appeal on emotions (the emotions of fear, wonder, and terror); from realism it derives the important principle of truth—not truth to fact, as in realism, but truth to human feeling. As a result, Lovecraft comes up with the somewhat startling deduction that "The imaginative writer devotes himself to art in its most essential sense."

In defending himself, and his writing, from charges of "unwholesomeness" and immorality (charges still made today against weird fiction), Lovecraft states that the weird, the fantastic, and even the horrible are as deserving of artistic treatment as the wholesome and the ordinary. No realm of human existence can be denied to the artist; everything depends upon the treatment, not the subject matter. Lovecraft cites Wilde's pretty paradox that

> a healthy work of art is one the choice of whose subject is conditioned by the tempermaent of the artist, and comes directly out of it. . . . An unhealthy work of art, on the other hand, is a work . . . whose subject is deliberately chosen, not because the artist has any pleasure in it, but because he thinks that the public will pay him for it. In fact, the popular novel that the public calls healthy is always a thoroughly unhealthy production; and what the public calls an unhealthy novel is always a beautiful and healthy work of art.

In this way Lovecraft neatly justifies his unusual subject-matter while simultaneously condemning the popular best-seller as a product of insincere hackwork. And yet, because Lovecraft realises that weird fiction is necessarily a cultivated taste, he is compelled to note repeatedly that he writes only for the "sensitive"—the select few whose imaginations are sufficiently liberated from the minutiae of daily life to appreciate images, moods, and incidents that do not exist in the world as we know and experience it. As a result, Lovecraft does not want to write for or about "ordinary people"— not only because, as he declares, he has no interest in them, but because they in turn have no particular interest in his imaginative work.

Lovecraft's defence of weird fiction as the literature of pure imagination and as the preserve of a select few is a compelling one, and we can see how well it justifies the work of such of his contemporaries and successors as Lord Dunsany, E. R. Eddison, Arthur Machen, Clark Ashton Smith, Ramsey Campbell, T. E. D. Klein, and Thomas Ligotti. The bestsellerdom of Stephen King, Clive Barker, and Anne Rice, on the other hand, seem motivated by exactly that sort of "unhealthiness" that Wilde detected in the popular novel, and there can hardly be a doubt as to which group of writers will survive as exponents of genuine literature and which will be banished to the oblivion of superficial, if lucrative, hackdom.

Although Lovecraft vindicates his own theories at length in these essays, he is well aware that the situation is not one of right and wrong but, fundamentally, of differing taste and outlook. Lovecraft summed up the matter in a note he wrote on a Circulator member's comment: ". . . Since all my 'literary' emanations are more or less grotesque and arabesque . . . it occurred to me that [they] might be rather boresome . . . [to] an audience predominantly pro-realistic."

It is not the case that Lovecraft's work was uniformly unpopular with the members of the Circulator; to some his stories were indeed powerful. Virtually all at least realised that Lovecraft was "a writer . . . undeniably possessed of fine powers of imagination and a really exceptional ability to say things in a striking way" (as John Munday commented in regard to "Dagon"), and Elsye Tash Sator even understood vaguely the cosmic quality that is the notable feature of Lovecraft's work when she hypothesised on the reasons for the final madness of the narrator of "Dagon": "Is it the immensity of space that overwhelms [him], or [his] feeling of powerlessness? Or is it loneliness in its intensest form that shatters the brain cells?" In a way she is right, although the crux of the tale lies in the narrator's (and the reader's) awareness of the "terrible and acknowledged antiquity of the earth and man's tenuous sinecure thereon," as Matthew H. Onderdonk termed it.

John Ravenor Bullen recognised the allegorical nature of "The White Ship" when he noted that it was a "powerful prose-poem in which the allegorist informs us somewhat sorrowfully that he was once an idealist but is now a materialist—that he once dwelt happily in the land of Sona-Nyl but foolishly forsook it and pushed on to explore forbidden territory—only to find the Cathuria of his hopes a hollow hell." The interpretation seems, however, somewhat unlikely, since—even judging solely from the passages in these essays—there is no indication that Lovecraft either was ever idealistic or ever regretted his materialistic stance.

Turning to the Circulator's opinion of Lovecraft's poetry, we find one comment by the poet Bullen on "Old Christmas" that is startlingly perceptive and may stand as one of the finer general comments passed on Lovecraft's verse:

> May I point out that poets of each period have forged their lines in the temper and accent of their age, whereas Mr Lovecraft purposefully "plates over" his poetical works with "the impenetrable rococo" of his predecessors' days, thereby running great risks. But it may be that his discerning eyes perceive that many modern methods are mongrel and ephemeral. His devotion to Queen Anne style may make his compositions seem artificial, rhetorical descriptions to contemporary critics, but the ever-growing charm of eloquence (to which assonance, alliteration, onomatopoeic sound and rhythm, and tone colour contribute their entrancing effect) displayed in the poem under analysis, proclaims Mr Lovecraft a genuine poet, and "Old Christmas" an example of poetical architecture well-equipped to stand the test of time.

This may be a somewhat charitable assessment of Lovecraft's poetry in general and of "Old Christmas" in particular, but it touches upon some important issues. Lovecraft indeed considered "modern methods" in poetry "mongrel and ephemeral" (see his comments on Whitman and T. S. Eliot), and did indeed choose to follow the Augustan poets of eighteenth-century England in form and substance. Much later, in the essay "Heritage or Modernism: Common Sense in Art Forms" (1935), Lovecraft attempted a justification for artistic archaism:

> When a given age has no new *natural* impulse toward change, is it not better to continue building on the established forms than to concoct grotesque and meaningless novelties out of thin academic theory?
>
> Indeed, under certain conditions is not a policy of frank and virile antiquarianism—a healthy, vigorous revival of old forms still justified by their relation to life—infinitely sounder than a feverish mania for the destruction of familiar things and the laboured, freakish, uninspired search for strange shapes which nobody wants and which really mean nothing? (*MW* 197)

This is sound enough in theory, but it cannot actually be used as a justification for Lovecraft's archaistic poetry (it should be pointed out that the above remarks were intended to apply not to poetry but to architecture); for no one could possibly maintain that eighteenth-century verse—at least the sort of quaint, mechanical eighteenth-century verse written by Lovecraft—was one of the "old forms still justified by their relation to life." Indeed, it was exactly because his poems were merely playful—and, to be honest, fundamentally insincere—excursions into antiquarianism that they fail as aesthetic products. Lovecraft ultimately realised this, and not only repudiated much of his earlier verse but, in *Fungi from Yuggoth* (1929–30), finally began using the language of his own day to convey his message.

Lovecraft's philosophical remarks in the *In Defence of Dagon* essays must also concern us, insofar as they occupy a large body of the text. It is unfortunate that no remarks of the Mr Wickenden whom Lovecraft so took to task survive; but the context allows us to assume that the matter must have been the familiar idealism vs. materialism debate in which Lovecraft and some of his other correspondents—Maurice W. Moe, James F. Morton, Rheinhart Kleiner—engaged. Just as his literary remarks represent the first significant enunciation of his theory of the weird, so do Lovecraft's philosophical remarks put forth—more vigorously and pointedly than even such essays as "Idealism and Materialism: A Reflection" (1919)—the secular, positivist world view that would, with some modifications, remain his dominant outlook for the whole of his life.

Several important features emerge in Lovecraft's comments which allow us to gauge exactly how far he had evolved certain facets of his metaphysics and ethics. By 1921 he had not only absorbed what were for him the most important branches of ancient thought—particularly Leucippus' determinism, the atomic theory of Leucippus and Democritus (probably through the *De Rerum Natura* of Lucretius), and (also in part through Lucretius) the ethical philosophy of Epicurus—but also such modern thinkers as Nietzsche, Thomas Henry Huxley, Ernst Haeckel (*The Riddle of the Universe*), and Hugh Elliot (*Modern Science and Materialism*). He had not yet, however, embraced Einstein or other advanced astrophysicists such as Planck, de Sitter, and Heisenberg, and therefore had yet to harmonise his old-style mechanistic materialism with the advances of modern science, as he would do in a later letter (see *SL* 2.266f.).

But Wickenden's repeated criticism of Lovecraft's use of the word "know"—how did Lovecraft "know" that there is no life after death?—forced him to shed belief in the absolute certainty of scientific discovery and to base all his arguments—on the existence of God or the soul; on survival after death; on the place of humanity in the universe—on *probability*. This belief in probability—i.e., a belief as to the *"is or isn'tness"* of things

(*SL* 3.307) as derived from the most up-to-date findings of science—
would serve as the foundation for Lovecraft's metaphysics for the rest of
his life.

In ethics Lovecraft had already accepted the teachings of Epicurus
that *pleasure*—interpreted widely as that which fosters well-being—as the
aim of terrestrial existence. Like Epicurus, Lovecraft saw pleasure as the
natural goal of all organisms, and later made pleasure the foundation for
his aesthetic thought as well:

> False or insincere amusement is the sort of activity which does not meet
> the real psychological demands of the human glandular-nervous system,
> but merely affects to do so. Real amusement is the sort which is based on
> a knowledge of real needs, and which therefore hits the spot. *This latter
> kind of amusement is what art is.* (*SL* 3.21)

Darwinian and Huxleyan evolution plays a considerable role in Lovecraft's debate with Wickenden, and he uses it as his trump-card in refuting
Wickenden's notion of the human soul: if human beings have a soul and
animals do not, exactly where along the course of our evolution from apes
to human beings did we acquire this mysterious element? In battling the
theist Wickenden, Lovecraft also relies upon anthropological work for a
natural account of the origin of religious belief in primitive man. Lovecraft
had by this time probably absorbed such seminal works as Edward Burnett
Tylor's *Primitive Culture* (1871), John Fiske's *Myths and Myth-Makers* (1872),
and James George Frazer's *The Golden Bough* (1890), which to his mind explained in a wholly satisfactory way the inevitable religiosity instilled in the
human race by ignorance of the true workings of natural phenomena,
thereby giving rise to notions of deity, soul, and immortality. Lovecraft
maintained that "This matter of the explanation of 'spiritual' feelings is
really the most important of all materialistic arguments; since the explana-
tions are not only overwhelmingly forcible, but so adequate as to shew that
man could not possibly have developed without acquiring just such false
impressions." There is, indeed, every reason to believe that Lovecraft is
correct on this point.

Works Cited

de Camp, L. Sprague. *Lovecraft: A Biography*. Garden City, NY: Doubleday,
    1975.
Onderdonk, Matthew H. "The Lord of R'lyeh" (1945). *Lovecraft Studies* No. 7
    (Fall 1982): 8–17.

The Rationale of Lovecraft's Pseudonyms

M uch has been written on the identification of Lovecraft's pseudonymous publication of stories, poems, articles, and letters, but
surprisingly little attention has been paid to the more essential
matter of *why* Lovecraft used pseudonyms at all or why he used any given
pseudonym for a given publication. The work of Robert H. Barlow, Willametta Keffer, George T. Wetzel, and several others had already resulted,
by the 1950s, in the identification of the overwhelming bulk of Lovecraft's
pseudonyms, although a few new ones came to light as recently as a few
years ago; but I have yet to find any discussion of the rationale of his pseudonyms.

In the first place, attention should be paid as to which works appeared
pseudonymously. It is significant that only two of Lovecraft's original
works of fiction did not appear under his own name: the humorous tale "A
Reminiscence of Dr. Samuel Johnson" (1917) and the prose-poem "Ex
Oblivione." The significance of this, however, may not be entirely obvious,
because the fact of his use of pseudonyms for various works must be con-
joined with the fact that virtually all his pseudonymous appearances were
in the amateur press, the most notable exceptions being his early letters
and articles for Providence *Evening News* (under the "Isaac Bickerstaffe, Jr."
pseudonym), for which he is not likely to have received payment. What
this means is that Lovecraft virtually stopped using pseudonyms at the very
time he ceased his extensive contributions to the amateur press—roughly
1923—and turned to professional publications. It is very likely that a
strong impetus for his use of pseudonyms was the very quantity of his
amateur writing, especially poetry: it seems clear that, his modesty being
what it was, he did not wish to give the appearance of flooding certain
amateur journals with his own work.

Which amateur journals received Lovecraft's pseudonymous contributions? There were a good many, but chief among them was the *Tryout*, in
which a large proportion of his poetry was published. Only three items in
Lovecraft's own amateur journal, the *Conservative*, were published pseudonymously: "Ye Ballade of Patrick von Flynn," "Inspiration" (both as by
"Lewis Theobald, Jun."), and "The Unknown" (for which see below). The
majority of Lovecraft's pieces in the *Conservative* (essays and editorials for
the most part) either appeared under his own name or were unsigned—
although in the latter case there was no especial secret as to his authorship.
Other amateur journals such as the *United Amateur*, the *Silver Clarion*, and

the *Wolverine* also received a fair number of Lovecraft's pseudonymous pieces.

This finally gets me back to the issue of why pseudonyms were used largely for poetry and not for stories or essays. It should not be assumed that Lovecraft used pseudonyms simply for works he did not value or whose authorship he did not wish to acknowledge. Firstly, such pseudonyms as "Ward Phillips" and "Henry Paget-Lowe" are scarcely very concealing, and it seems likely that most amateurs also knew of the "Lewis Theobald, Jun." pseudonym, which is by far the most extensively used. (It is under this pseudonym that Lovecraft's two collaborations with Winifred Jackson, "The Green Meadow" and "The Crawling Chaos," appeared; Jackson herself used her well-known pseudonym, "Elizabeth Berkeley.") Secondly, it became somewhat awkward for Lovecraft to publish his stories pseudonymously, since his first published amateur story, "The Alchemist" (*United Amateur*, November 1916), was his "credential" (i.e., a work that established his literary capability) for joining the United Amateur Press Association. The only odd thing is that this credential took so long in being published, since Lovecraft had joined the U.A.P.A. early in 1914 and had contributed voluminously over the next two and a half years. (Most credentials were published immediately upon a member's joining the association.) Then, when "The Tomb" was published in the *Vagrant* (November 1919), it was prefaced by an article by W. Paul Cook, "Howard P. Lovecraft's Fiction," which established Lovecraft in the amateur press as a fiction writer of note.

It is still a little puzzling that more essays did not appear pseudonymously, but it is interesting to see exactly what types of essays did so appear. The three most extensively used pseudonyms for Lovecraft's nonfiction are Isaac Bickerstaffe, Jr., El Imparcial, and Zoilus. The last is the easiest to deal with, since I have determined that, of the five Zoilus columns published in the *Wolverine* from 1921 to 1923, four are by Lovecraft and the other by Alfred Galpin. The name Zoilus needs no explanation, as it refers to the Greek critic of the fourth century B.C. who harshly criticised the Homeric poems. And yet, the Zoilus columns themselves are not especially harsh or polemical, and in fact one of them (by Lovecraft) is a paean to the amateur poet Lilian Middleton.

Willametta Keffer first tentatively identified El Imparcial as a Lovecraft pseudonym (Keffer 83). August Derleth doubted the attribution on the flimsy ground that "it is not the kind of pen-name HPL would normally have selected," whatever that is supposed to mean. But Keffer was right, and to date seven pieces by El Imparcial have been discovered, all of which concern amateur journalism. Keffer located four of them, and I admit with some embarrassment that one of these—an article on Winifred

Jackson—eluded my notice and failed to be incorporated in my bibliography of Lovecraft.

The Isacc Bickerstaffe, Jr. pseudonym does not require much elaboration, either, since Lovecraft himself provides a good account of it (see *SL* 1.4–5). He unearthed this Augustan pseudonym—used by both Jonathan Swift and Joseph Addison—to satirise the hapless astrologer J. F. Hartmann in the pages of the Providence *Evening News*. In addition to the three articles (actually two articles and a letter) published under this pseudonym, Lovecraft also wrote several articles attacking Hartmann under his own name, creating the impression that there were actually three individuals involved in the whole astrology controversy. Hartmann, clearly, never saw through the ploy, for in one of his responses he notes querulously: "Two recent articles in these columns, by an enemy falsely posing as an astrologer, are real 'gibberish,' the kind which our critic [i.e., Lovecraft] does not criticise."[1]

It is clear, then, that Lovecraft restricted his pseudonymous appearances of essays to very specific types: articles on amateur journalism (El Imparcial), attacks on astrology (Isaac Bickerstaffe, Jr.), a critical column under what is essentially a "house name" (Zoilus), and the like. Two items—"The Trip of Theobald" (1927), relating Lovecraft's visits to various New England sites in 1927, and "The Convention" (1930), an account of the 1930 N.A.P.A. convention in Boston—appeared in the *Tryout* as by "Theobald"; the very use of this laconic surname for what are clearly very autobiographical pieces indicates the degree to which Theobald was identified—and known by amateur readers to be identified—with Lovecraft. "Cats and Dogs" appeared posthumously in *Leaves* as by "Lewis Theobald, Jun.," but this was obviously R. H. Barlow's doing, as the manuscript is unsigned.

Lovecraft, accordingly, restricted his pseudonyms largely for poetry, and again I maintain that it was largely the sheer volume of poetry that he was writing at this time (1914–23) that largely spurred his use of pseudonyms, not some belief on his part that his poetry was inferior or embarrassing. We can, however, refine this idea still further by examining exactly which pseudonyms Lovecraft used for which poems.

Some pseudonyms—used for only one or two appearances—are easily dispensed with. The manuscript of the poem "Life's Mystery" was signed L. Phillips Howard; this fatuously bombastic poem was followed by a satirical response, "On Mr. L. Phillips Howard's Profound Poem Entitled 'Life's Mystery.'" I have no idea when this poem was written; it could conceivably be yet another attack on T. S. Eliot's *The Waste Land*, billed by its proponents

---

1. J. F. Hartmann, "A Defense of Astrology" (14 December 1914), rpt. in *Science versus Charlatanry*, ed. Scott Connors and S. T. Joshi (Madison, WI: Strange Co., 1979), p. 34.

as "a poem of profound significance," sparking Lovecraft's response in "Waste Paper," subtitled "A Poem of Profound Insignficance."

The pseudonym Alexander Ferguson Blair, used for the poem "North and South Britons" (1919), was identified by Tom Collins in *A Winter Wish*. No doubt Lovecraft wished to create the impression that this poem, urging unity of feeling between England and Scotland, was written by a Scotsman. No other work has been discovered under this pseudonym. Other pseudonyms were also used only once for various poems: Jeremy Bishop for the nasty satire "Medusa: A Portrait" (although the typescript bears the pseudonym "Theobaldus Senectissimus, Gent."); John J. Jones for the self-parody "The Dead Bookworm"; Richard Raleigh for "To a Youth" (a poem about Alfred Galpin); and Albert Frederick Willie for the parody, "Nathicana." Of the Richard Raleigh pseudonym Lovecraft states on a typescript of "To a Youth" (JHL): "How is this for an Elizabethan pseudonym?" HPL refers to the celebrated Elizabethan courtier Sir Walter Ralegh (whose name was formerly spelled "Raleigh"). Albert Frederick Willie is, in its first two names, an allusion to Alfred Galpin, and in its last name to Galpin's mother's maiden name, Willy. Galpin and Lovecraft actually cowrote the poem. The pseudonym Michael Ormonde O'Reilly was used when Lovecraft allowed his juvenile poem "To Pan" to appear in the *Tryout* for April 1919. This issue of the *Tryout* contained two other juvenile poems (all from *Poemata Minora, Volume II*, 1902), each printed under a pseudonym: "To the Old Pagan Religion" (as by Ames Dorrance Rowley) and "Ode to Selene or Diana" (as by Edward Softly). Still more curiously, the three poems were printed under titles different from those in the *Poemata* manuscript—"Pan," "The Last Pagan Speaks," and "To Selene." I imagine these titles changes were Lovecraft's.

Lawrence Appleton is again a transparent pseudonym. The two poems written under this pseudonym—"Hylas and Myrrha: A Tale" and "Myrrha and Strephon"—are among many directed toward Alfred Galpin, specifically relating to his various romantic involvements with girls in his hometown of Appleton, Wisconsin (all the "Damon and Delia" poems, as well as the play *Alfredo*, are on this subject). The Appleton surname clearly relates to Galpin's town of residence, while Lawrence refers to Lawrence College (now Lawrence University) in Appleton, which Galpin attended.

Wetzel speculated, somewhat laboriously, on the "Archibald Maynwaring" pseudonym, but failed to note the obvious origin of the name: Arthur Mainwaring, an obscure Augustan poet who translated a portion of "Garth's Ovid" (i.e., Ovid's *Metamorphoses* translated under the editorship of Sir Samuel Garth), which Lovecraft read as a boy. The three poems published under this pseudonym are all rather innocuous: a harmless pastoral poem, "The Pensive Swain"; a poem on the shared birthday of Alfred

Galpin and Margaret Abraham, "To the Eighth of November"; and, somewhat curiously, an explicitly religious poem entitled "Wisdom" (with the subtitle "The 28th or 'Gold-Miner's Chapter of Job, paraphrased from a literal translation of the original Hebrew text, supplied by Dr. S. Hall Young"). This poem appeared in the *Silver Clarion,* a journal known for its somewhat naive piety, and praised by Lovecraft as such (see his brief article "Comment" in the *Silver Clarion,* June 1918). The poem concludes:

> "Behold," He cries unto the mortal throng,
> "This is the Wisdom ye have sought so long:
> To reverence the Lord, and leave the paths of wrong!"

Henry Paget-Lowe, author of "On Religion," would certainly not have approved something like this! One can only imagine that Lovecraft wished to supply John Milton Samples, editor of the journal, with some copy to fill up his pages. It should be noted that the three "Archibald Maynwaring" poems all appeared in October or November 1919.

Humphry Littlewit, Esq. is somewhat of a curiosity. The name seems designed to be self-parodic or self-deprecating, but the three works for which this name was used are not exactly of this sort. To be sure, "A Reminiscence of Dr. Samuel Johnson" (1917) was written with tongue in cheek, and was in part intended as a send-up of Lovecraft's already well-known pose of extreme age and of his old-fashioned writing style ("Tho' many of my readers have at times observ'd and remark'd a Sort of antique Flow in my Stile of Writing . . ."); but what are we to make of the fact that the manuscript of "Waste Paper," Lovecraft's hilarious parody of T. S. Eliot, also bears this pseudonym? (I cannot imagine that the published version of the poem, in some still unlocated Providence newspaper, bore the pseudonym as well, although it may well have appeared anonymously.) This poem is certainly not a *self*-parody by any stretch of the imagination. But the most curious instance is the series of poems appearing under the title "Perverted Poesie or Modern Metre." This cycle is very early, dating possibly to 1914, and appeared posthumously in the amateur journal *The O-Wash-Ta-Nong,* edited by Lovecraft's old-time amateur colleague George W. Macauley; either Macauley or one of his associates must have worked from a manuscript supplied by Lovecraft. But what is most bizarre is that, of the four poems in the cycle—"The Introduction," "Unda, or, The Bride of the Sea," "The Peace Advocate," and "A Summer Sunset and Evening"—two had already appeared in Lovecraft's lifetime under pseudonyms other than "Humphry Littlewit, Esq." "Unda" appeared in 1916 as by "Lewis Theobald, Jr.," and "The Peace Advocate" appeared in the *Tryout* for May 1917—under the name "Elizabeth Berkeley"! This was the second instance of a Lovecraft poem appearing under the pseudonym of

Winifred Jackson, the other being the weird poem "The Unknown" (*Conservative*, October 1916); he explains in a letter that this occurred "in an effort to mystify the [amateur] public by having widely dissimilar work from the same nominal hand."[2] These poems, again, are not *self*-parodic, although they are certainly parodies—of the mawkishly romantic love lyrics of the Lord Byron or Thomas Moore type ("Unda"), of pacifism ("The Peace Advocate"), and of the vapid pastoral elegy ("A Summer Sunset and Evening").

Ames Dorrance Rowley is the one pseudonym of Lovecraft's that is meant as a parody of *someone else*—in this case, the amateur poet James Laurence Crowley. One would imagine that the poems appearing under this name would somehow be parodies of poems by Crowley, or at least of Crowley's manner, but I am not entirely convinced that this is the case. Certainly it is not the case for the juvenile poem "To the Old Pagan Religion" (published as "The Last Pagan Speaks"). Of the three other poems, perhaps only "Laeta; a Lament" can be considered a genuine parody of Crowley. It rather resembles "Unda, or, The Bride of the Sea" in tone:

> How sad droop the willows by Zulal's fair side,
> Where so lately I stray'd with my raven-hair'd bride:
> Ev'ry light-floating lily, each flow'r on the shore,
> Folds in sorrow since Laeta can see them no more!

The two other poems are both militaristic—"To Maj.-Gen. Omar Bundy, U.S.A." and "The Volunteer." I would certainly like to think that these are somehow parodic, but the sad fact is that they do not seem to be. Here is the final stanza of the former:

> So ever shine COLUMBIA'S brave,
>   First in the fray, unconquer'd still;
> Whose glories echo o'er the wave,
>   And ev'ry land triumphant fill!

The tone of these poems is scarcely different from that of such windy (but seriously intended) patriotic effusions as "An American to Mother England" or "Britannia Victura."

Among the most extensively used of Lovecraft's pseudonyms are Henry Paget-Lowe, Ward Phillips, Edward Softly, and Lewis Theobald, Jun. Of these, the easiest to deal with is Henry Paget-Lowe. I have already remarked how transparent the pseudonym is, and I cannot imagine that any amateur could have failed to recognise it. It is strange that all five works

---

2. Lovecraft to the Gallomo, 12 September 1921 (AHT).

written with this pseudonym appeared in 1920. "Poetry and the Gods," a tale with Anna Helen Crofts (not a pseudonym), is one of his few collaborative stories to appear pseudonymously. Of the four poems, two are innocuous paeans to seasons ("January" and "October"), one a neo-classic spasm ("On a Grecian Colonnade in a Park"—whose title, but nothing else, is obviously derived from Keats's "Ode on a Grecian Urn"), and one rather biting satire, "On Religion." Regardless of the merits of these poems, they were all clearly intended seriously and not self-parodically.

Ward Phillips is also scarcely much of a disguise, and it is under this name that Lovecraft's one original *weird* tale—the prose-poem "Ex Oblivione"—appeared. But it is of note that a good many of Lovecraft's very powerful weird *poems* also appeared under this pseudonym—"Astrophobos," "Bells," "The City," "A Cycle of Verse," "The Eidolon," and "The House." Other works by Ward Phillips are highly personal tributes to friends ("To Mr. Hoag, on His Ninetieth Birthday"; "In Memoriam: J. E. T. D.," an elegy to the deceased amateur Jennie E. T. Dowe; "Sir Thomas Tryout," on the death of C. W. Smith's cat) and a poignant philosophical poem ("Ambition"). As with Humphry Littlewit, Esq., the *name* "Ward Phillips" is somewhat self-parodic (recall the obviously parodic figure of that name in "Through the Gates of the Silver Key"), but the works appearing under the name are not.

The Edward Softly pseudonym derives from Joseph Addison's *The Tatler* No. 163 (25 April 1710), where a sentimental poem is attributed to one "Ned Softly." Accordingly, the pseudonym is used for a number of Lovecraft's parodic pastorals satirising Alfred Galpin's youthful love affairs ("Chloris and Damon," "Damon and Delia, a Pastoral," "The Dream" [subtitled: "Respectfully Dedicated to Master Consul Hasting," a Galpin pseudonym], and "To Delia, Avoiding Damon"). Otherwise it was used for a humorous poem about C. W. Smith ("Tryout's Lament for the Vanished Spider") and a perfectly pleasant little Christmas poem ("Christmas," an 8-line lyric not to be confused with the interminable 327-line "Old Christmas").

Lewis Theobald, Jun. is the most difficult of Lovecraft's pseudonyms to categorise, as it seems to have been used for a bewildering variety of works—essays, story collaborations, and poems alike. We have already remarked on the essays ("The Trip of Theobald" and "The Convention") and the collaborations ("The Green Meadow" and "The Crawling Chaos"), and also on the fact that the name seems to have become known very early on in the amateur world as a Lovecraft pseudonym: an unsigned "biography" of Theobald appeared in the "News Notes" section of the *United Amateur* for March 1918 (it was likely written by Verna McGeoch, Official Editor of the U.A.P.A. at the time). I am not sure that the origin of the *name* Lewis Theobald, Jun. has any particular bearing on the works published under that name. As is well known (see Boerem), the name derives from a celebrated eighteenth-century poet and critic (whose edition of Shakespeare [1733] is still highly regarded) who had the misfortune of earning the wrath of Alexander Pope (he severely—and rightly—criticised the errors in Pope's own 1725 edition of Shakespeare) and was accordingly pilloried in the first version of Pope's *Dunciad* (1728). But Lovecraft seems to have adopted the name, at least initially, as a sort of half-parodic reference to his own eighteenth-century inclinations and to the acknowledged mediocrity of his archaic poetry. But the name was used so frequently, from 1916 onward, that its original meaning and purpose seem to have been lost, and it became simply another Lovecraft alter ego like Henry Paget-Lowe and Ward Phillips.

If anything, the bulk of the Lewis Theobald, Jun. poems are humorous and mildly satiric, many directed at his own colleagues. Here again we have a number of poems about Galpin ("Damon—a Monody," "To Alfred Galpin, Esq.," "To Damon," "To Mr. Galpin, upon His 20th Birthday"), not all of which are by any means satirical; a number of parodies of or poems about Rheinhart Kleiner ("Cindy: Scrub-Lady in a State Street Skyscraper," "To Mistress Sophia Simple, Queen of the Cinema," "To Phillis," "To Rheinhart Kleiner, Esq., upon His Town Fables and Elegies");[3] a satire of both Kleiner and George Julian Houtain ("Ex-Poet's Reply"); a parody of a poem by Olive G. Owen ("The Nymph's Reply to the Modern Business Man"); more general parodies of romantic poetry ("The Poet of Passion," "The Poet's Rash Excuse," "Unda, or, The Bride of the Sea"); poems about Frank Belknap Long ("To Endymion") and Maurice W. Moe ("On the Return of Maurice Winter Moe, Esq., to the Pedagogical Profession"); and two birthday poems to Jonathan E. Hoag. All these poems are lighthearted and somewhat frivolous, but they are not all sharp satires, although "Ye Ballade of Patrick von Flynn" and, perhaps, "Monody on the Late King Alcohol" are. On the other hand, Lewis Theobald, Jun. was used for some undoubtedly serious and even some very touching poems, including the exquisite "Sunset," the pensive "Brotherood," "Inspiration," and "Sonnet on Myself," and two weird poems, "The Rutted Road" and— surprisingly late—"The Wood" (1929). It becomes evident, therefore, that this pseudonym was not used in any systematic way save perhaps for poems that perhaps had some special personal significance to Lovecraft.

---

3. It should be pointed out that Lovecraft's letter to Alfred Galpin (21 August 1918; ms., JHL) contains a number of parodies of poems by Kleiner, under such pseudonyms as "Kleinhart Reiner," "Edvardus Softleius," "Anacreon Microcephalos," and (my favourite) "A. Saphead."

In 1927 Lovecraft made an odd statement about pseudonyms in a letter to Zealia Bishop. "No one can advise another regarding the choice of a nom de guerre, since only one's self can fully grasp all the sentimentally associative factors concerned. . . . For my part, I have always used my own name as a matter of course—for sheer lack of any reason to use any other—except for hack work too poor to be acknowledged" (*SL* 2.161–62). This last sentence is clearly false: however little Lovecraft valued his early poems later on in life, he would never have wished to repudiate such things as "A Cycle of Verse" or "The House" (which was written about the same house in Providence that served as the setting for "The Shunned House"), or in any case would never have dismissed this material as "hack work." Still, it is evident that Lovecraft became increasingly disinclined to use pseudonyms, as they tended to violate his notions of writing as pure self-expression: "My only general objection to pseudonyms is that they tend to imply a sort of self-consciousness or self-dramatisation on the user's part, which is somewhat foreign to the process of impersonal, disinterested artistic creation. They imply that the user stands off and thinks of himself as an author, instead of being so wrapped up in his aesthetic vision that he never regards himself as a person at all" (*SL* 2.162). And yet, Lovecraft's early use of pseudonyms for a wide array of works—poetry, essays, fiction, collaborations, and even letters—points not merely to a tremendous fecundity in writing but to a careful awareness of the purpose and direction of a given work, whereby the use of a pseudonym enhances its general atmosphere and conveys a certain knowing wink to those readers who are in on the joke. The fact that so many of his pseudonyms—Isaac Bickerstaffe, Jr., Humphry Littlewit, Esq., Archibald Maynwaring, Lewis Theobald, Jun.—hark back to the eighteenth century once more emphasises the spiritual affinity to the Augustans that Lovecraft claimed from very early youth. It was that affinity which led him to write, in his best poetry, some of the most pungent satire and parody of his period, under pseudonyms that betrayed rather than concealed his authorship.

Works Cited

Boerem, R. "The First Lewis Theobald." In Darrell Schweitzer, ed., *Essays Lovecraftian* (1976); rev. ed. as *Discovering H. P. Lovecraft*. Mercer Island, WA: Starmont House, 1987, pp. 42–46.

Derleth, August. "New HPL Pseudonyms Rejected by Derleth." *Fossil* No. 159 (October 1958): 90.

Keffer, Willametta. "Howard P(seudonym) Lovecraft: The Many Names of HPL." *Fossil* No. 158 (July 1958): 82–84.

Wetzel, George T. "The Pseudonymous Lovecraft." *Xenophile* 3, No. 4 (November 1976): 3–5, 73.

The Dream World and the Real World in Lovecraft

I am perhaps not the only one who has been puzzled at the singular fashion in which sites, characters, and even gods from Lovecraft's "dream world" find their way into those of his tales that are presented as taking place in the "real" world. Why, for example, does Abdul Alhazred, in the passage from the *Necronomicon* cited in "The Dunwich Horror," refer to "Kadath in the cold waste" (*DH* 170) when the very title of *The Dream-Quest of Unknown Kadath* reveals that Kadath is in the world of dream? Why does Dr Willett mention the sign of Koth (*MM* 214) in *The Case of Charles Dexter Ward*—when Koth was a place where Randolph Carter had one of his most harrowing dream-experiences? How did Richard Upton Pickman go from the very real world of Boston's North End in "Pickman's Model" to meet Randolph Carter in the land of Deeper Slumber? Was Lovecraft merely amusing himself with playful interrelations that he knew to be impossible? Did he not realise the apparent paradoxes of such an intermingling? Or did he have a coherent system for effecting such an interpenetration of dream and reality? My own conclusion is that, while a certain method can be traced in this apparent madness, Lovecraft did in fact fail to detect some contradictions when—especially in *The Dream-Quest of Unknown Kadath*—he made attempts to show that the realms of dream and reality are not entirely distinct. That a certain element of playfulness entered into the matter seems also inescapable.

It is, in the first place, important to establish which of Lovecraft's tales occur in a dream-setting. The number is far fewer than many seem to have assumed. It can be demonstrated that only three (perhaps four) tales are conclusively set in a dream world; of these, two—when taken in conjunction with other tales—turn out not to be actual dream-narratives at all. It seems a common assumption that Lovecraft's "Dunsanian" tales all take place in a dream world, in spite of the fact that in at least one instance—"The Tree"—we are dealing with a very real if historical world (i.e., ancient Greece). There is in fact no justification, in the great majority of his "Dunsanian" tales, for the inference that they are set in a dream world. It may be true that the use of such imagined place-names as Ulthar, Nir, Lomar, Sona-Nyl, and the like—and the absence of overt references to places in the real world—seem to imply a "never-never land" existing only in the author's imagination; but the actual narratives of many of these tales are not postulated explicitly as being in a dream world, and testimony from other tales proves conclusively that many are not so situated. Dunsany himself rarely admitted openly that his narratives took place in a dream world: we find, for example, a mention of "Europeans" in "Bethmoora" (Dunsany 54, 56); and in "Poltarnees, Beholder of Ocean" we are told that "the name of the river is Oriathon, but men call it Ocean [here meaning the Greek concept of a single body of water surrounding all the land masses of the earth]" (Dunsany 6). It is true that in "Idle Days on the Yann" the narrator tells his ship-captain that "I came from Ireland, which is of Europe, whereat the captain and all the sailors laughed, for they said, 'There are no such places in all the land of dreams'" (Dunsany 60), but such a specific indication that a tale is set in a dream world is as rare in Dunsany as it is in Lovecraft.

"Polaris" (1918) appears manifestly to be in a dream setting, for the narrator remarks: "After the beams came clouds, and then I slept" (*D* 19); there follows his description of his adventures in Olathoë, in the land of Lomar. Indeed, it appears superficially that the narrator has so confused the worlds of dream and reality that he believes his "real-life" existence to be the dream: "My head, heavy and reeling, drooped to my breast, and when next I looked up it was in a dream, with the Pole Star grinning at me through a window from over the horrible swaying trees of a dream swamp. And I am still dreaming" (*D* 23). But we know, of course, that the narrator has somehow managed to tap a source of ancestral memory and actually go back to a prehistoric age; this is suggested by the poem in the tale (especially the lines ". . . till the spheres, / Six and twenty thousand years, / Have revolv'd" [*D* 23], which effectively places the fall of Lomar at c. 24,000 B.C.E.) and by the implication that the Esquimaux are the descendants of the "squat, hellish yellow" (*D* 22) Inutos who overwhelm Lomar. All later mentions of Lomar in Lovecraft's fiction (even in the *Dream-Quest*) confirm the impression that Lomar is postulated by Lovecraft as existing in the real world; note *At the Mountains of Madness*: "The ultimate blow, of course, was the coming of the great cold [i.e., the Ice Age] which . . . put an end to the fabled lands of Lomar and Hyperborea" (*MM* 73).[1] Note, too, that it is in "Polaris" where occurs the first citation of the Pnakotic Manuscripts (*D* 22), which are again universally regarded as being in the real world; even in the otherwise ambiguous *Dream-Quest* it is noted that "those inconceivably old Pnakotic Manuscripts [were] made by waking men in

---

1. The term "fabled" need not imply that Lomar is "fabulous" (i.e., existing only in fable), but merely that it is extremely old. An earlier passage in *At the Mountains of Madness* makes this clear: "Here sprawled a palaeogean megalopolis compared with which the fabled Atlantis and Olathoë in the land of Lomar are recent things of today—not even of yesterday" (*MM* 47).

forgotten boreal kingdoms" (*MM* 310). All this confirms that "Polaris" describes a "forgotten" civilisation in the real world before the birth of history. Indeed, in "Through the Gates of the Silver Key" it is implied that Lomar may in fact be the first true human civilisation (as opposed to those, such as Ib, whose inhabitants seem not to be fully human): "For this shape [i.e., 'Umr at-Tawil] was nothing less than that which all the world had feared since Lomar rose out of the sea" (*MM* 432).

It seems difficult to deny that "The White Ship" (1919) is a dream-journey; but it is odd that no explicit mention of such a thing occurs in the tale. The story was, of course, manifestly inspired by Dunsany's "Idle Days on the Yann," which takes place in a dream world; and the narrator of "The White Ship," as that in "Idle Days on the Yann," seems at least initially to be in the real world, although even this cannot be conclusively proven: "I am Basil Elton, keeper of the North Point light that my father and grandfather kept before me" (*D* 36).[2] When the White Ship comes Elton makes a supernatural ascent upon it ("I walked out over the waters to the White Ship on a bridge of moonbeams" [*D* 37]); but recall that Denys Barry seems to do roughly the same thing at the end of "The Moon-Bog," which is clearly set in the real world of Ireland. But the question of whether the events in "The White Ship" take place in the real or dream world becomes academic; for not only is the tale a virtual allegory, but none of the sites or characters mentioned in it recur anywhere in Lovecraft's fiction save in the ambiguous *Dream-Quest*.

In "The Doom That Came to Sarnath" (1919) we are explicitly told that the "grey stone city of Ib" stood "when the world was young" (*D* 43), and that Sarnath itself existed "ten thousand years ago" (*D* 43). Manifestly, then, the land of Mnar is in a prehistoric world, and not in a dream world; and in "The Nameless City" (1921) we are told that Sarnath was inhabited by early human beings while Ib was pre-human: ". . . I thought of Sarnath the Doomed, that stood in the land of Mnar when mankind was young, and of Ib, that was carven of grey stone before mankind existed" (*D* 100).

---

2. In the *Dream-Quest* allusion is made to the story, and Elton is now described as a "fellow-dreamer of earth—a lighthouse-keeper in ancient Kingsport" (*MM* 317). The evidence here is singularly ambiguous (does "fellow-dreamer" imply that Elton dreamed his journey on the White Ship or merely that he was given to dreaming?), but at least we know that Elton started from "earth." His location in Kingsport is merely an "in-joke," one supposes: Kingsport was not created until "The Terrible Old Man" (1920); and even so, Kingsport (along with Lovecraft's other "mythical" towns, Arkham, Dunwich, and Innsmouth) is not postulated as being in a dream world but in the "actual" world of New England.

In *At the Mountains of Madness* we learn that the great megalopolis of the Old Ones ranks "with such whispered pre-human blasphemies as . . . Ib in the land of Mnar" (*MM* 47). There may even be a veiled reference to Ib in "The Moon-Bog," where mention is made to tales "of an imagined city of stone deep down below the swampy surface" (*D* 119). Note that this tale seems to contain an allusion to "The Tree" ("that monotonous piping . . . made me think of some dance of fauns on distant Maenalus" [*D* 121]), so that such a reference to Ib is not impossible. All references, then, confirm that Mnar was actually a prehistoric land in the real world. If this is the case, then the other sites mentioned in the tale are no less real: "There were [in Sarnath] many palaces, the least of which were mightier than any in Thraa or Ilarnek or Kadatheron" (*D* 45).

We must briefly withhold judgment as to whether Lovecraft's next Dunsanian tale, "The Cats of Ulthar" (1920), is in the real or the dream world; let us note again that no explicit remark places the story in the land of dream. For the solution of the problem we must turn to "The Other Gods" (1921), where we learn that Barzai the Wise was "familiar with the Pnakotic Manuscripts of distant and frozen Lomar" (*D* 128). Barzai, it turns out, is from Ulthar (*D* 128), and the clear implication is that this tale too takes place in a prehistoric civilisation. Indeed, if—as seems indisputable—the Pnakotic Manuscripts were written in the "real" world, then not merely must Ulthar, Nir, Hatheg, and other towns mentioned in the tale be real, but so too must "Kadath in the cold waste" (*D* 127) and Mt. Hatheg-Kla, upon which the "gods of earth" (*D* 127) used to dance. Note this remark: "Now it is told in the mouldy Pnakotic Manuscripts that Sansu found naught but wordless ice and rock when he did climb Hatheg-Kla *in the youth of the world*" (*D* 131; my emphasis). It is to be noted that Atal, who was a mere "innkeeper's son" (*D* 58) in "The Cats of Ulthar," has now become a "young priest" (*D* 128) in "The Other Gods." In *The Dream-Quest of Unknown Kadath* he is "fully three centuries old" (*MM* 311).

"The Quest of Iranon" (1921) also makes reference to Lomar and to the sites mentioned in "The Doom That Came to Sarnath": "I [Iranon] have been to Thraa, Ilarnek, and Kadatheron on the winding river Ai, and have dwelt long in Olathoë in the land of Lomar" (*D* 114). As a result, the sites in "The Quest of Iranon"—Teloth, the river Zuro, etc.—must also be in the prehistoric world; although Iranon's city of Aira exists only in his imagination, since the name of Aira came only "from the lips of a playmate, a beggar's boy given to strange dreams" (*D* 117). Here the whole crux of the tale depends on the poignant distinction between a prosy real world (Teloth, Oonai, etc.) and the magical dream world imagined by Iranon. And recall the final sentence of he story, commenting on Iranon's death: "That night something of youth and beauty died in the *elder* world" (*D* 117; my emphasis).

"Celephaïs" (1920) resembles "Polaris" in that a sort of dream is employed in penetrating other worlds or other planes of reality; and since the tale so closely foreshadows the problematical *Dream-Quest* in theme, it is of the utmost importance to ascertain the precise nature of the realm of Celephaïs. It is true that, as in "The Quest of Iranon," the point of the tale consists in the dichotomy between the real world of London with its "indifferent millions" (*D* 83) and the imagined world of Celephaïs. The very opening of the tale tells us that Kuranes (and this was, after all, his dream name) saw Celephaïs "in a dream" (*D* 83); and that "when truth and experience failed to reveal [beauty], he sought it in fancy and illusion" (*D* 82–83)—but what does that "fancy and illusion" consist of? Nothing but the "nebulous memories of childhood tales and dreams" (*D* 84)—in other words, memories of the real world. The problematical nature of Celephaïs' existence is underscored by Kuranes' final (and permanent) journey there, for he initially starts the journey by a literal descent into time:

> . . . they . . . all rode majestically through the downs of Surrey and onward toward the region where Kuranes and his ancestors were born. It was very strange, but as the riders went on they seemed to gallop back through Time; for whenever they passed through a village in the twilight they saw only such houses and villagers as Chaucer or men before him might have seen . . . (*D* 88)

What seems to have happened is that Kuranes has somehow gone back in time to the town of his ancestors; Celephaïs is merely a name invented by Kuranes in his childhood fancies, but stands for some real locale (presumably in Surrey). It may be, indeed, that, like the narrator of "Polaris," Kuranes is prey to ancestral memory, and that his "dreams" are merely a means of escaping into a world that is very real, but which is merely set in the historical past. The fantastic or "dreamlike" details of Celephaïs may be merely the products of Kuranes' boyhood imagination.

It may well be that the fragment "Azathoth" (1922)—the last of Lovecraft's quasi-Dunsanian tales before the *Dream-Quest*—is the only tale in which an actual dream-journey is involved. Here the narrator is said specifically to have "travelled out of life on a quest into the spaces whither the world's dreams had fled" (*D* 357). Hence the character seems authentically to have fled the "real" world; but where precisely is the region "whither the world's dreams had fled"? The answer to this question may perhaps be found in the *Dream-Quest*, since Randolph Carter seems to have undertaken a journey very akin to that of the narrator of "Azathoth."

We have seen, then, that virtually all the characters and sites in Love-craft's "Dunsanian" tales can conclusively be set not in the world of dream but in a prehistoric (or, as in the case of "Celephaïs," an historical) land where a series of civilisations—Ib, Sarnath, Ulthar, Lomar, and the rest—have risen and fallen. There is striking uniformity in this conception, and—at least in the tales written before 1926—we have no justification for making any clear distinction between the "Dunsanian" tales and the real-world tales; there is nothing paradoxical about the intermixture of these worlds, since they can all be incorporated into a history of the planet that, though (obviously) imagined by Lovecraft, is postulated to be as "real" as the imagined cities of Dunwich, Arkham, Kingsport, and Innsmouth. Indeed, when in *At the Mountains of Madness* Lovecraft mentions a parade of lost civilisations—Atlantis, Lemuria, Commoriom, Uzuldaroum, Lomar, Valusia, R'lyeh, Ib, the Nameless City (*MM* 47)—he is, because they are cited in a definitely "real-world" tale, implicitly acknowledging their actual existence on this planet (for fictional purposes, it need hardly be added). It is, in fact, only with *The Dream-Quest of Unknown Kadath* and (to a lesser degree) "The Silver Key" that confusion enters into the picture.

We have already seen that Kadath, first mentioned in "The Other Gods" (*D* 127, 132), has been placed in the real world. This conception persists throughout the whole of Lovecraft's work except the *Dream-Quest* itself. Alhazred's mention of it—"Kadath in the cold waste hath known Them [the Old Ones], but what man knows Kadath?" (*DH* 170)—would not be paradoxical at all if, in the *Dream-Quest* (and only there), Kadath were not placed emphatically in the dream world. Even if we discount the title of the novel (and it was only the last of half a dozen titles devised by Lovecraft for the work, nearly all emphasising the dreamlike aspect of the narrative),[3] there is too much textual evidence in the novel to leave any doubt as to the dream-world status of Kadath. Carter, after being denied the sight of his sunset city, "prayed . . . to the hidden *gods of dream* that brood capricious above the clouds on unknown Kadath" (*MM* 307). Then, after Carter descends the "seventy steps" in "light slumber" (*MM* 307), he is told by the priests Nasht and Kaman-Thah that "not only had no man ever been to Kadath, but no man had ever suspected in what part of space it might lie" (*MM* 307–8). The mention of "space" here is slightly odd, apparently implying that Kadath occupies some space in the "real" world, but

---

3. The others are recorded on the verso of p. 1 of the A.Ms. (JHL): *The Dream-Quest of Randolph Carter; A Pilgrim in Dreamland; A Dreamland Quest/ Pilgrimage; The Seeking of Dreamland's Gods; Past the Gate of Deeper Slumber; In the Gulfs of Dream; A Seeker in Gulfs of Dream; The Quest of the Gods on Kadath.*

this implication is immediately dispelled by the subsequent remark—
"whether in the *dreamlands* around our own world, or in those surrounding
some unguessed companion of Fomalhaut or Aldebaran" (*MM* 308). This
is itself a little paradoxical, for if Kadath holds only the gods of earth (as
stated in "The Other Gods"), then there would presumably be no reason
why the gods (hence Kadath) would be anywhere but on or around our
planet. This confusion is cleared up by Atal the priest, who tells Carter that
the gods "are indeed only earth's gods, ruling feebly our own dreamland
and having no power of habitation elsewhere" (*MM* 311–12). It therefore
seems conclusive that Kadath is—in the *Dream-Quest*—in the dream world.

But if Carter has to descend the "seven hundred steps to the Gate of
Deeper Slumber" (*MM* 308) to find Kadath, then all his journeys described
in the novel must take place in the dream world. This means that nearly all
the sites invented in Lovecraft's earlier "Dunsanian" tales are suddenly
transported from the real (if prehistoric) world to the world of dream. Only
Lomar seems to preserve its real-world status, since we learn that the Pnakotic Manuscripts had been "made by waking men in forgotten boreal kingdoms . . . when the hairy cannibal Gnophkehs overcame many-templed
Olathoë and slew all the heroes of the land of Lomar" (*MM* 310). But these
very Pnakotic Manuscripts have now been "borne into the land of dream"
(*MM* 310). This copy of the Pnakotic Manuscripts has been taken to Ulthar
(*MM* 310), which means that it must now be in the land of dream. All the
other sites which Carter visits—the land of the zoogs (who "know many obscure secrets of the dream world and a few of the waking world" [*MM* 308]),
Dylath-Leen, Mt. Ngranek, Celephaïs, Inganok, and presumably Leng itself—must equally be in the dream world. The case of Leng is singularly bizarre. It was first cited in "Celephaïs," although nothing conclusive about its
existence in the real or dream world can be drawn from that mention; but in
"The Hound" (1922) we are clearly told that Leng is in "Central Asia" (*D*
174). It is true that its location here is dependent upon the testimony of Alhazred's *Necronomicon*, and Lovecraft takes the opportunity in *At the Mountains
of Madness* of transferring it to the Antarctic (*MM* 103); but nevertheless Leng
is always postulated as existing in the real world. Here again the *Dream-Quest*
flies in the face of all the testimony found in Lovecraft's other tales.

I maintain that Lovecraft never carefully thought out the *Dream-Quest*,
for there are certain internal inconsistencies in the novel that are puzzling
in the extreme. First, we learn from Atal that "at least twice in the world's
history the Other Gods set their seal upon earth's primal granite; once in
antediluvian times, as guessed from a drawing in . . . the Pnakotic Manuscripts . . ., and once on Hatheg-Kla when Barzai the Wise tried to see
earth's gods dancing by moonlight" (*MM* 312). We have seen that the Pna-

kotic Manuscripts, even in the *Dream-Quest,* are postulated as being written by people of the "waking" world (*MM* 310); therefore the mention of the first instance of the gods' setting their seal must also have taken place in the real world, and specifically in the ancient (perhaps prehistoric) world.[4] The incident with Barzai, if the *Dream-Quest* is here being consistent with "The Other Gods," must also have taken place in the real world; but of course this is contradicted by other parts of the novel, where Ulthar and Hatheg-Kla are set in the dream world. Similarly, it is remarked that "Ninety aeons ago, before even the gods had danced upon its [Ngranek's] pointed peak . . ." (*MM* 330), which tallies with a comment in "The Strange High House in the Mist": "the host grew timid when he spoke of the dim first age of chaos before the gods or even the Elder Ones [= the Great Ones of the *Dream-Quest*] were born, and when *the other gods* [Lovecraft's italics] came to dance on the peak of Hatheg-Kla in the stony desert near Ulthar" (*D* 282). As in all other tales, Hatheg-Kla (of which Ngranek is the name given to it by the gods—cf. "The Other Gods" [*D* 127]) is now set in the real world, along with the various gods who dwell or once dwelt upon it; but how can this be reconciled with the "gods of dream" (*MM* 307) whom Carter seeks in the dream world in the *Dream-Quest?* Finally, there is a stupendous internal contradiction when, after Carter escapes from the "almost-humans" who transport him to the moon to deliver him to Nyarlathotep, it is remarked that "on an unhallowed summit of the moon-mountains still vainly waited the crawling chaos Nyarlathotep" (*MM* 307). But how can Kadath (hence Leng), where Nyarlathotep must be waiting, be on the moon? As we know, the onyx castle is transferred back to the earth's dreamland at the conclusion of the *Dream-Quest.*

If we try to examine how precisely the dream world in the *Dream-Quest* is related to the real world, we will either discover more paradoxes and contradictions or be unable to integrate the relation into that found in other of Lovecraft's "Dunsanian" tales. There seem four ways in which we may conceive the dream world: 1) it is Carter's own dream world; 2) it is (literally) under the earth; 3) it is a prehistoric world (as in all the other "Dunsanian" tales) but Carter, by dreaming, has found a way to enter into it; 4) it is a "general" or "universal" dream world superimposed upon the real world. Let us examine each of these possibilities further.

The first hypothesis is ruled out almost automatically by Atal's remark that Carter's sunset city "probably . . . belonged to his [Carter's] especial dream world and not to the general land of vision that many know" (*MM*

---

4. It is unlikely that by "antediluvian" Lovecraft specifically means "before the Flood"; the adjective in Lovecraft means nothing more than "ancient."

312). Note, moreover, that the dream world continues to exist after Carter (at the end of the *Dream-Quest*) has woken up: "So . . . Randolph Carter leaped shoutingly awake within his Boston room. . . . And vast infinities away, past the Gate of Deeper Slumber and the enchanted wood . . . [etc.]" (*MM* 406). It appears, therefore, that the dream world in which Carter travels is a sort of "universal" dream world and not his own; and it is probably to this that the fragment "Azathoth" refers when it is said that the character there went on a "quest into the spaces whither the world's dreams had fled" (*D* 357). These dreams "that men have lost" (*D* 358) must similarly form a general body of dream accessible to all human beings (or, at least, to those who are powerful dreamers like Carter).

The case of Kuranes in the *Dream-Quest* is both enlightening and confusing in this regard. Although in "Celaphaïs" it was said that "it was he [Kuranes] who had created Ooth-Nargai in his dreams" (*D* 88), Ooth-Nargai and Celephaïs now appear to have become part of the general world of dream, while Kuranes now longs for the waking world and his boyhood memories of England. But "he could not go back to these things in the waking world because his body was dead; but he had done the next best thing and dreamed a small tract of such countryside in the region east of the city [sc. Celephaïs]" (*MM* 354). Kuranes has therefore created his own private world of dream in the land of dream. But why is Carter's similar private "sunset city" not in the (general) land of dream as well? Presumably (although this is never stated or even implied by Lovecraft) it is because Carter is not dead in the real world, so that all he has to do (and does do at the end of the novel) is to wake up and recapture his boyhood memories. But it is peculiar that Kuranes seems not to have any great control over his own dream world: "there hobbled to meet him [Carter] no robed and anointed lackey but a small stubby old man in a smock who spoke as best he could in the quaint tones of far Cornwall" (*MM* 355). If Kuranes, clearly an experienced dreamer, has created his own dream world, why can he not make the old man speak actually and perfectly in the tones of far Cornwall? And Kuranes furthermore was "seeking ever to teach them [the inhabitants of a "little Cornish fishing village" that Kuranes had dreamed] the dear remembered accents of old Cornwall fishers" (*MM* 354). But why do the people not know these accents already if they are merely creations of Kuranes? Here again Lovecraft has created, certainly, a poignant episode and one that clearly foreshadows Carter's discovery at the end of the novel, but he has not thought through the details of the concept very well. But whatever the situation with Kuranes, it is at least clear that there is both a general dream world and separate dream worlds that can be created by individual dreamers.

There are many indications that the general dream world into which

Carter enters is in some fashion under the earth.[5] We have already noted that Carter initially descends the seventy steps to the cavern of flame (*MM* 307) and then the 700 steps to the Gate of Deeper Slumber (*MM* 308). Indeed, as Maurice Lévy wryly remarked, "We could almost say that Carter moves more often vertically, in height or in depth, than horizontally" (Lévy 103). We know that the Enchanted Wood housing the zoogs "at two places touches the land of men" (*MM* 308), which implies that it is geographically very close to the surface of the real world; and recall Carter's apprehension that in the land of the ghouls "he was probably nearer the waking world than at any other time . . ." (*MM* 338)—this too seems to imply a vertical arrangement whereby the land of the ghouls is on the underside of the world. We may even draw support for this from "Pickman's Model," since we learn there that the ghouls have made a vast series of underground tunnels under Boston. That these tunnels are not, however, very far underground can be inferred from the fact that Pickman can presumably call upon and photograph the ghouls in his "cellar studio" (*DH* 25) by lifting "the circular brick curb of what was evidently a great well in the earthen floor" (*DH* 21). It is even remarked in the *Dream-Quest* that "these ghouls of the waking world would do no business in the graveyards of upper dreamland" (*MM* 338). It would be cumbrous to attempt to distinguish the various layers of Lovecraft's dream world (note, for example, that Sarkomand is "the valley *below* Leng" [*MM* 339]), but one remark may be significant. When the night-gaunts snatch Carter as he is ascending Mt. Ngranek, he suspects that they are taking him to the "primal mists of the earth's core" (*MM* 335); but Lovecraft's looseness of terminology—there is throughout the novel a confusion as to whether "earth" means the real world or the dream world—does not allow us to ascertain whether the literal earth's core is meant.

Nevertheless, the evidence seems overwhelming that the dream world is literally situated below the earth. But this theory encounters apparently insuperable obstacles. If Carter is actually under the earth, how can he see in the sky such galaxies and constellations as the Milky Way (*MM* 334), Charles' Wain, and the Little Bear (*MM* 357)? How can there be a sky at

---

5. This was realised by Wetzel, who compared the dream world to the Hades of Greek myth, since Kuranes has died in the real world to descend into the dream world (see Wetzel 84–85). The comparison to Hades is interesting, but Kuranes is the only one in the dream world of whom we know who is dead in the real world. There is no sign that Richard Upton Pickman died on earth, for the narrator of "Pickman's Model" merely remarks: "He's gone—back into the fabulous darkness he loved to haunt" (*DH* 24–25).

all? Most paradoxically, how can the black galley suddenly leap into space and go to the (apparently real) moon? How can the cats make similar leaps to and from the moon? Finally—and this seems to be a major obstacle to this theory and the next—if the "dream world" in the *Dream-Quest* is only a loose way of referring to a portion of the real world, what are we to make of the fact that the leader of the cats on the moon recognised Carter "as the sworn friend of his kind on earth and in the land of dream" (*MM* 324)? What is the distinction being drawn here? and did Lovecraft not realise that nearly all his other Dunsanian tales seem to take place in the real world? But here we are faced with yet another internal inconsistency: if Ulthar has now been placed in the dream world in this novel, how are we to understand the remark that "it was fortunate that the moon was not up, so that all the cats were *on earth*" (*MM* 346)? How can this be? Are not the cats in the dream world? or does "earth" merely refer to the dream world? If this is so, the distinction between "earth" and the "land of dream" noted above can have no meaning. Clearly Lovecraft is guilty of either extreme inconsistency or extreme looseness and vagueness of language.

When we turn to the third hypothesis—that the dream world is actually in the prehistoric past, as with nearly all the other "Dunsanian" tales, and that dream is simply a means of reaching this realm—we are in no better situation; for the theory seems not only inherently inappropriate to the *Dream-Quest* but may be tacitly contradicted by it at various points. First, we note that the law forbidding the killing of cats in Ulthar is now regarded as "ancient and significant" (*MM* 311); one cannot be sure what scope to give to the term "ancient," but just previous to this we are told that the stone bridge across the river Skai was built "thirteen-hundred years before [sc. Carter's arrival there]" (*MM* 311); presumably the law is much more ancient than this. Parts of the Pnakotic Manuscripts are now regarded as "too ancient to be read" (*MM* 312)—although it must be noted that they were termed "mouldy" in "The Other Gods" (*D* 131)—and Sarkomand's ruins are said to have "bleached for a million years before the first true human saw the light" (*MM* 371), which at least hints that we are far from the prehistoric age. In sum, although there is nothing explicitly forbidding the belief that the dream world is merely the prehistoric past, there is nothing in the novel to suggest such a view. In any case, the repeated hints that we are either literally or figuratively under the earth could not be incorporated into this scheme. We seem manifestly to be in a world not temporally distant from our own; moreover, the artist Pickman does not seem to have penetrated into the dream world by dreaming (as with Carter), but literally through one of the openings between the real world of the surface and the dream world below.

We are then left only with the theory that the dream world is somehow superimposed upon the real world, but how this is done is never explained (save in the curious remark about "dreamlands *around* our own world" [*MM* 308], which seems to imply some sort of outer membrane or atmosphere). Moreover, this would force us to ignore the very frequent hints that the dream world is underground ("the inner world has strange laws" [*MM* 337). I can only conclude that Lovecraft never clearly thought out the relations between the real world and the dream world in this novel, and—in wilfully ignoring the fact that his previous "Dunsanian" stories had clearly been set in the prehistoric past of the real world—subsumed all his previous Dunsanian sites into the dream world in order to make Carter's discovery of the real-world nature of his "sunset city" the more poignant. One could live with the mere failure of the *Dream-Quest* to tally with Lovecraft's other "Dunsanian" tales, for Lovecraft was not obliged to be uniformly systematic from one story to the next; but we may well express a certain irritation in not being able to ascertain even an internally consistent dream world within the confines of the *Dream-Quest* itself.

It remains to explore some later tales where Lovecraft seems consciously to have modified his previous conceptions of his "Dunsanian" sites and characters. Of the mention of the sign of Koth in *The Case of Charles Dexter Ward* ("It was the sign of Koth, that dreamers see fixed above the archway of a certain black tower standing alone in twilight—and Willett did not like what his friend Randolph Carter had said of its powers" [*MM* 214]) we need take little notice: this seems a completely frivolous and joking reference that, in any case, has no bearing on the outcome of the novel. More important is Alhazred's remark that "Kadath in the cold waste has known Them [i.e., the Old Ones]" (*DH* 170). But who are the Old Ones? or rather, how can Kadath have known them? If the Ones Ones are to be identified with any gods in the *Dream-Quest*, it must be with the Other Gods, for the Great Ones are merely the "mild gods of earth" (*MM* 399), hardly to be equated with the titanic entities depicted by Alhazred. This harmonises both with the *Dream-Quest*—since Nyarlathotep is there called "the soul and messenger" (*MM* 308) of the Other Gods, a designation commonly applied to him in other tales—and with "Through the Gates of the Silver Key," where the Old Ones or Other Gods have not merely been given yet another name but have returned to their dreamlike state: "He [Carter] wondered at the vast conceit of those who babbled of the *malignant* Ancient Ones, as if They could pause from their everlasting dreams to wreak a wrath on mankind" (*MM* 433). It appears that both Nyarlathotep and the Old Ones/Other Gods/Ancient Ones have the power of dwelling simultaneously in the dream world and the real world, although it is inevitably never explained how this is possible.

At the Mountains of Madness (1931) both clarifies and casts further confusion upon the whole picture. We have seen that the novel confirms the real-world existence of Lomar and Ib by incorporating them into Lovecraft's history of life on this planet; and we have also seen that Kadath has been transferred from Central Asia to the Antarctic (although this shift was anticipated in "The Mound" [1929–30], where we are told that the underground denizens of K'n-yan "had had some remarkable civilisations, especially one at the South Pole near the mountain Kadath" [*HM* 131]). But note Lovecraft's terminology when he makes the shift in *At the Mountains of Madness*: "For this far violet line could be nothing else than the terrible mountains of the forbidden land . . . the unknown *archetype* of that dreaded Kadath in the Cold Waste beyond abhorrent Leng whereof *primal legends* hint evasively" (*MM* 103). Kadath has now become merely a "legend," hence presumably has no concrete existence at all. Leng is similarly transformed: "Mythologists have placed Leng in Central Asia" (*MM* 20); ". . . I thought again of the eldritch primal *myths* . . . of the daemoniac plateau of Leng" (*MM* 45). What seems to be going on in this novel is a general "de-mythologising" (see Price) of the myth-cycle evidenced by the fact that the very real barrel-shaped entities are themselves "the originals of the fiendish elder myths which things like the Pnakotic Manuscripts and the *Necronomicon* affrightedly hint about. They were the great 'Old Ones' that had filtered down from the stars . . ." (*MM* 59). Hence not merely Kadath and Leng, of which Alhazred had spoken, but the Old Ones themselves whom he had deemed divine, are all myths and legends—or rather, there were very real causes or "archetypes" that gave rise to these myths. How we are to reconcile this with the fact that, in "Through the Gates of the Silver Key" (1932–33), the Old Ones or Ancient Ones seem to have regained their ethereal divinity is anyone's guess. But Kadath at any rate has evolved from a real site in the prehistoric past ("The Other Gods") to a dream site (*The Dream-Quest of Unknown Kadath*) to a mere myth whose real model is the range of unexplored mountains in the Antarctic. Indeed, Lovecraft in *At the Mountains of Madness* may be trying to imply that all his previous tales about Kadath, Ulthar, Lomar, and the rest are merely fragments of this body of legend.

The results of this investigation are, inevitably, tentative and confused. In nearly all the tales before the *Dream-Quest*, the characters and sites of Lovecraft's "Dunsanian" tales seem to be emphatically placed in a prehistoric setting; the *Dream-Quest* causes great confusion to this schema, placing most of the sites in the dream world but doing so in a paradoxical and self-inconsistent fashion; finally, in later tales Lovecraft develops or changes his conceptions at will, and finally transforms them into myth or legend in the manner of a J. G. Frazer or Margaret Murray. All this is, doubtless, somewhat strange for a writer who is otherwise remarkably self-consistent; but this investigation—aside from indicating that *The Dream-Quest of Unknown Kadath* cannot be used indiscriminately as a source for many aspects of the Lovecraft Mythos unless its internal inconsistencies be resolved—shows the singular fertility of Lovecraft's mind, not content to let the smallest details of his various invented characters, gods, and civilisations go unaltered in the course of his fictional career. I suspect, however, that Lovecraft would have been comparatively unconcerned at the non-synchronisation of all aspects of his fictional geography, for he knew that

> the final criterion of authenticity [in a weird tale] is not the dovetailing of a plot but the creation of a given sensation. . . . The one test of the really weird is simply this—whether or not there be excited in the reader a profound sense of dread, and of contact with unknown spheres and powers; a subtle attitude of awed listening, as if for the beating of black wings or the scratching of outside shapes and entities on the known universe's utmost rim. (*Supernatural Horror in Literature* [*D* 368–69])

There can hardly be any question that, judged from these standards, Lovecraft's tales succeed as few others ever have.

Works Cited

Dunsany, Lord. *A Dreamer's Tales*. 1910. Rpt. Boston: John W. Luce, [1917].

Lévy, Maurice. *Lovecraft: A Study in the Fantastic*. Trans. S. T. Joshi. Detroit: Wayne State University Press, 1988.

Price, Robert M. "Demythologizing Cthulhu." *Lovecraft Studies* No. 8 (Spring 1984): 3–9, 24.

Wetzel, George T. "The Cthulhu Mythos: A Study" (1972). In S. T. Joshi, ed., *H. P. Lovecraft: Four Decades of Criticism*. Athens: Ohio University Press, 1980.

Lovecraft's Alien Civilisations:
A Political Interpretation

In a chapter of *H. P. Lovecraft: The Decline of the West* (1990) I attempted to outline the major tenets of Lovecraft's political and economic thought, particularly as they evolved toward the end of his life, when, with the onset of the Depression, his attention became directed more and more to the problems of employment, social organisation, and particularly the place of aesthetics in modern society. But these views are not only reflected in his letters and in such essays as "Some Repetitions on the Times" (1933), but also in his later fiction. Fritz Leiber was among the earliest to hint that Lovecraft's later tales—notably *At the Mountains of Madness* (1931) and "The Shadow out of Time" (1934–35)—contain much discussion of the political, social, and cultural aspects of his alien civilisations (see Leiber, "Through Hyperspace"); but it is now clear that in several of Lovecraft's late narratives—not only the two mentioned but other such tales as "The Mound" (1929–30),[1] "The Whisperer in Darkness" (1930), "The Shadow over Innsmouth" (1931), and "In the Walls of Eryx" (1936)[2]—these alien civilisations either represent a sort of Lovecraftian utopia or are predictions of the possible future of mankind. The six extra-terrestrial races involved—the Great Race, the Old Ones, the mound denizens,[3] the fungi from Yuggoth, the Innsmouth folk, and the Venusians—are, in varying degrees, embodiments of Lovecraft's political and economic views; but while some are utopias, others are very much dystopias.

It is interesting to note, however, that all the alien civilisations involved are in many ways superior to human beings—or, at least, to human beings in their present state. Lovecraft declares flatly that the Great Race

---

1. It need not concern us that the tale was "revised" (or, rather, ghostwritten) for Zealia Bishop, since it is obvious that Lovecraft not only wrote but conceived the entire tale. See my article, "Who Wrote 'The Mound'?," *Nyctalops* No. 14 (March 1977): 41–42; rev. ed. *Crypt of Cthulhu* No. 11 (Candlemas 1983): 27–29.

2. Here the amount of work that can definitely be ascribed to Lovecraft (as opposed to his collaborator, Kenneth Sterling) is less certain; but the descriptions of the natives of Venus seem to be Lovecraft's. Nevertheless, caution must be exercised.

3. They too are curiously called the "Old Ones"; I shall, however, not use this designation for the mound dwellers but shall restrict it to the alien race in *At the Mountains of Madness*.

(which probably represents his quintessential utopia, since it is called "the greatest race of all," having "learned all things that ever were known or ever would be known on earth" [*DH* 385]) had an intelligence "enormously greater than man's" (*DH* 393). Similarly, the "scientific and mechanical knowledge" of the Old Ones in *At the Mountains of Madness* "far surpassed man's today" (*MM* 62) (the final word is to be noted), while the "brain capacity [of the fungi from Yuggoth] exceeds that of any other surviving life-form" (*DH* 240). (This appears to be hyperbole, since the Great Race and the Old Ones—despite the fact that the latter were defeated in warfare by the fungi at the dawn of our planet's history [see *MM* 68]— seem clearly superior to the fungi in pure intelligence; but as this remark is found in a letter to Wilmarth written by one of the fungi themselves, one may legitimately suspect that it is an instance of self-congratulatory egotism.) The mound denizens can also boast superiority in intelligence to human beings: they have gained the power of dematerialisation, converse purely by telepathy, and have also conquered old age.

This last quality is an interesting one; for while the incredible longevity of the Great Race and the Old Ones seems to be a product of their anatomical structures, the mound denizens have triumphed over old age apparently through sheer strength of mind. In a less intellectual way, the Innsmouth folk have become immortal by returning to the sea, the original habitat—so Lovecraft has Zadok Allen declare[4]—of all terrestrial life. The longevity of the fungi from Yuggoth is not stated, and is thus probably not notable.

Lovecraft conveys the great intelligence of his alien races in other ways. Several of them possess more (or keener) senses than human beings: the Great Race "had but two of the senses which we recognise—sight and hearing . . . [but] of other and incomprehensible senses . . . they possessed many" (*DH* 398); the protagonists of *At the Mountains of Madness* have difficulty in understanding some of the bas-reliefs that they see, since "certain touches here and there gave vague hints of latent symbols and stimuli which another mental and emotional background, and a fuller or different sensory equipment, might have made of profound and poignant significance to us" (*MM* 57); while even the Venusians seem to have a "special sense" (*D* 293) for the crystals which they worship.

The ability for space-travel is noted for all the races save the Innsmouth folk and the Venusians. Both the Old Ones and the fungi from Yuggoth are said to have flown through the aether on their "vast membranous" (*MM* 61) wings. This idea has been ridiculed by Richard L. Tierney;

---

4. "Seems that . . . everything alive come aout o' the water onct": "The Shadow over Innsmouth" (*DH* 331).

and perhaps Lovecraft himself saw the improbability of the device, for he declares that the Great Race flew through space and time by projecting their minds forward (or, more rarely, backward) through time with "suitable mechanical aid" (*DH* 386) (presumably the curious mechanism of "rods, wheels, and mirrors" [*DH* 374] seen in Peaslee's home just before the end of his "amnesia"). In "The Mound" it is said that the people of K'n-yan "had come from a distant part of space where physical conditions are much like those of the earth" (*HM* 131); this idea is still harder to swallow, particularly in view of Lovecraft's condemnation of the use of anthropomorphic alien races in such essays as "Some Notes on Interplanetary Fiction." Lovecraft adds the qualification, "All this . . . was legend now; and one could not say how much truth was in it" (*HM* 131); but, we wonder, if the origin of the mound denizens were not extra-terrestrial, how could they have had such notions of extra-terrestriality to begin with? Suffice it to say that, with the exception of "The Shadow out of Time," Lovecraft's conceptions of space travel were somewhat primitive.

Three of Lovecraft's alien civilisations possess the power of hypnosis and telepathy. The mound denizens not only converse telepathically but control their slaves by "streams of thought" (*HM* 119). The Old Ones maintain a similar control over their slaves, the shoggoths. In "The Whisperer in Darkness" the "undoubted telepathic and hypnotic powers of the hill creatures and their agents" (*DH* 231) is noted.

Scientific research is high among several of Lovecraft's alien races. The prodigious scientific intelligence required to build the "mechanical aid" that permits mind-exchange certainly argues a high development of physics, electronics, astronomy, and perhaps psychology on the part of the Great Race. As for the Old Ones, not only does Lovecraft say (as noted above) that their "scientific and mechanical knowledge" greatly exceeded that of human beings, but remarks that the information revealed in their maps and diagrams is "uncannily close to the latest findings of mathematics and astrophysics" (*MM* 60). The pseudo-Akeley in "The Whisperer in Darkness" tells Wilmarth: "You can't imagine the degree to which those beings [i.e., the fungi from Yuggoth] have carried science" (*DH* 253). Among the mound denizens "scientific curiosity . . . was keen," and "science had been profound and accurate, and all-embracing save in the one direction of astronomy" (*HM* 132, 135).

The Venusians seem to have excelled in only a single branch of science (or art)—that of architecture. The narrator of "In the Walls of Eryx" categorically states: "They haven't any skill except building" (*D* 293). Indeed, we cannot place the Venusians too high on the intellectual scale; for if we believe (as the narrator comes to do) that they had constructed their invisible labyrinth solely to entrap human beings greedy for their crystals, we can only wonder at the stupendous waste of energy and effort. Lovecraft's other civilisations are, however, also notable builders: Zamacona is stupefied at the sight of the "monstrous, gigantic, and omnipotent city of Tsath" (*HM* 143), while the two protagonists of *At the Mountains of Madness* experience still greater amazement at the site of the Old Ones' immemorial megalopolis. Peaslee admires the imposing and Cyclopean architecture of the Great Race's city, remarking that "the principle of the arch was known as fully and used as extensively as by the Romans" (*DH* 379). On Yuggoth the fungi have built "great houses and temples"; although the "mysterious Cyclopean bridges . . . [were] built by some elder race extinct and forgotten before the beings came to Yuggoth from the ultimate voids" (*DH* 254). Even the Innsmouth denizens (clearly at the bottom of the scale among Lovecraft's alien civilisations) have a distinctive architecture, but only in their underwater homes: who can forget the conclusion of the tale, when the narrator longs to behold "Cyclopean and many-columned Y'hanthlei" (*DH* 367)?

History is a major pursuit among the alien races in Lovecraft, particularly the Great Race, in whose "vast libraries were volumes of texts and pictures holding the whole of earth's annals—histories and descriptions of every species that had ever been or that ever would be, with full records of their arts, their achievements, their languages, and their psychologies" (*DH* 386). Lovecraft emphasises the "abnormal historic-mindedness" (*MM* 57) of the Old Ones, adding somewhat dryly that the continental drift theory of Taylor, Wegener, and Joly received "striking support from [the] uncanny source" (*MM* 66) of the Old ones' maps. History was certainly a high priority among the mound denizens, although it was "more and more neglected" (*HM* 136) at the time of Zamacona's visit. Even the fungi from Yuggoth have some interest in history or ethnography, since "they like to take away men of learning once in a while, to keep informed of the state of things in the human world" (*DH* 218). One senses, however, that this curiosity is not so much academic as practical and even strategical.

Finally, medicine has been carried to a high level by many of the aliens. Here the fungi from Yuggoth seem to be paramount, since "surgery is an incredibly expert and every-day thing among them" (*DH* 240). In other tales this medical capacity is only implied: certainly the mound denizens must be skilled in surgery to create their bizarrely composite reanimated slaves, while the Old Ones, if not skilled in medicine, are at least curious about the human and canine anatomies (cf. *MM* 37, 86). No particular mention is made of the Great Race's medical capacities.

In social organisation Lovecraft's alien civilisations are in some respects strikingly similar and in others notably divergent. In the final analysis the

Great Race clearly emerges as the most enlightened and "model" race in Lovecraft, with the Old Ones some distance back and the mound denizens well behind. The social structure of the fungi, the Venusians, and the Innsmouth folk is scarcely described, but we can assume that all these societies—despite the intelligence of the fungi—represent Lovecraftian dystopias in greater or lesser degrees. Lovecraft's attitude toward the social and political structure of his alien races will be studied in greater detail later.

It is a fact of no small interest that all three of Lovecraft's comparatively utopian societies have done away with sex in the normal human fashion. This is understandable in the cases of the Great Race and the Old Ones, since both these races are totally non-human in biology and could thus hardly propagate like humans. Both reproduce by spores; consequently there is little place for family life in the two civilisations. Normal family life has also been done away with among the mound denizens (cf. *HM* 344).[5] In the early period of the mound denizens' history, the "ruling type" had practised "selective breeding" (*HM* 134) to gain supremacy; and long before Zamacona's visit "births had ceased," since people "could easily become young again when they felt like it" (*HM* 132). Indeed, the "naturally inferior members of the ruling race" (*HM* 134) became slaves so that the ruling type remained uncorrupted. Similarly, the Great Race disposed of its "defective individuals . . . as soon as their defects were noticed" (*DH* 399), while the Old Ones did away with any "bothersome forms" (*MM* 65) which they happened to create. A particularly surprising detail is that the inferior stock of the mound denizens not only became slaves but actually contributed to the meat supply (*HM* 139).

That Lovecraft was essentially reflecting his own social views when writing such passages is obvious from the manifestly sympathetic tone in which they are written. While, certainly, Lovecraft would surely not have wished to make a feast of such of his characters as Joe Slater in "Beyond the Wall of Sleep," it is clear that the idea of racial purity and the elimination of "bad blood" remained central to his thought even at the end of his life (as the correspondence to J. Vernon Shea indicates), and is all of a piece with his comparative admiration of Hitler. Both the Old Ones and the mound denizens make extensive use of slaves; and while slavery has no place in the socialistic order embraced by Lovecraft in his later years, he was nonetheless sympathetic to slavery: in "Medusa's Coil" he wrote that "to hear [negro slaves upon a southern plantation] singing and laughing

---

5. The resemblance in this detail to Plato's utopia in the *Republic* need not be stressed, since Lovecraft, having no great respect for Plato, probably derived his ideas independently of him—largely through keen observation of the political and social developments of his own time.

and playing the banjo at night was to know the fullest charm of a civilisation and social order now sadly extinct" (*HM* 169). It is true that both the Old Ones and the mound denizens went into a decline, and that the former were actually extirpated by the slaves of their own creation; but the causes of their decline (to be examined in greater detail later) were not restricted to their being a slave-owning society, hence we can infer no moral condemnation of slavery by Lovecraft in these cases.

In more minor particulars of social organisation, we may note that the Great Race does without sleep altogether (*DH* 398) and no longer hunts for its food, it being wholly "vegetable and synthetic" (*DH* 397). In these details—which allow the beings to engage the more extensively in intellection—the Great Race again asserts its superiority to the other alien civilisations in Lovecraft. Even the Old Ones continue to hunt and practise herding (*MM* 65), while the same holds true for the mound denizens. Both the Old Ones and the Innsmouth folk are fishermen. Little is said on the eating habits of the Venusians or the fungi (although the pseudo-Akeley's refusal to share a dinner with Wilmarth at the conclusion of "The Whisperer in Darkness" may imply that the fungi cannot eat human food); but they presumably require some sort of sustenance, probably gained from the land through rudimentary agriculture.

It is in the political structure of some of Lovecraft's alien civilisations that we trace the clearest reflections of his own political views. The Great Race in particular seems to represent the governmental utopia toward which Lovecraft wished mankind to strive:

> The Great Race seemed to form a single, loosely knit nation or league, with major institutions in common, though there were four definite divisions. The political and economic system of each unit was a sort of fascistic socialism, with major resources rationally distributed, and power delegated to a small governing board elected by the vote of all able to pass certain educational and psychological tests. (*DH* 399)

I have elsewhere pointed out the startling similarities of these remarks to Lovecraft's views as crystallised in "Some Repetitions on the Times." In that essay Lovecraft clearly advocates the limiting of franchise to those "able to pass rigorous educational examinations (emphasising civic and economic subjects) and scientific intelligence tests" (*MW* 283), the limiting of power to a small "oligarchy of intelligence," the wider distribution of wealth (including government control "over large accumulations of resources"), and other such measures.

The two stories, "The Mound" and *At the Mountains of Madness*, provide interesting insights into the gradual development of Lovecraft's political and economic thought. "The Mound" (1929–30), the first tale where political remarks (and even satire) are inserted, shows that Lovecraft had not yet evolved the views codified in "Some Repetitions on the Times." The mound denizens' government "was a kind of communistic or semi-anarchical state; habit rather than law determining the daily order of things" (*HM* 135). This is most surprising, since Lovecraft was never sympathetic to communism, much less anarchism; writing in 1931: "I think no conceivable system of communism could bring civilised people any possible recompense for the damage its establishment would inevitably involve" (*SL* 3.377). But it appears that the mound denizens had drifted into communism through "paralysing ennui" (*HM* 135) rather than through the violent revolution predicted by Marx and realised in the Russia of 1917. Indeed, the mound society is hardly communistic, but rather aristocratic; hence Lovecraft's frequent mentions of the "ruling race" or the "ruling type." It is precisely the aristocratic temperament—whose noblest features were, as Lovecraft wrote, "good manners, taste, intelligence, responsibility, and a certain sense of honour" (*SL* 4.423)—that makes possible a government ruled by "habit rather than law." "The Mound," then, indicates that Lovecraft had yet to abandon the vestigial predilection for aristocracy gained through his early readings and upbringing, and had not yet fully adopted socialism. His aristocratic or elitist views never in fact left him; for even the socialistic Great Race has four "definite" classes. But Lovecraft easily reconciled aristocracy with socialism, since to the end of his life he believed that progress in intellectual and aesthetic life—in effect, the distinctive features of civilisation—were determined by a very small segment of the population.[6] But Lovecraft's "oligarchy of intelligence" (which might better have been called an oligarchy of specialists) does not necessarily consist of these intellectual leaders; for in "Some Repetitions on the Times" he writes: "No non-technician, be he artist, philosopher, or scientist, can even begin to judge the labyrinthine governmental problems with which . . . administrators must deal" (*MW* 283).

The political system of the Old Ones in *At the Mountains of Madness* is quite different from that of the mound denizens. Lovecraft flatly declares that their "government was evidently complex and probably socialistic"; adding, however, that "no certainties in this regard could be deduced from the sculptures we saw" (*MM* 65). Lovecraft's comparative lack of detail on the governmental structure of the Old Ones may be explained not only through the exigencies of plot—since, as he wrote, it would be exceedingly difficult to ascertain an entire social system merely from bas-reliefs, however extensive and detailed—and not only through his imperfect adoption

---

6. Here he is an agreement with, among others, Bertrand Russell; see his essay "Western Civilization" in *In Praise of Idleness and Other Essays* (1935).

of socialism, but through a lack of conviction as to the necessity for social reform in his own time. "Some Repetitions on the Times," however—written in the bleakest days of the Depression, just before the inauguration of Roosevelt—burns with a sense of urgency for reform lest we "starve and goad the people into an uprising," which "is likely to mean bolshevism in the end . . . a thing worth going to any length to escape" (*MW* 277–78). This sense of urgency not only colours his letters from the period but also accounts for the notably detailed presentation of the Great Race's political and social structure in "The Shadow out of Time."

It is noteworthy that two of Lovecraft's three highly evolved races—the Old Ones and the mound denizens—had passed through a stage of mechanised culture but had discarded it because they found it unsatisfying (*MM* 62, *HM* 343). This is in strict accordance with Lovecraft's loathing of the rampant mechanisation which was altering the whole structure of his society: "The future civilisation of mechanical standardisation of life and thought is a monstrous and artificial thing which can never find embodiment either in art or in religion" (*SL* 2.104–5). What, then, are we to make of the fact that the Great Race still maintains its mechanised society? "Industry, highly mechanised, demanded but little time from each citizen; and the abundant leisure was filled with intellectual and aesthetic activities of various sorts" (*DH* 399). Here again we must look to "Some Repetitions on the Times": Lovecraft had there suggested a rational distribution of work to solve unemployment; hence, given the "radically increased leisure among all classes of society . . . education . . . will require amplification. . . . It is possible that the number of persons possessing a sound general culture will be greatly increased, with corresponding good results to the civilisation" (*MW* 282).

The development of Lovecraft's views now becomes clear: when he wrote "The Mound" and *At the Mountains of Madness,* he still felt it possible to reverse the tide of mechanisation and return to the rural-based aristocracy of the past;[7] but with the writing of "Some Repetitions on the Times" and "The Shadow out of Time," we see that Lovecraft has accepted the inevitability of a mechanised future—though by no means sympathising with it—and feels that proper education and the reorganisation of society (particularly the abolishment of democracy and capitalism) could perhaps provide

---

7. "Granted the machine-victim has leisure. What is he going to do with it? What memories and experiences has he to form a background to give significance to anything he can do? What can he see or do that will mean anything to him? If he takes an aeroplane trip to the country, what will such a glimpse mean to one whose natural connexion to the rural landscape is hopelessly shattered?" (*SL* 2.308).

a meaningful and aesthetically satisfying existence. Lovecraft had ceased to want a *restoration* of the past, but now looks to *reform* for the future.

Lovecraft notes that "crime was surprisingly scant" among the Great Race, "and was dealt with through highly efficient policing" (*DH* 400). Indeed, the Great Race seems to be the only one of Lovecraft's alien races to have a police force: none is mentioned in *At the Mountains of Madness,* while the lack of one among the mound denizens is implied by the fact that Zamacona was given ten slaves to "protect him from thieves and sadists and religious orgiasts on the public highways" (*HM* 146). The government of the mound people must have been anarchical, indeed!

All the alien civilisations—with the exception, perhaps, of the Innsmouth folk[8]—seem to deal in warfare on a lesser or greater level; and the Great Race, the Old Ones, and the fungi from Yuggoth all battled one another in massive wars long before the emergence of humanity. All the races, however, conduct their wars in a roughly similar fashion—through the use of a vast army. The use of such a large force is interesting, for it implies the failure on the part of the races to develop weapons that—as with modern nuclear weapons—would render the use of large bodies of men needless. True, the Great Race has "camera-like weapons which produced tremendous electrical effects," but it also has an "enormous army" (*DH* 400). The mound denizens had sent a "suitably armed and equipped exploring party . . . to Yoth" (*HM* 141), while the fungi from Yuggoth "could easily conquer earth, but have not tried so far because they have not needed to. They would rather leave things as they are to save bother" (*DH* 218); and their battles with Akeley imply that they fight largely through the strength of numbers than through any powerful devices. It is true that the Old Ones "used curious weapons of molecular disturbance" (*MM* 67) against both the shoggoths and their extra-terrestrial rivals; but these seem to have availed them little, since the Old Ones were defeated not only by the Cthulhu spawn and the fungi from Yuggoth but ultimately by the shoggoths themselves. Lovecraft thus apparently failed to predict the revolutionary effect upon warfare which such weapons as the atomic bomb (the physical effects of which were so precisely if accidentally predicted in "The Colour out of Space") would have, for in "Some Repetitions on the Times" he continues to emphasise the need for "an army and navy of great strength," possibly involving "universal training" (*MW* 282). Of course, even today nuclear weapons seem to be used largely as a strategic tool, and

---

8. There are, however, a few hints of the Innsmouth folk's warlike tendencies: their alliance with the shoggoths (see below) may imply that they use those entities for militaristic purposes; while the Innsmouth folk pursue the narrator in a "limitless stream" (*DH* 360), though apparently lacking any real coordination or organisation.

the need for conventional weapons and a large standing army has by no means diminished.

All the alien races—the Venusians apparently excepted—practise trade or commerce in one form or another. The Innsmouth folk subsist on "fishing and lobstering. Everybody trades mostly either here [i.e., Newburyport] or in Arkham or Ipswich" (*DH* 306), and they also sell their "queer foreign kind of jewellery . . . on the sly" (*DH* 309). The fungi appear to do no trading with human beings, but have come to earth "to get metals from mines that go deep under the hills" (*DH* 218). The mound denizens once traded extensively with the surface civilisations, but "traffic with the lands of sun and starlight abruptly ceased" (*HM* 131) when the mound people gained a sudden prejudice of the men of the outer earth. Among the Old Ones "there was extensive commerce, both local and between different cities; certain small, flat counters, five-pointed and inscribed, serving as money" (*MM* 65). Trade among the Great Race is curiously not mentioned by Lovecraft, although it must have existed; perhaps it was conducted along the same lines as that of the Old Ones.

Aesthetic activity is high among each of Lovecraft's alien civilisations, although the fungi can only boast of their Cyclopean architecture upon Yuggoth. The Innsmouth folk produce a fascinating type of jewellery that "clearly belonged to some settled technique of infinite maturity and perfection," but which ultimately inspires dread in the narrator because it was "overflowing with the ultimate quintessence of unknown and inhuman evil" (*DH* 312). As for the invisible labyrinth on Venus, the narrator of "In the Walls of Eryx" is so impressed with its construction that he refuses to believe that the Venusians could have built it: "There must have been another race aeons ago, of which this is perhaps the last relique" (*D* 301). The art of the Old Ones "was mature, accomplished, and aesthetically evolved to the highest degree of civilised mastery. . . . In delicacy of execution no sculpture I have ever seen could approach it" (*MM* 56). As for the Great Race, "art was a vital part of [their] life" (*DH* 399).

The mound denizens are.among the most interesting in this regard, for their whole lives are conducted in a quest for "pleasure-seeking" (*HM* 135)—the traditional perversion of Epicureanism.[9] Indeed, even their intellectual activities—science, history, and philosophy—seem to be carried out rather in the pursuit of amusement than of knowledge:

---

9. "Remember that the goal of the great Epicurus was not an earthly *hedone* (Hedonism), or pleasure, but a lofty *ataraxia*, or freedom from cares and trivial thoughts" (*SL* 1.87).

Science had been profound and accurate. . . . Of late, however, it was falling into decay, as people found it increasingly useless to tax their minds by re- calling its maddening infinitude of details and ramifications. It was thought more sensible to abandon the deepest speculations and to confine philoso- phy to conventional forms. . . . History was more and more neglected . . . [but] it was still an *interesting* [my italics] subject. . . . In general, though, the modern tendency was to feel rather than think; so that men were now more highly esteemed for inventing new diversions than for preserving old facts or pushing back the frontier of cosmic mystery. (*HM* 135–36)

Which view comes closest to Lovecraft's own—the quest for pleasure or the quest for knowledge? There is no denying that, on occasion, Lovecraft confessed himself more given toward the former than the latter:

The truth is, that I am really most emphatically non-intellectual, if not positively anti-intellectual. I abhor mathematics, take no interest in feats of mental sprightliness, have no especial quickness of apprehension, and am certainly not at all distinguisht for holding in my head the many simul- taneous threads of a complex matter. What liking I have for logick and analysis is purely an aesthetick one—a wish to *arrange* and *classify* things in patterns whose configuration shall possess, in the realm of ideas, that decorative *beauty of form* possesst by tangible objects of art and nature in the realm of matter. (*SL* 2.52)

I have already discussed, in a previous essay ("'Reality' and Knowledge"), Lovecraft's devotion to knowledge; the statement above—made, perhaps, when he was still under the influence of the Decadent philosophy of his earlier years, and betraying disingenuousness with its use of pretentious ar- chaisms—can perhaps be contrasted with one made only a few years later:

The process of delving into the black abyss is to me the keenest form of fascination, and it is my conviction that this process demands the exercise of those parts of the human organism which represent the latest and most complex degrees of evolution. I burn, I admire, I respect . . . and what I crave, admire, and respect is the pure and abstract abyss-plunging which enthralled Anaxagoras, Anaximines, and Anaximander. Dry, utilitarian mechanism? John L. Sullivan's ass! Don't make an old man hee-haw! I want the straight dope on the clear *is or isn't* proposition as far as it can be pushed, and a weeding out of all silly, unmotivated, and gratuitous guess- work and lie-faking in the unknown gulph beyond the present radius of the *is or isn't* searchlight. (*SL* 3.299)

It is clear that Lovecraft valued intellection for his own sake; and the inference we must draw from the relevant passages of "The Shadow out of Time," *At the Mountains of Madness,* and "The Mound" is that, in his mind, the Great Race and the Old Ones are significantly higher on the cultural scale for practising *both* intellection and aesthetics than the mound denizens, who practise a type of intellection *because* of their aesthetic tastes.

The conclusion is confirmed when we note that the normal activities of the mound denizens do not consist in intellectual activity but in "games, intoxication, torture of slaves, day-dreaming, gastronomic and emotional orgies, religious exercises, exotic experiments, artistic and philosophical discussions, and the like" (*HM* 135). The student of Lovecraft will readily acknowledge that few of these activities found sympathy with him. Indeed, the "torture of slaves" immediately brings to mind the gladiator displays that formed part of the *panem et circenses* of the later Romans: "[There were] many amphitheatres where curious sports and sensations were provided for the weary people of K'n-yan" (*HM* 145).

In the end Lovecraft condemns the mound denizens' lifestyle—and in the process declares his ultimate rejection of the Decadent philosophy:

> He [Zamacona] felt that the people of Tsath were a lost and dangerous race—more dangerous to themselves they they knew—and that their growing frenzy of monotony-warfare and novelty-quest was leading them rapidly toward a precipice of disintegration and horror. . . . As time progressed, he noticed an increasing tendency of the people to resort to dematerialisation as an amusement; so that the apartments and amphitheatres of Tsath became a veritable witches' sabbath of transmutations, age-adjustments, death-experiments, and projections. With the growth of boredom and restlessness, he saw, cruelty and subtlety and revolt were growing apace. There was more and more cosmic abnormality, more and more curious sadism, more and more ignorance and superstition, and more and more desire to escape out of physical life into a half-spectral state of electronic dispersion. (*HM* 147–48)

The significance of this decadence—as well as the less complete decline of the Great Race and the Old Ones—shall be examined later.

The final aspect of social life upon which Lovecraft dwells in his tales of extra-terrestrial races is religion. Lovecraft's views on religion are well known, and it is interesting to note that only the Great Race seems almost wholly free of religious tendencies. It is true that their "dead were incinerated with dignified ceremonies" (*DH* 399), but no religious connotation need be drawn from this fact. The closest that the Great Race comes to any sense of religion is a quasi-superstitious dread or "fear of the basalt ruins and trap-doors," since it was "the one subject lying altogether under a taboo among the Great Race" (*DH* 400). Even this fear is understandable, however, since the trap-doors concealed "elder beings" whose "successful irruption" would "one day . . . send millions of keen minds [of the Great Race] across the chasm of time to strange bodies in the safer future" (*DH* 402).

The Old Ones have not banished religion from their sphere of existence—a curiosity considering their supreme intellectual achievements.
Not only do they regard the Antarctic as a "sacred spot" (*MM* 70), but
their city has "great temples" (*MM* 74) and, "in the decadent days," they
"made strange prayers" to the vast mountains to the west representing the
"fabled nightmare Plateau of Leng" (*MM* 70). The Venusians, of course,
seem irrationally to worship their crystals, not realising that they are a
source of energy: "They have no use for the crystals except to pray to" (*D*
293).

The three other alien races—the mound denizens, the fungi from
Yuggoth, and the Innsmouth folk—are all related in their religious prac-
tices, since they worship either Cthulhu ("Tulu" in "The Mound") or
Tsathoggua or Nyarlathotep. Indeed, a strange linkage between the
Innsmouth folk and the shoggoths is implied in "The Shadow over
Innsmouth" (cf. *DH* 340, 367), and may confirm William Fulwiler's view
that "The Shadow over Innsmouth" is a partial sequel to *At the Mountains of
Madness*. Moreover, this connexion with the shoggoths—a species toward
which Lovecraft has no sympathy whatever—further condemns the Innsmouth folk as representatives of a Lovecraftian dystopia. The religious
practices of the three races are, indeed, quite odious in their superstitiousness, mysticism, and barbarity; and it is clear that Lovecraft is passing a
negative judgment upon the races, as they show themselves to be similar to
the "degraded and ignorant" worshippers in Louisiana described in "The
Call of Cthulhu" (*DH* 139).

The religion of the mound denizens is of particular interest, and is in
fact the key to understanding the decadence of the race. Lovecraft initially
describes their religion before the decline set in: "Religion was a leading
interest in Tsath, though very few actually believed in the supernatural.
What was desired was the aesthetic and emotional exaltation bred by the
mystical moods and sensuous rites which attended the colourful ancestral
faith" (*HM* 136). This aesthetic religiosity was, indeed, approved after a
fashion by Lovecraft, and he spoke of the Roman Catholic church in a
similarly sympathetic vein:

> It seems to me—an atheist of Protestant ancestry—that Catholicism is
> really an admirable faith for those artists whose tastes are wholly Gothic
> and mystical without any mixture of the classic or the intellectual. It is the
> inheritory of ancient and beautiful rhythms of thought, cadence, and ges-
> ture which thousands of years of human feeling have woven symbolically
> and expressively around the various significant points of mortal experi-
> ence; and as such it cannot help having a profound and genuine artistic
> importance and satisfyingness. It is the oldest continuously surviving
> poem of life that the races of Western Europe possess, and as such has an

authority which no other one system of symbolic expression can claim. It seems to me that if one is to have anything so extra-rational as religion of any sort the Catholic and Episcopal systems are the only two sects with enough roots and anchors in the past to make them worthy of the affiliation of the artist. (*SL* 2.104)[10]

But the mound religion does not remain in this enlightened and artistic spirit for long: "The more Zamacona studied these things the more apprehensive about the future he became. . . . Rationalism degenerated more and more into fanatical and orgiastic superstition, centreing in a lavish adoration of the magnetic Tulu-metal" (*HM* 149). As with the Romans of the late Empire (whose Stoic philosophy is curiously reflected in the mound denizens[11]), the mound people's increasing religiosity is a testimony to their decay; and they thus fully deserve the condemnation that Lovecraft the atheistic rationalist dealt them.

Lovecraft's attitude toward his own alien civilisations is not always clear, since we obviously cannot impute to Lovecraft all the remarks made by his narrators. "The Mound" is a case in point: initially we note a tone of sarcasm directed toward Zamacona for his lack of perspective and pious horror at the mound civilisation:

> Zamacona found difficulty in describing conditions so unlike anything he had previously known; and the text of his manuscript proved unusually puzzling at this point. . . . He himself never participated in any of the rites save those which he mistook for perversions of his own faith; nor did he ever lose an opportunity to convert the people to that faith of the Cross which the Spaniards hoped to make universal. (*HM* 135–36)

But as the narrative proceeds, more and more sympathy is accorded to Zamacona; and Lovecraft, after describing the decadent (or, rather, Decadent) lifestyle of the mound denizens, agrees with Zamacona's attitudes and identifies with him. In "The Whisperer in Darkness" the reverse is the case: Akeley is obviously Lovecraft's mouthpiece, and the reader's sympa-

---

10. One wonders whether Lovecraft gained this view from George Santayana, who acknowleged a belief in Roman Catholicism for somewhat analogous reasons. Lovecraft had, indeed, encountered Santayana at this time (see *SL* 2.226). It may also be possible that in the above passage, written to August Derleth, Lovecraft was attempting to deal gingerly with Derleth's own religious beliefs.

11. "Temples to Great Tulu, a spirit of universal harmony, anciently symbolised as the octopus-headed god who had brought all men down from the stars, were the most richly decorated objects in K'n-yan" (*HM* 136). The similarity to the Stoic philosophy—which also emphasised the brotherhood of all human beings, and which Lovecraft probably encountered in the work of the younger Seneca—is striking.

thy for him continues to grow as the fungi engage in increasingly vicious battles with him; but the final letter from "Akeley"—and particularly Wilmarth's meeting of the pseudo-Akeley—reverses the situation. "Akeley's" defence of the fungi—"All that the Outer Ones wish of man is peace and non-molestation and an increasing intellectual rapport" (*DH* 239)—only confirms our opinion of their loathsomeness; for to physical horror is added a sinister deceitfulness which makes all "Akeley's" words have a double meaning and which causes us to be repelled by them just as we are by the decadent mound denizens, the Innsmouth folk, and the Venusians. Hence only the Great Race and the Old Ones appear as "model" civilisations in Lovecraft's mind.

But not one of Lovecraft's alien races fails to inspire horror within the human characters in the story—hence, to a certain degree, in Lovecraft. The Great Race and the Old Ones, however benign and enlightened, are nonetheless a source of terror in the tales in which they appear. The fact that Peaslee "waked half of Arkham with [his] screaming" when, in his "dreams," he found himself in the "monstrous form" (*DH* 394) of his extra-terrestrial captor is a sufficient indication of the terror which the Great Race's *outré* appearance inspires in him; while the equally bizarre outlines of the Old Ones, with their "stench" and "noisome dark-green ichor," cause the narrator at one point to declare them not merely horrible but "blasphemous" (*MM* 95). We need quote no passages to convey the loathsomeness of the Innsmouth folk, the fungi from Yuggoth, and the Venusians: the narrators' distaste is evident on every page. Only the mound denizens—so uncannily like human beings for all their extra-terrestrial origin— seem to have inspired no horror in the narrator; instead, their ugliness is entirely moral.

How do we account for the horror that even the two "model" races inspire in Lovecraft's characters? Several factors must here be considered. Note, firstly, Wilmarth's comment in "The Whisperer in Darkness": "Close contact with the utterly bizarre is often more terrifying than inspiring" (*DH* 249). To this we may add Lovecraft's celebrated explanation of his predilection for fantasy: "I *know* that my most poignant emotional experiences are those which concern the lure of unplumbed space, the *terror* [my italics] of the encroaching void" (*SL* 3.197). All Lovecraft's alien races are, in greater or lesser degree, embodiments of the "encroaching void," and as such are a source of terror.

In a certain way, moreover, Lovecraft adhered to the dictum that "man is the measure of all things," that the human scale is the standard of measure upon this world; hence his remark in "The Shadow out of Time" that "it is not wholesome to watch monstrous objects doing what we had known only human beings to do" (*DH* 392). The belief connects with Lovecraft's political and racial views, and made him write to J. Vernon Shea:

> The *primary* reason [for racial segregation] is simply a sensible wish to keep *every* settled culture (Nordic or not) true *to itself* for the sake of human values involved. No one wishes to force Nordicism on the non-Nordic—indeed, a real friend of civilisation wishes merely to make the Germans *more German*, the French *more French*, the Spaniards *more Spanish*, and so on. (*SL* 4.253)

While such a statement hardly indicates (as some have believed) that Lovecraft "feared" or even "hated" other races and cultures, it nevertheless helps us to understand that his narrators' terror at the sight of aliens stems from the latter's sheer difference from human beings—what the pseudo-Akeley called "man's eternal tendency to hate and fear and shrink away from the *utterly different*" (*DH* 238).

Furthermore, the Great Race is an added source of terror because it has robbed the narrator of his own body—although for no nefarious purpose—and thus forces the narrator to feel that "loss of identity" than which, as is written in "Through the Gates of the Silver Key," "no death, no doom, no anguish can arouse [greater] despair. . . . To be aware . . . that one no longer has a *self*. . . is the nameless summit of agony and dread" (*MM* 438).[12]

But in mitigation we can note that the horror inspired by the Great Race and the Old Ones lessens gradually as the respective narratives advance—to the point that Lovecraft can make his celebrated declaration that the Old Ones were "scientists to the last. . . . Whatever they had been, they were men!" (*MM* 96). Indeed, in both tales we notice that the horror is slowly transferred from the extra-terrestrial races to the even more *outré* beings—the Blind Beings and the shoggoths, respectively—who are their enemies; as Fritz Leiber said, "The author shows us horrors and then pulls back the curtain a little farther, letting us glimpse the horrors of which even the horrors are afraid!" (Leiber, "Copernicus" 57). No such mitigation occurs in respect to the four other entities concerned—the Innsmouth folk, the Venusians, the fungi, and the mound denizens. Instead, the horror they inspire grows at every moment; culminating in "The Whisperer in

---

12. This passage was originally written by Lovecraft's collaborator E. Hoffmann Price (see his original sequel to "The Silver Key," entitled "The Lord of Illusion"; *Crypt of Cthulhu* No. 10 [1982]: 47–56). But the sentiment was frequently expressed by Lovecraft elsewhere; indeed, the fact that this was one of the few passages by Price which Lovecraft retained in "Through the Gates of the Silver Key" indicates his approval of the sentiment.

Darkness" with the pseudo-Akeley and in "The Shadow over Innsmouth" with the metamorphosis of the narrator himself into a monster.

* * *

We must now give attention to Lovecraft's ideas on the decadence of civilisations. In four of the six tales under consideration—"The Shadow out of Time," *At the Mountains of Madness*, "The Mound," and "The Shadow over Innsmouth"—the alien races undergo a greater or lesser decline. It is now well known that Lovecraft quickly adopted the theory of the successive rise and fall of world civilisations as propounded by Oswald Spengler in *The Decline of the West*, the first volume of which he read around 1927 (see *SL* 2.103). The idea of decadence is so strong in Lovecraft that it has led some commentators to believe that he actually took a "pleasure uncertain even in himself over [the] collapse of [Western civilisation] and the rages of excess that the calamity would unloose" (Buhle 204). Barton L. St Armand (11) quotes the following letter as proof of Lovecraft's "fascination with decadence":

> There may be some—such as the 19th century decadents in France—who can derive a sort of pleasurable tragic exaltation from the picture of themselves as the crew of a sinking ship—a ship which is sinking, no matter how many other ships may later put to sea from other ports. To be a Psamettichus in a dying Egypt, a Lucian in a fading Hellenistic world, a Boëthius or a Venantius Fortunatus in a doomed Rome—there is quite a kick in the idea for those who like that kind of thing. (*SL* 3.41)

That such a passage reveals a "fascination with decadence" is clear; but that it implies a "pleasure" at the prospect is a more debatable matter. Indeed, the passage quoted above leads one to believe that Lovecraft would *not* have been one of those who might enjoy the experience of witnessing civilisation's collapse. In balance to the above we can quote his remark that "no civilisation has lasted for ever, and perhaps our own is perishing of natural old age. If so, the end cannot well be deferred" (*MW* 166)—a remark that reveals an historical awareness of the impermanence of any civilisation, from the greatest to the worst.

It is precisely this awareness that explains the decadence of the two "model" civilisations in Lovecraft. The Great Race, indeed, has scarcely declined at all; and Lovecraft's only remark to that effect is that its art had "at the period of [Peaslee's] dreams . . . passed its crest and meridian" (*DH* 399). The vast intelligence of the Great Race will prevent it from a wholesale decadence such as that of the mound denizens; and the species will simply transfer itself into the bodies of other beings as soon as its present habitat becomes too dangerous. This comparative absence of decadence on the part of the Great Race not only underscores Lovecraft's relative distaste for the decline of civilisation—a distaste that helps us to understand his remarks on racial purity—but again establishes the Great Race as the supreme example of a Lovecraftian utopia.

The Old Ones have declined rather more significantly: not only do they have difficulty in controlling their synthetic slaves, but "with the march of time . . . the art of creating new life from inorganic matter had been lost" (*MM* 67); they are no longer able to "sally forth into the planetary ether" (*MM* 68), and, like the Great Race, their art has become "decadent," although even "these latest carvings had a truly epic quality" (*MM* 75); they have even gained some of the irrational superstitiousness of the later mound denizens. The conclusion to be drawn is that the decadence of the Great Race—slight as it was—and of the Old Ones was due largely to inevitable historical forces.

It is quite otherwise for the mound denizens and the Innsmouth folk: their decadence is manifestly caused by a moral and social collapse. The mound civilisation declined because it reacted "with mixed apathy and hysteria against the standardised and time-tabled life of stultifying regularity which machinery had brought it during its middle period" (*HM* 149). As with the Great Race and the Old Ones, "art and intellect . . . had become listless and decadent" (*HM* 135). As for the Innsmouth folk, their decadence is, interestingly, due to the unnatural inbreeding instigated by Obed Marsh—we need not be reminded that the Great Race, the Old Ones, and even the mound denizens do without the normal forms of sexuality. But rather than engaging in superficial Freudianism, we may note instead that the Innsmouth folk's decline—labelled a "biological degeneration" (*DH* 314)—not only is similar to the decline of the Martense family in "The Lurking Fear" and the Catskill denizens in "Beyond the Wall of Sleep,"[13] but again indicates Lovecraft's desire for racial purity. Throughout the novelette we can detect parallels between the Innsmouth folk and the "foreigners" with whom Lovecraft was so concerned: the ticket agent remarks significantly that the fear of the Innsmouth folk by the surrounding populace is largely a matter of "race prejudice," and draws an important parallel with the Innsmouth folk: "You've probably heard about the Salem man that came home with a Chinese wife, or maybe you know there's still a bunch of Fiji Islanders somewhere around Cape Cod" (*DH* 307). He also makes note of the "foreign talk" (*DH* 309) heard in the Gilman House. The narrator once speculates, "Just what foreign blood was in him [Joe Sargent] I could not even guess" (*DH* 314), and goes on to say that the

---

13. It is significant that both the Catskill folk and the Innsmouth residents are given the label "'white trash'"; see "The Shadow over Innsmouth" (*DH* 309) and "Beyond the Wall of Sleep" (D 26).

"people . . . had certain peculiarities of face and motions which I instinc-
tively disliked" (*DH* 317), and, finally, that there is an "alien strain" (*DH*
325) in the Innsmouth folk.

What is more interesting about the Innsmouth folk is that their decline
is not merely a "strange and insidious disease-phenomenon" (*DH* 321), but
a sort of reversion to type. As Zadok Allen says: "Seems that human folks
has got a kind o' relation to sech water-beasts—that everything alive came
aout o' the water onct, an' only needs a little change to back agin" (*DH*
331). Hence the Innsmouth folk are returning gradually to the state which
Walter de la Poer reached instantly at the conclusion of "The Rats in the
Walls." On a political level we can relate this decline to Lovecraft's belief
that miscegenation can lead to the collapse of civilisation: "It is easy to see
the ultimate result of the wholesale pollution of highly evolved blood by
definitely inferior strains. It happened in ancient Egypt—and made a race
of supine fellaheen out of what was once a noble stock" (*SL* 4.230).

It is clear from the above analyses that, in the depiction of his alien civilisations—notably the Great Race, the Old Ones, the mound denizens, and
the Innsmouth folk—Lovecraft was either making predictions on the fate of
modern society or was creating enlightened cultures toward the realisation of
which human beings ought to strive. A unified examination of each of these
four civilisations will the more clearly reveal Lovecraft's intentions.

By all accounts the Great Race deserves its appellation as "the greatest
race of all" (*DH* 385). They are unreservedly at the top of Lovecraft's pantheon of bizarre entities. The reasons for their supremacy are equally clear:
they are not merely intelligent but are filled with a thirst for knowledge that
is far greater than that of any other civilisation or race, and that is so vigorous that it impels them to make hazardous trips through time and space in
order to learn about civilisations "from every corner of the solar system"
(*DH* 395). Their political system—fascistic socialism with all its ramifications—is precisely the one Lovecraft declared to be the only workable system in a mechanised age. Art "was a vital part of life" (*DH* 399), crime and
warfare were scant. Their only failings were a slight decline of artistic excellence at the time of Peaslee's visit and their fear—well founded, indeed—
of the Blind Beings. They are the Lovecraftian utopia par excellence.

The Old Ones are not very far behind; for they too have a keen thirst
for knowledge—especially science and history—and have a keen sense of
aesthetics, perhaps greater than that of the Great Race. Their political system
seems roughly akin to that of the Great Race, although Lovecraft does not
describe it in any great detail. They passed through a stage of mechanisation,
but ultimately rejected it as aesthetically unsatisfying; and now no longer use
their knowledge, as Lovecraft sarcastically remarked of modern science, to

"serve useful ends in a civically acceptable fashion" (*SL* 3.298). They have, however, declined more than the Great Race: their power to create new forms of life is gone, they cannot fly through space, they have become more superstitious, and their art has declined. Nevertheless, "they were men!"

"The Mound," the first of Lovecraft's major tales to include a significant amount of political and social speculation, is the more interesting because in it he draws obvious parallels between the development of the mound denizens and the development of modern human society. At first their civilisation seems as nearly utopian as that of the Great Race or the Old Ones: they have conquered old age, have the power of dematerialisation, use religion merely as an aesthetic ornament, practise selective breeding to ensure the vigour of the "ruling type," and—like the Old Ones— have abandoned a life of mechanisation. But this utopia very quickly turns to a dystopia. Lovecraft makes us realise the similarity of the mound denizens to modern American and European civilisation, then presents a bleak picture of the development of that civilisation:

> The nation [had] gone through a period of idealistic industrial democracy which gave equal opportunities to all, and thus, by raising the naturally intelligent to power, drained the masses of all their brains and stamina. . . . Physical comfort was ensured by an urban mechanisation of standardised and easily maintained pattern. . . . Literature was all highly individual and analytical. . . . The modern tendency was to feel rather than to think. . . . (*HM* 134–36)

The cause of their decline was obviously mechanisation—and, perhaps more importantly, their inability to overcome it as had the Old Ones:

> The dominance of machinery had at one time broken up the growth of normal aesthetics, introducing a lifelessly geometrical tradition fatal to sound expression. This had soon been outgrown, but had left its mark upon all pictorial and decorative attempts; so that except for conventionalised religious designs, their was little depth or feeling in any later work. Archaistic reproductions of earlier work had been found much preferable for general enjoyment. (*HM* 135)

The similarity of these remarks to those on modern art and architecture as found in "Heritage or Modernism: Common Sense in Art Forms" (1935) is clear:

> They [the modernists] launch new decorative designs of cones and cubes and triangles and segments—wheels and belts, smokestacks and streamlined sausage moulders—problems in Euclid and nightmares from alcoholic orgies—and tell us that these things are the only authentic symbols of the age in which we live. (*MW* 196)

Lovecraft makes it obvious that it was precisely the mound civilisation's reaction "against the standardised and time-tabled life of stultifying regularity which machinery had brought it during its middle period" (*HM* 149) that caused its decline; adding significantly that in "bygone eras . . . K'n-yan had held ideas much like those of the classic and renaissance outer world, and had possessed a natural character and art full of what Europeans regard as dignity, kindness, and nobility" (*HM* 149).

These identical sentiments are found in Lovecraft's letters: remarking that "nothing good can be said of that cancerous machine-culture" (*SL* 2.304), he speculates bitterly on the fate of the masses in such an age:

> We shall hear of all sorts of futile reforms and reformers—standardised culture-outlines, synthetic sports and spectacles, professional play-leaders and study-guides, and kindred examples of machine-made uplift and brotherly spirit. And it will amount to just about as much as most reforms do! Meanwhile the tension of boredom and unsatisfied imagination will increase—breaking out with increasing frequency in crimes of morbid perversity and explosive violence. (*SL* 2.309)

Enough has been said on the rather different dystopia predicted in "The Shadow over Innsmouth"—a dystopia caused not by mechanisation but by unhealthy inbreeding. Maurice Lévy rightly remarked that the Innsmouth denizens could be seen as a "testimonial to the failure of America's politics of racial assimilation, a deliberate rejection of the notion of the 'melting pot,' which forms so integral a part of the American dream" (Lévy 61). That they so correspond with Lovecraft's views of "foreigners" is at least suggestive.

The political and social systems of the two other alien races here considered—the fungi from Yuggoth and the Venusians—is little described, and we can draw few conclusions from them. The former seem rather more highly evolved than the latter, who—despite their ingenuity in building the invisible maze—seem to have risen hardly above a primitive level. Rather than being reflections of the future development of Western man, they are pure embodiments of the "terror of the encroaching void" that Lovecraft sensed so keenly. They seem not quite as loathsome as the Innsmouth folk, but cannot claim even the few virtues of the mound denizens.

In conclusion, we can single out three traits which distinguish Lovecraft's higher alien civilisations—pure intelligence, sound political organisation, and aesthetic sensibility—and which in turn represent the goals for which Lovecraft wished modern society to aim. That these utopian concerns entered his fiction precisely at the time of the Depression—for "The Mound" was begun in late 1929—is of no small interest; and the extensive political, economic, and social speculation that fills not only his letters but his later fiction reveals the widening scope of his intellectual horizons. No longer concerned solely with Augustan England or Imperial Rome or colonial New England, Lovecraft consolidated his extensive historical and philosophical knowledge with keen observations of his own time; and, in "The Shadow out of Time," depicted a utopian society that—in brutal contrast with modern America—was as enlightened and aesthetically developed as the great cultures of Greece and Rome to which Lovecraft was ever allied and which he ever held up as great and model civilisations.

Works Cited

Buhle, Paul. "Dystopia as Utopia: Howard Phillips Lovecraft and the Unknown Content of American Horror Literature" (1976). In S. T. Joshi, ed., *H. P. Lovecraft: Four Decades of Criticism*. Athens: Ohio University Press, 1980.

Joshi, S. T. *H. P. Lovecraft: The Decline of the West*. Mercer Island, WA: Starmont House, 1990. Rpt. Berkeley Heights, NJ: Wildside Press, [2001].

Leiber, Fritz. "A Literary Copernicus." In S. T. Joshi, ed., *H. P. Lovecraft: Four Decades of Criticism*. Athens: Ohio University Press, 1980.

———. "Through Hyperspace with Brown Jenkin: Lovecraft's Contribution to Speculative Fiction" (1966). In Peter Cannon, ed., *Lovecraft Remembered*. Sauk City, WI: Arkham House, 1998.

Lévy, Maurice. *Lovecraft: A Study in the Fantastic*. Trans. S. T. Joshi. Detroit: Wayne State University Press, 1988.

St Armand, Barton Levi. *H. P. Lovecraft: New England Decadent*. Albuquerque: Silver Scarab Press, 1979.

Tierney, Richard L. Letter to the editor. *Nyctalops* 1, No. 5 (October 1971): 51.

Topical References in Lovecraft

The myth that H. P. Lovecraft was completely detached from the political, social, literary, and philosophical movements of his day is one whose death has been anomalously slow, despite the volumes of comment on the contemporary scene found not merely in his letters but also in his essays from so early as "The Crime of the Century" (1915). Lovecraft is in a way partially to blame for this state of affairs, since he was fond of portraying himself (more often than not with tongue in cheek) as an eighteenth-century gentleman with allegiance to the traditions of Republican Rome, and could also write such a line as "I know always that I am an outsider; a stranger in this century and among those who are still men" ("The Outsider" [*DH* 52]). And while there can be no question of Lovecraft's sincere adherence to the standards of the past, there can equally be no doubt, as Robert Bloch wrote, "but that H. P. Lovecraft was very much alive in the Twentieth Century of Picasso, Proust, Joyce, Spengler, Einstein, and Adolf Hitler" (Bloch [1959] 174).

Bloch himself, however, felt that Lovecraft's fiction was almost wholly—and quite consciously—devoid of reference to the political and social upheavals of the time. "Lovecraft ignores the post WWI Jazz Age in its entirety: Coolidge, Hoover, FDR, Lindbergh, Babe Ruth, Al Capone, Valentino, Mencken, and the prototypes of Babbitt have no existence in H. P. L.'s realm. It is difficult to believe that Howard Phillips Lovecraft was a literary contemporary of Ernest Hemingway" (Bloch [1972] 159). This remark itself is not correct in its details, and I maintain that it may not even be entirely true in the general sense in which Bloch meant it. The fact is that there are many topical references in Lovecraft's fiction, and these references—sometimes glancing, sometimes more or less central to the tale—are echoes of lengthier and more detailed remarks on modern literature, politics, and society as found in his letters and essays.

It is, of course, true that Lovecraft's tales frequently seem so remote from the time in which they were written that certain topical references become almost jarring in their abruptness. "The Rats in the Walls" (1923) is a classic example; and although we are at the outset told that the tale takes place in 1923 ("On July 16, 1923, I moved into Exham Priory after the last workman had finished his labours" [*DH* 26]), we tend to forget the date as the tale becomes involved in the ancient past of the mansion, reaching back even beyond the Roman foundations. Then, as if out of nowhere, we are given this allusion: "As we all took the train for Anchester I felt myself poised on the brink of frightful revelations, a sensation symbolised by the air of mourning among the many Americans at the unexpected death of the President on the other side of the world" (*DH* 40). This of course refers to Warren G. Harding, who died on 2 August 1923—a date that harmonizes perfectly with the chronology of the tale, and which makes me wonder whether the story was actually being written during this event. Lovecraft did indeed take notice of Harding's death, remarking rather cynically: "Harding was a handsome bimbo—I'm sure sorry he had the good luck to get clear of this beastly planet" (*SL* 1.253). Another odd and unexpected allusion occurs in "Out of the Aeons" (1933), where it is noted that the curious mummy on display in the Cabot Museum "formed—for imaginative people—a close rival to the depression as chief topic of 1931 and 1932" (*HM* 271). This is the only direct reference to the Great Depression I have found in all Lovecraft's fiction—a circumstance the more unusual in that his later letters are filled with discussions on possible means for the alleviation of unemployment and for general economic recovery.

Many other references to the political scene are not so irrelevant to a tale. World War I receives much mention in the fiction, and one of the most poignant references is at the end of "Dagon" (1917), where the narrator reflects: "I dream of a day when they [the things of the deep sea] may rise above the billows to drag down in their reeking talons the remnants of a puny, war-exhausted mankind" (*D* 19). The remark is vaguely echoed in the final paragraph of "The Call of Cthulhu" (1926), although here the reference is made broader and cannot actually be deemed topical: "Loathsomeness waits and dreams in the deep, and decay spreads over the tottering cities of men" (*DH* 154). It may be going too far to read into these references an indication of Lovecraft's adherence to the Spenglerian notion of a "decline of the west" (although he did ascribe generally to Spengler's notions on this subject), and even the reference at the opening of "The Call of Cthulhu" ("... the peace and safety of a new dark age" [*DH* 125]) cannot be adduced in favour of the idea, since there Lovecraft postulates (for fictional purposes, obviously) that the "piecing together of dissociated knowledge" will bring about the dark age, while in his letters he notes (as Spengler himself did) that mechanisation will perhaps be the ultimate cause of the collapse of Western civilisation. Still, the references in "Dagon"— observe that the very premise of the tale is that a man has escaped from a "German sea-raider" when "the great war was . . . at its beginning, and the ocean forces of the Hun[1] had not completely sunk to their later degrada-

---

1. In the first appearance of the tale (*Vagrant*, November 1919) the text read "Kaiser."

tion" (*D* 14)—are to be noted. "Dagon" is, as we know, only the second
tale of Lovecraft's mature fictional career; and its realism of setting and
employment of a major "current event" place it in an entirely different
category from the intentionally archaic and Poesque "The Tomb."

Most of the other mentions of World War I are brief and insignificant,
but in three stories the references are a little more vital to the tale's import.
"The Temple" (1920) purports to be the document of a commander of a
German submarine, and tries ironically to present the war from his point
of view; but the satire against the German is so clumsily handled that the
tale never amounts either to a penetrating social and political commentary
or to a successful weird tale. In "Herbert West—Reanimator" (1921–22)
one of the six episodes is set in Flanders in early 1915, since, like the narrator of "The Loved Dead," Herbert West and his companion were "one
of many Americans to precede the government itself into the gigantic
struggle" (*D* 153). This of course was true, although I have not been able
to discover any figures on how many Americans actually entered the war
before the United States' declaration of war in April 1917.[2] We have a dim
connexion with Lovecraft's continual criticisms of American pacifism in
the early stages of the war (see especially the essay "The Renaissance of
Manhood" [1915]), although later in the story we find that West "secretly
sneered at my occasional martial enthusiasms and censures of supine neutrality" (*D* 154—"craven pacifism" in "The Renaissance of Manhood"),
which may indicate that by 1921 Lovecraft was finding his earlier words on
the subject somewhat embarrassing. Finally, in "The Mound" (1929–30)
we find that interest in the mound has been rekindled by "the daredeviltry
of some of the youths back from service in France" (*HM* 103). It is precisely two of these "prematurely hardened young veterans"—the Clay
brothers—who meet horrible fates on the mound. Here, then, is certainly a
moderately significant social commentary used for horrific purposes.

Prohibition enters two stories, and in at least one is important for the
development of the plot. In *The Case of Charles Dexter Ward* we learn of an
anomalous event in conjunction with bootlegging: "In a lonely spot near
Hope Valley had occurred one of the frequent sordid waylayings of trucks
by 'hi-jackers' in quest of liquor shipments, but this time the robbers had
been destined to receive the greater shock" (*MM* 180). What they find are
coffins being delivered to Ward. In "The Shadow over Innsmouth" (1931)
a significant moment occurs when the narrator entices Zadok Allen with a

---

2. Edwin W. Morse, one contemporary writer, speaks of "hundreds of young
Americans" going abroad before America's declaration of war. See *The Vanguard of
American Volunteers: In the Fighting Lines and Humanitarian Service, August, 1914–April,
1917* (New York: Scribners, 1918), p. 4.

bottle of bootleg whiskey. Lovecraft's comment is illuminating: "A quart bottle of whiskey was easily, though not cheaply, obtained in the rear of a dingy variety-store just off the Square in Eliot Street" (*DH* 327). This single sentence vividly conveys the furtiveness, expense, and sordidness of purchasing alcohol during those fourteen long years when it was illegal. Lovecraft's attitude on the subject is well-known: having begun as an emphatic supporter of Prohibition (see such essays as "More *Chain-Lightning*" [1915] and "A Remarkable Document" [1917]), he later realised that Prohibition was simply too clumsy a means to cure the problem, although he continued to regard the consumption of alcohol a disgusting practice and maintained a strict teetotalism to the end of his life.

Certain other references apply more particularly to the New England region in which Lovecraft lived and travelled. In *The Case of Charles Dexter Ward* he makes reference to such things as the "vast new Christian Science dome" (*MM* 115) on Prospect Street in Providence, built between 1906 and 1913; and the mention of the State House earlier in the text (*MM* 113) could conceivably provide a *terminus post quem* for the story (if we needed one), since it was completed only in 1901. In "Pickman's Model" (1926) there are telling references to the Boston subways and the horrors that may be lurking there; indeed, the subways seemed to affect Lovecraft powerfully, and one of his most brilliant horrific strokes was in *At the Mountains of Madness*, when Danforth begins a crazy series of utterances after seeing the shoggoth: "'South Station Under—Washington Under—Park Street Under—Kendall—Central—Harvard . . .' The poor fellow was chanting the familiar stations of the Boston-Cambridge tunnel that burrowed through our peaceful native soil thousands of miles away in New England" (*MM* 100). One can still travel this exact subway route today, and Lovecraft must have ridden the line countless times. Indeed, it can be argued that the very notion of the shoggoth was inspired by the subway, since the shoggoth's "nearest comprehensible analogue is a vast, onrushing subway train as one sees it from a station platform—the great black front looming colossally out of infinite subterranean distance, constellated with strangely coloured lights and filling the prodigious burrow as a piston fills a cylinder" (*MM* 101). Here, then, is certainly one example of a modern—even prosaic—device inspiring Lovecraft's imagination!

In "The Colour out of Space" (1927) we find mentions of the "new reservoir" (*DH* 54) that is being designed for western Massachusetts. This is of course the Quabbin Reservoir, plans for which were undertaken by a special commission of the Massachusetts legislature in 1926, and work on which was begun as early as the fall of 1926, continuing sporadically for the next twenty years (see Clark, passim). Again, it is possible that Lovecraft's hearing of this impending project began his imagination working.

And then there is the very familiar reference to the Vermont floods of November 1927 which provides the starting point for the events in "The
Whisperer in Darkness" (1930). Lovecraft had visited Vermont earlier that
year, and must have kept close watch of the floods as he read about them
in the newspaper. Finally, that anomalous reference in "The Shadow over
Innsmouth" (1931)—"'Maybe you know there's still a bunch of Fiji Islanders somewhere around Cape Cod'" (*DH* 307)—has a real source, as Lovecraft wrote to his aunt in 1930 that "The drive to Onset was uneventful—
though it was interesting to have [Frank] Belknap [Long] point out a colony of *Fiji-Islanders* near Onset."[3] I do not know what has happened to this
colony, but presumably it has since become mingled with the surrounding
population.

Some topical references are not so much central to a tale as rather amusing indications that we are in fact in the early decades of the twentieth century. In "Facts Concerning the Late Arthur Jermyn and His Family" (1920)
occur several charming references. Recall that Sir Alfred Jermyn, father of
Arthur Jermyn, who "at thirty-six had deserted his wife and child to travel
with an itinerant American circus" (*D* 77), suffered so hideous an end that
the "members of 'The Greatest Show on Earth' do not like to speak" (*D* 77)
of it. This glancing allusion to the Barnum and Bailey circus is the more revealing in that Lovecraft clearly intends the reader to understand the reference without his having to mention the circus by name. Later in the story we
are told that the "once mighty N'bangus were now the submissive servants
of King Albert's government" (*D* 80), an obvious reference to the annexa-
tion of the Congo by Belgium in 1908; Albert himself became king in 1909
and ruled until his death in 1934. This obviously accounts for the Belgian
agent, M. Verhaeren, who sends the strange "white ape" to Jermyn. In *The
Case of Charles Dexter Ward* there is one particularly succulent reference,
where at the end of the novel Curwen (pretending to be Ward) "could recall
how the creaking of Epenetus Olney's new signboard . . . was exactly like the
first few notes of the new jazz piece all the radios in Pawtuxet were playing"
(*MM* 188). Here again the very point of the modern reference is not merely
to place the novel in the contest of the 1920s, but to indicate in a particularly
vivid way the unnatural longevity of the wizard Curwen: the implication is
that only a person who has actually lived in the eighteenth and the twentieth
centuries could make such a comparison.

Some indications of the modernity (or, rather, contemporaneity) of
Lovecraft's fiction can be derived from his reference to previous epochs.
Hence there are frequent references to the Victorian age in the tales, and
these occur in such a fashion as to suggest that that age is hopelessly out-

3. Lovecraft to Mrs. F. C. Clark, August 15–16, 1930 (ms., JHL).

moded and antiquated. Lovecraft here actually shares the outlook of his time in his rejection of nineteenth-century standards, although he claimed to do so simply so as to return to (what he felt were) the truer and more rationally based attitudes of the eighteenth century. This stance was, however, a little disingenuous, since part of the initiative for Lovecraft's condemnation of nineteenth-century values was his adoption of very advanced philosophical views from Nietzsche, Haeckel, T. H. Huxley, Spengler, Russell, and Santayana. Hence part of Lovecraft's scorn of the "pathetic Puritanism" (*D* 140) of Dr. Allan Halsey in "Herbert West—Reanimator" is in its acceptance of "sins like . . . anti-Darwinism [and] anti-Nietzscheism." The Darwin controversy is, of course, still with us, amazing as it may seem; and it may be well to note that Nietzsche died only in 1900. The very remoteness of the Victorian age is hinted more directly in "The Silver Key" (1926), where Randolph Carter decides to refurbish his home "as it was in his early boyhood—purple panes, Victorian furniture, and all" (*MM* 413). And note the description of Old Man Marsh in "The Shadow over Innsmouth," who "*still* [my italics] wore the frock-coated finery of the Edwardian era" (*DH* 323). This emphatically places the tale in at least the late 1920s, since the reign of Edward VII spanned the years 1901 to 1910.

I have elsewhere briefly discussed some elements of social satire found in Lovecraft's later tales, especially "The Mound," *At the Mountains of Madness*, and "The Shadow out of Time."[4] Some earlier examples of it may, however, be noted. We can hardly fail to note the acidity of his allusion to the "notably fat and especially offensive millionaire brewer" (*D* 89) who has taken over Trevor Towers after the death of Kuranes in "Celephaïs"; this, certainly, is an instance where Lovecraft reveals his adherence to the aristocratic standards of a previous epoch. A similar sort of satire, more topical this time, is found in "The Moon-Bog" (1920), where it is said of Denys Barry: "For all his love of Ireland, America had not left him untouched, and he hated the beautiful wasted space [i.e., the bog] where peat might be cut and land opened up" (*D* 119)—a reference that accidentally relates the story to the theme of Lord Dunsany's later novel, *The Curse of the Wise Woman* (1933). Here again it is precisely this "modern" stance of Barry's that leads directly to his doom.

Lovecraft's references to modern literature, art, and the general aesthetic movements of his time are surprisingly scant in the fiction, although they are of course voluminously recorded in his letters and essays. One odd mention occurs as early as "The Crawling Chaos" (1920/21): "My mind wandered back to an ancient and classical story of tigers which I had

---

4. See my "Humour and Satire in Lovecraft" (*Crypt of Cthulhu* No. 61 [Yuletide 1988]) and "Lovecraft's Alien Civilisations: A Political Interpretation."

read; I strove to recall the author but had difficulty. Then in the midst of
my fear I remembered that the tale was by Rudyard Kipling; nor did the
grotesqueness of deeming him an ancient author occur to me" (*HM* 13).
All this is a bit clumsy, but we may at least note that the very point of the
reference is that Kipling is a contemporary author (he would not die until
1936). The attack on free verse in "Poetry and the Gods" (1920) is somewhat more amusing, and Lovecraft's remarks tally with those found in his
essays and letters: "It was only a bit of *vers libre*, that pitiful compromise of
the poet who overleaps prose yet falls short of the divine melody of numbers" (*D* 350). I have elsewhere speculated that the actual examples of free
verse in the story may have been provided by Lovecraft's collaborator,
Anna Helen Crofts.[5]

References to the "Yellow Nineties" are tolerably frequent in Lovecraft, but are ambivalent in import: Lovecraft was probably repelled by the
general excesses of the period, but had fondness for individual writers such
as Machen, Wilde, Huysmans, Chambers, and others. Hence the decadence
of the two protagonists of "The Hound" (1922) is typified by the remark
that "Baudelaire and Huysmans were soon exhausted of thrills" and that
"the enigmas of the symbolists and the ecstasies of the pre-Raphaelites all
were ours in their time" (*D* 171). Huysmans is mentioned to no especial
purpose in "The Rats in the Walls" (*DH* 42), but some significant mentions occur in "Medusa's Coil" (1930). Here the phrase "yellow nineties" is
actually used (*HM* 170), and the painter Frank Marsh is said to be a "disci-
ple of Lafcadio Hearn and Gaugin and Van Gogh" (*HM* 170). The mention of Hearn is a little odd, but at least serves to give a *terminus ante quem* to
the events of the tale, since Hearn died in 1904. A later reference is still
more significant, when Marsh is said to be "like a Durtal or a des Esseintes
at the most jaded point of his curious orbit" (*HM*, 278). These are the central characters of Huysmans' *Là-Bas* (1891) and *À Rebours* (1884), respectively. Again the very allusiveness of the reference implies their familiarity
in Lovecraft's day, at least among the circle of *littérateurs*. The various mentions of Sidney Sime and Clark Ashton Smith fall more into the class of
"in-jokes" than actual topical references.

Lovecraft's disapproval of the general radical trend of modern literature—particularly its abandonment of traditional form and its excessive
dwelling on the day-to-day realities of mundane life—comes out frequently
in both early and late ficton. "Celephaïs" (1920) provides perhaps the first
example, and pungent remarks are made about modern writers who "strove
to strip from life its embroidered robes of myth, and to shew in naked ugli-

---

5. See "Lovecraft's Revisions: How Much of Them Did He Write?", in *Selected Papers on Lovecraft* (West Warwick, RI: Necronomicon Press, 1989).

ness the foul thing that is reality" (*D* 83). The theme is refined in "Azathoth" (1922), where we find that "learning stripped earth of her mantle of beauty, and poets sang no more save of twisted phantoms seen with bleared and inward-looking eyes" (*D* 357). This is actually not an inaccurate description of the obscurity and subjectivity of modern poetry, although the remark was made just before Lovecraft read the most celebrated and revolutionary of modern poems, *The Waste Land* of T. S. Eliot. Lovecraft seems to have read this almost immediately upon first American publication (*The Dial*, November 1922), and jumped upon it in an editorial in the *Conservative* of March 1923. The parody "Waste Paper" probably dates to about this time, although its appearance in "the newspaper" (*SL* 4.159)—presumably the *Providence Journal* or the *Providence Evening Bulletin*—has yet to be located. In any case, the most celebrated reference to Eliot in all Lovecraft is the mention at the end of *The Case of Charles Dexter Ward* where Willett, in the basement of Ward's bungalow, tries to calm himself by muttering the Lord's Prayer, "eventually trailing off into a mnemonic hodge-podge like the modernistic *Waste Land* of Mr. T. S. Eliot" (*MM* 197). The very use of the word "Mr." implies a reference to a living contemporary.

But Lovecraft's hostility to the sort of literary realism epitomised by Ben Hecht's teeth-gnashing *Erik Dorn* or the novels of Sinclair Lewis emerges more pungently in "The Silver Key," where Carter "did not dissent when they told him that the animal pain of a stuck pig or dyspeptic ploughman in real life is a greater thing than the peerless beauty of Narath" (*MM* 409)—a position that, if stripped of its vicious satire, is certainly a legitimate one (recall the triumphant first sentence of the preface to Wilde's *Picture of Dorian Gray:* "The artist is the creator of beautiful things"), although certainly out of tune with its time. Later a more general condemnation of the "Bohemian" or "Greenwich Village" sect is made, in a passage both virulent and noble:

> But when he [Carter] came to study those who had thrown off the old myths, he found them even more ugly than those who had not. They did not know that beauty lies in harmony, and that loveliness of life has no standard amidst an aimless cosmos save only its harmony with the dreams and the feelings which have gone before and blindly moulded our little spheres out of the rest of chaos. They did not see that good and evil and beauty and ugliness are only ornamental fruits of perspective, whose sole value lies in their linkage to what chance made our fathers think and feel, and whose finer details are different for every race and culture. Instead, they either denied these things altogether or transferred them to the crude, vague instincts which they shared with the beasts and peasants; so that their lives were dragged malodorously out in pain, ugliness, and disproportion, yet filled with a ludicrous pride at having escaped from something no more un-

> sound than that which still held them. They had traded the false gods of fear
> and blind piety for those of licence and anarchy. (*MM* 410)

Nearly every sentence here has an analogue in Lovecraft's correspondence.
Lovecraft could even parody more directly the literary fashions of his day;
"Waste Paper" is certainly a brilliant example, but it can be wondered
whether Lovecraft was trying to have fun at the expense of the "stream-of-
consciousness" school in "Hypnos" (1922) when he wrote at one point:
"Clocks—time—space—infinity . . ." (*D* 169).

The glancing allusion to the art of the pulp magazines in "Pickman's
Model" (1926) may be worth noting ("Any magazine-cover hack can
splash paint around wildly and call it a nightmare or a Witches' Sabbath or
a portrait of the devil" [*DH* 13]). Note the significant difference in "The
Colour out of Space": "It was too much like a landscape of Salvator Rosa;
too much like some forbidden woodcut in a tale of terror" (*DH* 54), where
"tale of terror" refers to the Gothic novels of the late eighteenth and early
nineteenth centuries. Here a modern allusion would have been inappropriate, since this introductory passage depicts timelessly a hoary land where
horrors have been lurking for hundreds of years. Then, of course, there is
that curious mention in "The Unnamable" (1923), where a magazine containing one of Randolph Carter's stories was taken "off the stands at the
complaints of silly milksops" (*D* 202). We immediately think of the similar
temporary banning of *Weird Tales* when it published C. M. Eddy's "The
Loved Dead"; but since that tale did not appear until the issue for May–
June–July 1924, we must either believe that the parallel is coincidental or
that Lovecraft revised the tale before its appearance in *Weird Tales* for July
1925 to include the reference.

It is, however, in the realms of science and philosophy that Lovecraft's
tales gain their greatest sense of topicality; for, as his letters amply testify,
Lovecraft kept closely abreast of the latest findings in astronomy, astrophysics, anthropology, and many other of the sciences, and was also very
well read in contemporary philosophy. Bloch himself came to this conclusion when he wrote that the fundamental link between Poe and Lovecraft
was "their mutual interest in science," and that this interest "softens the
charge that the two writers were totally unaware of the actual world and
unrealistic in their treatment of their times" (Bloch [1972] 159). Bloch
made no attempt to treat this topicality in detail, but we shall try to provide
at least a few hints here.

As with the political and literary references, some of Lovecraft's allusions to current science and philosophy are merely by the way, but in their
very allusiveness serve to root the works in their time. Hence the two references to the Piltdown man in Lovecraft ("The Tomb" [*D* 18] and "The

Rats in the Walls" [*DH* 42]) force us to date the events of these tales to after 1912, when it was first brought to public attention. Lovecraft, of course, had no way of knowing that it was a hoax, since nearly all leading anthropologists accepted the finding as genuine, if anomalous and difficult to place within the framework of primitive man's history. Only in 1949 did widespread scepticism emerge, and in 1953 the hoax was finally uncovered. Another brief archaeological note in "The Rats in the Walls" may be of interest, where it is remarked that Sir William Brinton's "excavations in the Troad excited most of the world in their day" (*DH* 40). The very nature of the reference places these excavations well before 1923, the date of the tale's events, and Brinton's work must surely have occurred after Schliemann's spectacular discovery of the site of Troy in 1867. Schliemann's last work at Troy dates to 1890, and from then until the early 1930s little of consequence was done, although the discovery received wide publicity through books by Schliemann and others; hence Brinton's excavations could plausibly be placed in the first decade of the twentieth century.

Some other anthropological references are of interest as well. Fritz Leiber recognised that the "authors Akeley lists [in "The Whisperer in Darkness"] to prove his competency in those fields are a nice selection" (Leiber 144); the list includes E. B. Tylor, Sir John Lubbock, Sir J. G. Frazer, Jean Louis Armand de Quatrefages de Breau, Margaret Murray, Henry Fairfield Osborn, Sir Arthur Keith, Pierre Marcellin Boule, and G. Elliott Smith (*DH* 216). All these are rough contemporaries of Lovecraft, although several did their best work in the last two decades of the nineteenth century. Tylor, incidentally, aside from writing the seminal *Primitive Culture* (1871), which may have given Lovecraft much of his information on anthropology, primitive man, and the origin of religion, also wrote the article on "Magic" in the 9th edition of the *Encyclopaedia Britannica,* which Lovecraft pillaged for "The Horror at Red Hook" (1925). Lovecraft read Margaret Murray's *Witch-Cult in Western Europe* (1921) a few years after it came out—apparently in 1924, since he wrote to Clark Ashton Smith in October 1925: "Meanwhile let me urge you, as I did over a year ago, to read *The Witch-Cult in Western Europe.* . . . It ought to be full of inspiration for you" (*SL* 2.28). That it was full of inspiration for Lovecraft is abundantly clear, since it receives first mention in "The Horror at Red Hook" (*D* 249). It is then cited in "The Call of Cthulhu" (1926), but let us recall that that tale was conceived more than a year previously: in October 1926 Lovecraft notes that "I've written two new tales, one of which is the sunken-land thing I described in advance last year" (*SL* 2.77). In his diary for 1925, under the dates of August 12–13 (only a day after the writing of "He" and about two weeks after writing "The Horror at Red Hook") Lovecraft notes: "Write out story plot—'The Call of Cthulhu'" (ms., JHL). Indeed, the tale is set generally in March–April 1925, so perhaps Lovecraft had sketched out a timetable of events in the story plot and maintained it when he wrote the tale—he seems to have done something similar in "The Whisperer in Darkness" (1930), most of which is set in late 1927 and 1928.

Mentions of modern occultist works can perhaps be noted here. The mention of Charles Fort in "The Descendant" (*D* 361) does not help much to date that fragment. Fort had written two of his major books by this time, *The Book of the Damned* (1919) and *New Lands* (1923); Lovecraft, however, did not read the latter until late 1927, when he notes that he "didn't find it as interesting as *The Book of the Damned*" (*SL* 2.174); I have not been able to determine when Lovecraft read that volume. The mention of "Ignatius Donnelly's chimerical account of Atlantis" (*D* 361) in the same fragment is of even less help, since Donnelly's *Atlantis: The Antediluvian World* was published so early as 1882. In "Out of the Aeons" (1933) we have mentions of Colonel Churchward and Lewis Spence (*HM* 269). Churchward's books on the lost continent Mu all date to the 1920s and 1930s;[6] Lovecraft confessed, however, that "I've never seen [Churchward's] books, but have read fairly indicative reviews of them."[7] These reviews must at least have told Lovecraft of the ancient Naacal language that Churchward claimed to have discovered, since Naacal is mentioned extensively in "Through the Gates of the Silver Key" and "Out of the Aeons." As for Spence, Lovecraft owned his *Encyclopedia of Occultism* (1920), and may have been familiar with such other of his books as *Atlantis in America* (1925) and *The Problem of Lemuria* (1932). No doubt Lovecraft, if he read any of these books at all, would have done so only because of their possible imaginative stimulus: he says of Fort that he "scraped up all sorts of press anecdotes of a certain type—which in turn were typical misstatements, misinterpretations, exaggerations, and distortions of actually observed things, or else hallucinations or fabrications" (*SL* 5.172–73).

References to modern psychology enter into only a few tales, but in a telling manner. It is interesting to note that both "Beyond the Wall of Sleep" (1919) and "From Beyond" (1920) were revised after initial publication to incorporate some rather snide references to Freud. In the former tale, as Wetzel long ago pointed out, the cynical insertion "—Freud to the contrary with his puerile symbolism—" (*D* 25) was added subsequent to the tale's appearance in *Pine Cones* (October 1919). Wetzel did not realise that a similar addition was made in "From Beyond": in the original manuscript the sentence "I laugh at the shallow endocrinologist, fellow-dupe

---

6. Cf. *The Lost Continent of Mu* (1926); *The Children of Mu* (1931); *The Sacred Symbols of Mu* (1933); *Cosmic Forces of Mu* (1934).

7. Lovecraft to E. Hoffmann Price, 15 February 1933 (ms., JHL).

and fellow-parvenu of the Freudian" (*D* 93) is missing, and must have been added at some point preceding the tale's first appearance in the *Fantasy Fan* (June 1934). Can we date these insertions? They may well have occurred quite early, for in June 1921 Lovecraft announces: "Dr. Sigmund Freud of Vienna, whose system of psycho-analysis I have begun to investigate, will probably prove the end of idealistic thought" (*SL* 1.134). Lovecraft was unfortunately mistaken in his prediction (just as he was wrong when he noted that "a mere knowledge of the approximate dimensions of the visible universe is enough to destroy forever the notion of a personal godhead" [*SL* 1.44], even though this knowledge seems to have had such an effect upon him), and no contradiction need be assumed between the tolerably favourable mentions of Freud in the letters and the rather sarcastic ones in the two tales in question: Lovecraft is merely criticising Freud's single-minded attribution of all human impulses to the libido (a position that most modern Freudians have themselves abandoned), since, as he remarked, "I am inclined to accept the modifications of Adler, who in placing the ego above the eros makes a scientific return to the position which Nietzsche assumed for wholly philosophical reasons" (*SL* 1.136). The glancing reference to the "big three" of early twentieth-century psychology in "The Trap" (1931)—"Even the most prosaic scientists affirm, with Freud, Jung, and Adler, that the subconscious mind is most open to external impression in sleep" (*HM* 384)—can be noted in brief.

It is, actually, somewhat curious that pure philosophers do not receive much notice in the fiction. We have observed the passing reference to "anti-Nietzscheism" in "Herbert West—Reanimator"; and in the same story Lovecraft notes that West believed "with Haeckel that all life is a chemical and physical process, and that the so-called 'soul' is a myth" (*D* 134). Ernst Haeckel (1834–1919) was probably the greatest of the biologist-philosophers of the late nineteenth and early twentieth centuries, and the great apostle for materialistic monism in his time (although Santayana could note, as early as 1923, that "In natural philosophy I am a decided materialist— apparently the only one living";[8] certainly Santayana would have amended his statement if he had read Lovecraft's trenchant essay, "Idealism and Materialism: A Reflection"!) and Lovecraft was greatly influenced by Haeckel's seminal volume, *The Riddle of the Universe* (1899; English translation 1900), which he seems to have read in late 1919 or 1920 (*SL* 1.87, 141). But of other philosophers we find no mention.

Einstein, however, runs through Lovecraft's fiction like an elusive thread, although here, of course, we are treading the borderline between as-

---

8. Santayana, "Preface" to *Scepticism and Animal Faith* (1923). Lovecraft later read this volume.

trophysics and metaphysics (as, indeed, physics since Einstein has tended increasingly to do). The first—and very allusive—citation occurs so early as "Hypnos" (1922), where it is remarked that "one man with Oriental eyes has said that all time and space are relative, and men have laughed" (*D* 165); this mention is actually anomalously early, for only in May 1923 does Lovecraft announce: "My cynicism and scepticism are increasing, and from an entirely new cause—the Einstein theory. . . . All is chance, accident, and ephemeral illusion—a fly may be greater than Arcturus, and Durfee Hill may surpass Mount Everest—assuming them to be removed from the present planet and differently environed in the continuum of space-time" (*SL* 1.231). Indeed, Lovecraft's remark here that "All the cosmos is a jest" is peculiarly reminiscent of what he had written a year before in "Hypnos": "The cosmos of our waking knowledge, born from such an universe as a bubble is born from the pipe of a jester, touches it only as such a bubble may touch its sardonic source when sucked back by the jester's whim" (*D* 165).

Loveraft first cites Einstein in a letter to the Gallomo that probably dates to April 1920 (ms., AHT). He then took note of the eclipse observations in May 1923 (reported on the front page of the *New York Times*) that, in the minds of most physicists, definitively confirmed the truth of the theory. Another sentence from "Hypnos"—"But even that man with Oriental eyes has done no more than suspect"—suggests that Lovecraft (along with most members of the intelligentsia) felt that the theory of relativity was, in 1922, still a theory, lacking empirical proof. In any event, Lovecraft's immediate reaction to Einstein is typical of that of many intellectuals, especially those lacking technical training in physics; indeed, it is precisely this sort of misunderstanding and false application of the theory of relativity that led many philosophers to reject the positivism of the later nineteenth century and to usher in a new age of idealism and mysticism. Lovecraft, of course, snapped out of his naive perceptions of the Einstein theory quite early, and by 1929 was telling Frank Belknap Long: "If any mystic thinks that matter has lost its known properties because it's been found made of invisible energy, just let him read Einstein and try to apply his new conception by butting his head into a stone wall" (*SL* 2.267)—which is amusingly reminiscent of Dr. Johnson's refutation of Berkeley. Lovecraft knew, however, that in the "nearer heavens" the "given area *isn't big enough* to let relativity get in its major effects"—hence he wisely warned Long: "Don't let the Einstein-twisters catch you here!" (*SL* 2.265). All this reveals an admirable grasp of the Einstein theory and its integration into a positivist and even materialist scheme, at least partially similar to that produced by Russell and Santayana.

In any case, Einstein reappears in vivid fashion in "The Whisperer in Darkness" (1930), where the pseudo-Akeley boldly announces: "'Do you know that Einstein is wrong, and that certain objects and forces *can* move with a velocity greater than that of light?'" (*DH* 253). One wonders whether this remark was inspired by Frank Belknap Long's "The Hounds of Tindalos," where the protagonist notes: "What do we know of time, really? Einstein believes that it is relative, that it can be interpreted in terms of space, of *curved* space. But why must we stop there?" And compare pseudo-Akeley's statement—"With the proper aid I expect to go backward and forward in time" (*DH* 253)—with the remark of Long's character: "With . . . the aid of my mathematical knowledge I believe that I can *go back through time*" (Long 94–95). Lovecraft almost certainly read "The Hounds of Tindalos" in manuscript, and even if he did not he could have read it in its appearance in *Weird Tales* (March 1929) in time to use it in his own tale.

But the two most interesting citations of the Einstein theory—as well as other advances in modern physics—occur in "The Shunned House" (1924) and "The Dreams in the Witch House" (1932). The former is particularly interesting in that it reinterprets the traditional vampire legend in terms of modern physics. Note these passages:

> To say that we actually believed in vampires or werewolves would be a carelessly inclusive statement. Rather must it be said that we were not prepared to deny the possibility of certain unfamiliar and unclassified modifications of vital force and attenuated matter; existing very infrequently in three-dimensional space because of its more intimate connexion with other spatial units, yet close enough to the boundary of our own to furnish us occasional manifestations which we, for lack of a proper vantage-point, may never hope to understand. . . .
>
> Such a thing was surely not a physical or biochemical impossibility in the light of a newer science which includes the theories of relativity and intra-atomic action. One might easily imagine an alien nucleus of substance or energy, formless or otherwise, kept alive by imperceptible or immaterial subtractions from the life-force or bodily tissue and fluids of other and more palpably living things into which it penetrates and with whose fabric it sometimes completely merges itself. (*MM* 251–52)

The overt mention of relativity is to be observed, and the mention of "intra-atomic action" presumably alludes to the quantum theory. What Lovecraft actually made of the quantum theory is not easy to deduce from the letters, where neither the theory itself nor Max Planck is mentioned at all frequently. Like the Einstein theory, Planck's findings were hailed by idealists as spelling the downfall of determinism and a *carte blanche* for all sorts of previously outmoded notions about the universe and humanity's relation to it. Lovecraft knew better, and by the time he assimilated the quantum theory he felt that it posed no real threat to determinism. "What most physicists take the quantum theory, at present, to mean, is *not that any cosmic uncertainty exists* as to which of several courses a given reaction will take; but that in certain instances *no conceivable channel of information can ever tell human beings which course will be taken*" (*SL* 3.228). Lovecraft thus seems to regard the "uncertainty" revealed by the quantum theory as epistemological and not ontological—i.e., it is simply our inability to predict the movement of sub-atomic particles that produces the "uncertainty," but the uncertainty does not inhere in Nature. This conclusion (although also adopted by Einstein, who made the celebrated remark that "God does not play dice with the universe") does not appear to be correct, since, in the words of Russell:

> In quantum theory, individual atomic occurrences are not determined by the equations; these suffice only to show that the possibilities form a discrete series, and that there are rules of determining how often each possibility will be realized in a large number of cases. There are reasons for believing that this absence of complete determinism is not due to any incompleteness in the theory, but is a genuine characteristic of small-scale occurrences. The regularity which is found in macroscopic phenomena is a statistical regularity. Phenomena involving large numbers of atoms remain deterministic, but what an individual atom may do in given circumstances is uncertain, not only because our knowledge is limited but because there are no physical laws giving a determinate result. (Russell 23–24)

Nevertheless, determinism as a philosophical position is by no means undermined, since "the crucial but so far unanswered question is whether there are processes by which random sub-atomic occurrences trigger larger scale neural processes and so introduce some randomness into them" (Mackie 220). Hence Lovecraft's belief that "the future, though wholly determinate, is . . . essentially unknown" (*SL* 3.31)—where again the distinction is made between ontological determinism and human epistemological uncertainty—is still viable, although the case for determinism now tends to be based rather on psychological than metaphysical foundations.

The point of all these reflections is that Lovecraft could use the findings of modern physics to produce an "updated" or "modernised" version of such standard supernatural themes as the vampire in "The Shunned House." A similar transformation occurs in "The Dreams in the Witch House," where witchcraft and time travel are reinterpreted through Einstein. At the very beginning of the tale is a mention of "quantum physics" (*MM* 263)—nowadays called quantum mechanics—and shortly after we are given a hint as to the possible sources of Keziah Mason's powers: "some circumstance had more or less suddenly given a mediocre old woman of the seventeenth century an insight into mathematical depths perhaps beyond the utmost modern delvings of Planck, Heisenberg, Einstein, and de Sitter" (*MM* 264).

The mention of Einstein and Planck is not unusual, but the other two call for some notice. Willem de Sitter (1872–1934) was chiefly known for having been instrumental in introducing the theory of relativity into the English-speaking world in a series of articles published during 1916–17, and he worked extensively on the relation of relativity to cosmology; in so doing he evolved a view of the universe sufficiently different from Einstein's as to earn it the nickname of the "De Sitter Universe." Lovecraft heard a lecture by him on 9 November 1931 (*SL* 3.437), which probably accounts for the mention of him in "The Dreams in the Witch House," written in February 1932. The mention of Werner Karl Heisenberg (1901–1976) is even more interesting; for, basing his work on the quantum theory, he produced in 1927 the celebrated Indeterminacy Principle, whereby "natural laws" previously thought to be fixed were reduced to mere statistical averages. It might be thought that Lovecraft would be highly inspired by this theory, since his whole aesthetic of weird fiction centred on the depiction of "the illusion of some strange suspension or violation of the galling limitations of time, space, and natural law" (*MW* 113); but in fact the reverse would be the case, since Lovecraft's "suspension or violation" of the laws of Nature could be aesthetically effective only if those laws were assumed to be immutable and eternal. In any case, I am not certain how well Lovecraft ever explored the Indeterminacy Principle, although it is certainly rather curious that Heisenberg was awarded the Nobel Prize for Physics in the very year (1932) Lovecraft wrote "The Dreams in the Witch House."

The discussions of time travel and hyperspace travel later in the tale have already been examined by Fritz Leiber, and we need remark on only a few particulars. Compare, for example, the bold statement "Time could not exist in certain belts of space" (*MM* 285) and the subsequent logical development of the idea with the earlier, nebulous, and poetic expression of the same idea in "The White Ship": "In the land of Sona-Nyl there is neither time nor space, neither suffering nor death; and there I dwelt for many aeons" (*D* 39). Granted that the intent of the two tales is wholly dissimilar, and that in the earlier tale a scientific exposition would be entirely inappropriate, it may still be observed how the discoveries of modern physics—and Lovecraft's early and intelligent absorption of them—have led to a tightening of the intellectual and philosophical foundations of his later tales, and even perhaps to an expansion in imaginative scope, since, as Lovecraft knew, "the more we learn about the cosmos, the more bewildering does it appear" (*SL* 4.324).

As we move to the realm of pure astronomy, we may examine the one great example of Lovecraft's topicality: the mention of the discovery of

Pluto in "The Whisperer in Darkness." Although the core of the tale was inspired by Lovecraft's trips to Vermont in 1927 and 1928, it may be of interest to note that the actual writing of the tale was begun on 24 February 1930. The discovery of Pluto was made by C. W. Tombaugh at the Lowell Observatory on 23 January 1930, but the earliest announcement of the discovery that I can find is the front page of the *New York Times* for 14 March 1930; it was announced in various scientific journals shortly thereafter. It cannot, therefore, precisely be said that the discovery impelled the actual commencement of a tale whose genesis had occurred several years earlier, but it is still clear that Lovecraft was eager to incorporate this great discovery into his story. It may also be of some interest to note that the search for a trans-Neptunian planet was instigated as early as 1915 by Percival Lowell (with whose work Lovecraft was quite familiar) in a manner not wholly dissimilar to that advised by Lovecraft himself in his letter to the *Scientific American* of July 1906.

The last example of Lovecraft's scientific topicality to be considered here is his mention of the continental drift theory in *At the Mountains of Madness*. I have elsewhere noted that one example of Lovecraft's attempts to keep this tale "up to date" was the elimination of some references to an incorrect theory that the Antarctic continent was actually two land masses separated by a frozen strait between the Weddell and Ross Seas;[9] this elimination must have been made just prior to the submission of the tale to *Astounding Stories* in late 1935 (*SL* 5.209–10). I had, however, previously thought that these changes were triggered by information derived from Admiral Byrd's expedition to the Antarctic (1933–35); it now appears that the widely held theory of the frozen strait was effectively refuted by a plane flight from the Weddell to the Ross Sea made by Lincoln Ellsworth and Herbert Hollick-Kenyon in late 1934 and early 1935 (see Chapman 240). Whatever the situation, it is clear that Lovecraft was intent on eliminating any obsolete scientific references in the novel—perhaps he did so in March 1935, when he told Emil Petaja that "Before long I'll try to dig it [the novel] up and shoot it along" (*SL* 5.120).

But it is fortunate that Lovecraft did not alter the two references to the continental drift theory, which he actually notes had been "lately advanced by Taylor, Wegener, and Joly" (*MM* 66). For the fact is that the continental drift theory was very controversial throughout the 1920s and 1930s, and the majority of scientists tended to reject it; only after World War II did it gain widespread acceptance (although in a slightly altered form from that expounded by its originators). Lovecraft was here re-

---

9. See "Textual Problems in Lovecraft," *Lovecraft Studies* No. 6 (Spring 1982): 28.

markably advanced and prophetic in embracing the theory.[10] Even the order in which Lovecraft mentions the three proponents of the theory is
chronologically correct. Frank Bursley Taylor (1860–1938) published a paper on the theory in 1910 but did not himself expand upon it. The major
advocate and elaborator of the theory was Alfred Lothar Wegener (1880–
1930), who himself announced the theory in 1912 and went on to write a
volume on the subject translated as *The Origin of Continents and Oceans*
(1924). Wegener's work was adopted by John Joly (1857–1933), who published his *Surface History of the Earth* in 1925; but Joly does not seem to have
advanced the theory much farther than Wegener. I do not believe that
Lovecraft actually read either Wegener's or Joly's book, but he was certainly conversant with the major principles of the theory and uses it in a
brilliant and clever fashion in his novel, remarking wryly that the theory
"receives striking support from [the] uncanny source" (*MM* 69) of the Old
Ones' bas-reliefs in their millennia-abandoned megalopolis.

Lovecraft, then, was not merely very much alive in the era of Hitler,
T. S. Eliot, and Einstein (as his letters clearly prove), but he was not above
making overt references to contemporary political, social, literary, and scientific movements in his fiction. It is true that these references rarely occupy a large or central place in his tales, and we have nothing akin to the
minute descriptions of life in seventeenth- and eighteenth-century Providence forming the sub-narrative about Curwen in *The Case of Charles Dexter
Ward;* but it is clear that Lovecraft assumes knowledge of the culture in
which he was writing and makes few attempts to depict a consciously archaic environment or to write in an archaic idiom. Indeed, the belief that
Lovecraft's work is "antiquated" either in theme or in style has been greatly
exaggerated by critics. The very allusiveness of many of the references—
note the mention of "the President" and not "President Harding" in "The
Rats in the Walls"—signifies a shared body of information that Lovecraft
expected of his reader. Even if Lovecraft intended his fiction to be, as with
Thucydides, a "possession for all time," there can be no doubt but that it is
firmly rooted in the culture of the inter-war years in America and Europe
which Lovecraft observed so perceptively in his life and letters.

Works Cited

Bloch, Robert. "Out of the Ivory Tower." In Lovecraft's *The Shuttered Room and
Other Pieces*. Sauk City, WI: Arkham House, 1959.
———. "Poe and Lovecraft" (1972). Rpt. in S. T. Joshi, ed., *H. P. Lovecraft:
Four Decades of Criticism*. Athens: Ohio University Press, 1980.

---

10. I am grateful to John Shaw for first alerting me to this circumstance.

Chapman, Walker. *The Loneliest Continent: The Story of Antarctic Discovery*. Green-wich, CT: New York Graphic Society, 1964.

Clark, Walter E. *Quabbin Reservoir*. New York: Hobson Book Press, 1946.

Leiber, Fritz. "Through Hyperspace with Brown Jenkin: Lovecraft's Contribu-tion to Speculative Fiction" (1966). Rpt. in S. T. Joshi, ed., *H. P. Lovecraft: Four Decades of Criticism*. Athens: Ohio University Press, 1980.

Long, Frank Belknap. "The Hounds of Tindalos." In *The Hounds of Tindalos*. New York: Jove/HBJ, 1978.

Mackie, J. L. *Ethics: Inventing Right and Wrong*. Harmondsworth: Penguin, 1977.

Russell, Bertrand. *Human Knowledge: Its Scope and Limits*. New York: Simon & Schuster, 1948.

III. Studies on Individual Works

Lovecraft, Regner Lodbrog, and Olaus Wormius

Those few fortunate souls who have seen the *Acolyte* for Summer 1944 have presumably observed the editors' note by Francis T. Laney and Samuel D. Russell prefacing the first publication of Lovecraft's curious poem, "Regnar Lodbrug's [*sic*] Epicedium: (An 8th Century Funeral Song . . . . Translated from Olaus Wormius":

> This interesting item presents to *Acolyte* readers what was to us, at least, an entirely new facet of HPL's writings. Written about 1920, *The Epicedium* is probably one of the very earliest attempts to "translate" a mythical manuscript, and is also notable for the first reference to the redoubtable Olaus Wormius, who later became renowned as a translator and publisher of the diabolic writings of the mad Arab, Abdul Alhazred. The various gaps in the poem are, we assume, deliberate; and probably are meant to convey the idea that only portions of so ancient and battered a vellum could be deciphered. So far as we know, *Regnar Lodbrug's Epicedium* is new to print.

Through no fault of their own, nearly the entirety of this utterance by Laney and Russell is false: 1) "Regner Lodbrog's Epicedium" (to give it its exact title) dates not to 1920 but to 1914; 2) it was not translated from "a mythical manuscript"; and 3) while the poem indeed contains the first reference to Olaus Wormius in Lovecraft, the apparent implication here that Wormius is himself mythical is also false.

The solution to this entire affair begins with a letter by Lovecraft to Maurice W. Moe, dated 17 December 1914:

> I recently tried the "Hiawatha" type of blank verse in translating a curious bit of primitive Teutonic martial poetry which Dr. Blair quotes in his "Critical Dissertation on the Poems of Ossian." This fragment is a funeral song composed in Runes by the old Danish monarch Regner Lodbrok (eighth century A.D.). In the Middle Ages Olaus Wormius made the rather incoherent Latin version which Blair uses. It is in stanzas, each headed by the words "Pugnavimus ensibus." In translating, I end each stanza with a rhyming couplet. (AHT)

This tells us much that we need to know. Hugh Blair (1718–1800), whose landmark *Lectures on Rhetorick and Belles-Lettres* (1784) Lovecraft owned, published *A Critical Dissertation on the Poems of Ossian, the Son of Fingal* in 1763. This work, noted for its defence of the claims by James Macpherson that the poems of "Ossian" were authentic (i.e., were actually written by an ancient Scottish bard rather than fabricated by Macpherson himself), contains a lengthy disquisition on ancient Runic or "Gothic" poetry in general. At one point Blair writes:

> Our present subject leads us to investigate the ancient poetical remains, not so much of the east, or of the Greeks and Romans, as of the northern nations; in order to discover whether the Gothic poetry has any resemblance to the Celtic or Galic, which we are about to consider. Though the Goths, under which name we usually comprehend all the Scandinavian tribes, were a people altogether fierce and martial, and noted, to a proverb, for their ignorance of the liberal arts; yet they too, from the earliest times, had their poets and their songs. Their poets were distinguished by the title of *Scalders*, and their songs were termed *Vyses*. Saxo Grammaticus, a Danish historian of considerable note, who flourished in the thirteenth century, informs us, that very many of these songs, containing the ancient traditionary stories of the country, were found engraven upon rocks, in the old Runic character, several of which he has translated into Latin, and inserted into his history. But his versions are plainly so paraphrastical and forced into such an imitation of the style and the measures of the Roman poets, that one can form no judgment from them of the native spirit of the original. A more curious monument of the true Gothic poetry is preserved by Olaus Wormius, in his book de Literatura Runica. It is an Epicedium, or funeral song, composed by Regner Lodbrog; and translated by Olaus, word for word from the original. This Lodbrog was a king of Denmark, who lived in the eighth century, famous for his wars and victories; and, at the same time, an eminent *Scalder* or poet. It was his misfortune to fall at last into the hands of one of his enemies, by whom he was thrown into prison, and condemned to be destroyed by serpents. In this situation, he solaced himself with rehearsing all the exploits of his life. The poem is divided into twenty-nine stanzas, of ten lines each; and every stanza begins with these words, Pugnavimus ensibus. We have fought with our swords. Olaus's version is in many places so obscure as to be hardly intelligible. I have subjoined the whole below, exactly as he has published it; and shall translate as much as may give the English reader an idea of the spirit and strain of this kind of poetry. (Blair 143–47)

There follows, in a footnote, the entire twenty-nine stanzas of Olaus' Latin translation of Regner Lodbrog's epicedium; in the text Blair translates, in prose, the second through the seventh stanzas (for some reason he omits the first). It is no accident that Lovecraft's own translation from Olaus extends only to these exact seven stanzas.

I now append first Olaus' Latin translation, then Blair's prose translation (I have divided it into paragraphs corresponding to each stanza), then Lovecraft's poetic translation (corrected from the *Acolyte* appearance by consultation with the autograph manuscript):

Olaus Wormius:

> ### 1.
>
> Pugnavimus ensibus
> Haud post longum tempus
> Cum in Gotlandia accessimus
> Ad serpentis immensi necem
> Tunc impetravimus Thoram
> Ex hoc vocarunt me virum
> Quod serpentem transfodi
> Hirsutam braccam ob illam ceem
> Cuspide ictum intuli in colubrum
> Fero lucidorum stupendiorum.
>
> ### 2.
>
> Multum juvenis fui quando acquisivimus
> Orientem versus in Oreonico freto
> Vulnerum amnes avidae serae
> Et flavipedi avi
> Accepimus ibidem sonuerunt
> Ad sublimes galeas
> Dura ferra magman escam
> Omnis erat oceanus vulnus
> Vadavit corvus in sanguine Caesorum.
>
> ### 3.
>
> Alte tulimus tunc lanceas
> Quando viginti annos numeravimus
> Et celebrem laudem comparavimus passim
> Vicimus octo barones
> In oriente ante Dimini portum
> Aquilae impetravimus tunc sufficientem
> Hospitii sumptum in illa strage
> Sudor decidit in vulnerum
> Oceano perdidit exercitus aetatem.

4.

Pugnae facta copia
Cum Helsingianos postulavimus
Ad aulum Odini
Naves direximus is ostium Vistulae
Mucro potuit tum mordere
Omnis erat vulnus unda
Terra rubefacta Calido
Frendebat gladius in loricas
Gladius findebat Clypeos.

5.

Memini neminem tunc fugisse
Priusquam in navibus
Heraudus in bello caderet
Non findit navibus
Alius baro praestantior
Mare ad portum
In navibus longis post illum
Sic attulit princeps passim
Alacre in bellum cor.

6.

Exercitus abjecit clypeos
Cum hasta volavit
Ardua ad virorum pectora
Momordit Scarforum cautes
Gladius in pugna
Sanguineus erat Clypeus
Antequam Rafno rex caderet
Fluxit ex virorum capitibus
Calidus in loricas sudor.

7.

Habere potuerunt tum corvi
Ante Indiorum insulas
Sufficientem praedam dilaniandam
Acquisivimus feris carnivoris

> Plenum prandium unico actu
> Difficile erat unius facere mentionem
> Oriente sole
> Spicula vidi pungere
> Propulerunt arcus ex se ferra.

Hugh Blair:

We have fought with our swords. I was young, when, towards the east, in the bay of Oreon, we made torrents of blood flow, to gorge the ravenous beast of prey, and the yellow-footed bird. There resounded the hard steel upon the lofty helmets of men. The whole ocean was one wound. The crow waded in the blood of the slain.

When we had numbered twenty yers, we lifted our spears on high, and every where spread our renown. Eight barons we overcame in the east, before the port of Dominum; and plentifully we feasted the eagle in that slaughter. The warm stream of wounds ran into the ocean. The army fell before us.

When we steered our ships into the mouth of the Vistula, we sent the Helsingians to the hall of Odin. Then did the sword bite. The waters were all one wound. The earth was dyed red with the warm stream. The sword rung upon the coats of mail, and clove the bucklers in twain.

None fled on that day, till among his ships Heraudus fell. Than him no braver baron cleaves the sea with a ship; a cheerful heart did he ever bring to the combat.

Then the host threw away their shields, when the uplifted spear flew at the breasts of heroes. The sword bit the Scarfian rocks; bloody was the shield in battle, until Rafno the king was slain. From the heads of warriors the warm sweat streamed down their armour.

The crows around the Indirian islands had an ample prey. It were difficult to single out one among so many deaths. At the rising of the sun I beheld the spears piercing the bodies of foes, and the bows throwing forth their steel-pointed arrows. Loud roared the swords in the plains of Lano.—The virgins long bewailed the slaughter of that morning.

H. P. Lovecraft:

> *With our swords have we contended!*
> Come but new to Gothland's shore
> For the killing of the serpent
> We have gain'd from Thor ( )
> (   )
> From this deed they call me man

Because I have transfix'd the adder:
Shaggy breeches from that slaughter.
(   )
I have thrust a spear into the serpent
With metal brighter (   )

With our swords have we contended!
But a youth was I when eastward
In the channel of Oreon
With our foemen's gore in torrents
We the ( ) and wolves delighted;
And the yellow-footed buzzard.
There the harden'd steel resounded
On the high-wrought hostile helmets.
One vast wound was all the ocean
And the hungry raven waded
Searching for its carrion food
Deep in dead men's thick'ning blood.

With our swords have we contended!
Ere two score of years we counted
High we bore our glist'ning lances
Wide we heard our fame and praises.
In the east before the harbour
(Barons eight we overcame;)
We the rav'ning eagle glutted;
Dripping wounds fill'd up the ocean.
Weary of the hopeless fray,
All the host dissolved away.

With our swords have we contended!
When the Vistula we enter'd
With our ships in battle order
We unto the hall of Woden
Sent the bold Helsingian foemen.
Then the sword-points bit in fury;
All the billows turn'd to life-blood
Earthg with streaming gore was crimson'd;
Reeking sword with ringing note
Shields divided; armour smote.

(With our swords have we contended!)

(None had fallen on that day)
(Till on his ship Heraudus fell:)
(Than him before no braver baron)
Cleft the sea with ships of battle;
Never after him was chieftain
Lighter hearted in the fighting.

With our swords have we contended!
Now the host flung down their buckles;
Flying spears tore heroes' bosoms
Swords on Scarfian rocks were striking.
Gory was his shield in slaughter
Till the royal Rafno perish'd.
Sweat from weary hands and pale
Trickled down the suits of mail.

With our swords have we contended!
Copious booty had the ravens
Round about th' Indirian islands,
In that single day of action
(One in many deaths was little.)
(The rising sun grew bright on spears)
In the forms of prostrate warrior-men.
Arrows from their bows ejected;
(Weapons roared on Lano's plain.   )
(Long the virgin mourned that slaughter)

In spite of the fact that Blair has failed to translate the first stanza, it can readily be seen that Lovecraft was otherwise much dependent on Blair for his own rendition of this very peculiar Latin; indeed, Lovecraft has also versified the two final sentences in Blair, which actually derive from the first few lines of the eighth stanza of the Latin text. I am not entirely clear what the gaps and parentheses in Lovecraft's text are meant to signify; the gaps may indicate places where he (not surprisingly) cannot make much sense of the Latin and suspects something missing.

While this poem is indeed the first mention of Regner Lodbrog in Lovecraft, it is not the only one. The last four lines of stanza 4, the fourth and fifth lines of stanza 23, and the last four lines of stanza 29 of Olaus' Latin version as printed in Blair are cited as an epigraph to the poem "The Teuton's Battle-Song" (*United Amateur,* February 1916). The poem itself, of course, is written in Lovecraft's usual heroic couplets. I know of no other mention of Regner Lodbrog in any text by Lovecraft.

Olaus Wormius is a different story, and I think we are now in a position to understand why Lovecraft habitually dated him to the thirteenth
century when in fact Olaus (Ole Wurm, 1588–1654) is clearly a figure of
the seventeenth century. It does not appear as if Lovecraft knew of him
other than in this mention by Blair, who never supplies his life dates or
even the approximate period in which he wrote. What I believe has happened is that Lovecraft has confused Olaus with Saxo Grammaticus,
whom Blair places in the thirteenth century, or merely assumed that Olaus
and Saxo were contemporaries. The fact that Lovecraft mentions in the
letter to Moe that Olaus flourished in the "Middle Ages" clearly means that
he thought Olaus to date to this time, and that his repeated dating of
Olaus' purported Latin translation of the *Necronomicon* to 1228 is simply the
result of an error, not a deliberate change on Lovecraft's part.

After this poem, Lovecraft cites Olaus in "The Festival" (1923), referring to "the unmentionable *Necronomicon* of the mad Arab Abdul Alhazred,
in Olaus Wormius' forbidden Latin translation" (*D* 211). In "History of the
Necronomicon" (1927) he writes: "After this [i.e., the banning of the Greek
text in 1050] it is only heard of furtively, but (1228) Olaus Wormius made
a Latin translation later in the Middle Ages . . ." In "The Dunwich Horror"
Lovecraft refers to "the hideous *Necronomicon* of the mad Arab Abdul Alhazred in Olaus Wormius' Latin version, as printed in Spain in the seventeenth century" (*DH* 169); this would be an historically plausible mention
had he not already dated Olaus to the thirteenth century.

Wormius himself is an interesting figure in his own right. He was a
Danish philologist and historian who did valuable work in the collection of
texts and other materials pertaining to his native land. The volume referred
to by Blair as *De Literatura Runica* appears to be a work published as *Runir;
seu, Danica Literatura Antiquissima, vulgo Gothica Ducta Luci Reddita* (1636)
[Runes; or, The Most Ancient Danish Literature, Commonly Called Gothic
Poems, Brought to Light]. He also wrote a book on the philosopher's
stone—*Liber Aureus Philosophorum* (1625)—but, even though it would make
Olaus a more likely candidate for the translator of the *Necronomicon,* I can
find no evidence that Lovecraft knew of this work.

All this may seem much ado about nothing, and it probably is; but it is
one more small indication of the trouble Lovecraft could get into when he
relied upon second-hand erudition. The poem "Regner Lodbrog's Epicedium" is actually a rather striking piece of work, and it is remarkable that it
was one of the earliest poems of Lovecraft's mature literary career; had he
written more poems of this sort, and not been fatally lured by the swan
song of the eighteenth-century heroic couplet, he might have amounted to
something as a poet. And if he had done a little more research on Olaus

Wormius, he would have saved himself a small but embarrassing error in the otherwise ingenious "history" of his most celebrated mythical tome.

Works Cited

Blair, Hugh. *A Critical Dissertation on the Poems of Ossian, the Son of Fingal.* 1763. Rpt. in *The Poems of Ossian.* Leipzig: Gerhard Fleischer, 1826, Vol. 3.

Lovecraft, H. P. "Regner Lodbrog's Epicedium." A.Ms., JHL, Brown University. T.Ms. (prepared by R. H. Barlow), JHL. Printed in *The Acolyte* 2, No. 3 (Summer 1944): 14–15.

On "Polaris"

> "Polaris" is rather interesting in that I wrote it in 1918, *before* I had ever read a word of Lord Dunsany's. Some find it hard to believe this, but I can give not only assurance but absolute proof that it is so. It is simply a case of similar types of vision facing the unknown, and harbouring similar stores of mythic and historical lore. Hence the parallelism in atmosphere, artificial nomenclature, treatment of the dream theme, etc. (*SL* 2.120)

This revealing passage, written in a letter of 1927, tells us many important things; in particular, the fact that not only Lovecraft himself but his colleagues were taken aback at the manner in which "Polaris" seemed to have anticipated Lovecraft's later "Dunsanian" imitations, beginning in late 1919 with "The White Ship." Modern scholars have not merely echoed Lovecraft's remarks about this remarkable instance of parallelism, but have used it to defend Lovecraft's "Dunsanian" tales from charges of derivativeness. Dirk W. Mosig unhesitatingly declared that "'Polaris' was written a whole year prior to his encounter with Lord Dunsany and his work, and clearly shows that Lovecraft's mind, at the time, was running in a parallel channel to Dunsany's. It is quite possible that, had Lovecraft never come across Lord Dunsany, he would still have written most of his 'Dunsanian' tales" (Mosig 186).

But both Lovecraft and his later critics seem to have been content with acknowledging this "proto-Dunsanianism" in "Polaris" and have not tried to ascertain whence it may have derived. An examination of the possible literary and philosophical sources of "Polaris" may help to place the tale in proper perspective and perhaps to render it a little less anomalous.

The fact is that both Lovecraft and Dunsany had one common and very powerful influence: Edgar Allan Poe. But whereas Lovecraft was primarily influenced by Poe's "pure" horror tales (he ranked "The Fall of the House of Usher" and "Ligeia" as Poe's two finest tales [see *D* 399]), Dunsany seems conversely to have been affected by some of Poe's more "poetic" narratives. In his autobiography, Dunsany makes no secret of the effect of Poe's stories and poems on his early imaginative development: "the haunted desolation and weird gloom of the misty mid-region of Weir remained for many years something that seemed to me more eerie than anything earth had" (Dunsany 32). Lovecraft himself conjectures that Poe's prose-poems (especially "Silence—a Fable" and "Shadow—a Parable"), which "employ[ed] that archaic and Orientalised style with jewelled phrase, quasi-Biblical repetition, and recurrent burthen," had left their mark upon such "later writers [as] Oscar Wilde and Lord Dunsany" (*D* 398). Can it be, then, that Poe's prose-poems were at least an indirect influence upon "Polaris"?

A very good case could be made for such an influence. Poe's prose-poems seem to have made a great impression upon Lovecraft in his early fiction. It has not been observed even by the defenders of Lovecraft's "Dunsanian" tales that "Memory"—which could well be classed as "proto-Dunsanian"—was written several months before Lovecraft's first encounter with the Irish fantaisiste.[1] Here too we have imaginary place-names (the "valley of Nis" [*MW* 31])[2] and a generally dreamlike and poetic atmosphere. But this tale almost certainly derives from Poe's "Silence—a Fable"; both tales contain a "Demon" as a character ("'Listen to me,' said the Demon" is the first sentence of Poe's tale; Lovecraft introduces us to a "Daemon of the Valley"), while the "Genie that haunts the moonbeams" in Lovecraft's tale may be paralleled by the mention of "Genii" in Poe's. Indeed, the very structure of the tale—a dialogue between two bizarre supernatural beings which takes on an unreal, almost allegorical air—may have found its source in such of Poe's tales as "The Conversation of Eiros and Charmion" and "The Colloquy of Monos and Una." Lovecraft's tale certainly contains that "quasi-Biblical repetition" which he observed in Poe's tales ("The Genie . . . spake to the Daemon of the Valley, saying, 'I am old, and forget much'"). Finally, in "The Picture in the House" (1920) Lovecraft borrowed a memorable phrase from the end of Poe's "Shadow—a Parable" ("I am SHADOW, and my dwelling is near to the Catacombs of Ptolemais"; "Searchers after horror haunt strange, far places. For them are the catacombs of Ptolemais" [*DH* 116]).

Poe's influence, then, was pervasive in Lovecraft's early tales, and "Polaris" may well fit into the pattern. It contains the same sort of Biblical style that is at the heart of both Poe's prose-poems and Dunsany's early work, and its inclusion of a ten-line poem ("Slumber, watcher, till the spheres . . .") is reminiscent of the poetic snatches in some of Poe's tales, notably "The Haunted Palace" in "The Fall of the House of Usher" and "The Conqueror Worm" in "Ligeia." Lovecraft had already used the device in the hilarious drinking-song in "The Tomb" (1917) but never again employed it, although "The Nameless City" (1921) and "Under the Pyramids"

---

1. It was published in the June 1919 issue of the *United Co-operative;* Lovecraft first read Dunsany in October 1919.

2. "The Valley Nis" is in fact an early title for Poe's poem "The Valley of Unrest," although Lovecraft may have been unaware of the fact. Nis, in any event, is mentioned in the poem.

(1924) contain some lines of poetry by other hands (in both cases Thomas Moore). A claim might even be made that Lovecraft's other original fictional work of 1918—the lost "dime-novel" "The Mystery of Murdon Grange"—owed something to Poe's detective tales, although in the absence of the actual text such a claim is tenuous.

The most unusual feature of "Polaris"—or, rather, the feature that links it most closely with the work of Dunsany—is the use of mythical names. Here too we may find in Poe the common source of this technique in Lovecraft and Dunsany. Many of the names invented by Lovecraft in "Polaris" are pseudo-Greek coinages—Olathoë, Sarkis (reminiscent of Sardis, the ancient capital of Lydia in Asia Minor), Noton, Kadiphonek, Alos, Zobna, Thapnen, and perhaps even the Gnophkehs. Poe, in fact, in "Shadow—a Parable" uses actual Greek names (Oinos, Corinnos, Zoilus, etc.), while the names in "The Colloquy of Monos and Una" are derived, respectively, from the Greek masculine and Latin feminine adjectives meaning "one." Lovecraft himself recognised that Dunsany's "amazing facility for devising musical, alluring, and wonder-making proper names . . . [derives from] classical and Oriental models" ("Lord Dunsany and His Work" [*MW* 106]), but he seems not to have made the connexion that Poe's Hellenic names may at least have helped to inspire his own and Dunsany's mythical coinages.

Finally, it must be noted that Lovecraft is in fact incorrect in believing that the "treatment of the dream theme" (*SL* 2.120) in "Polaris" finds a parallel in Dunsany. Few of Dunsany's tales are postulated as occurring in a dream; rather, they simply employ a mythical terrain and completely ignore its possible relations to the "real" world. Moreover, Dunsany seems not to have based many of his stories upon his own dreams: his most celebrated tale, "Idle Days on the Yann" (in *A Dreamer's Tales*), was written in anticipation (what Lovecraft might have called "adventurous expectancy") of a journey he was to take down the Nile. Indeed, Dunsany seems to have had few vivid dreams at all. We now know, however, that "Polaris" was founded upon a dream that Lovecraft had in May 1918:

> Several nights ago I had a strange dream of a strange city—a city of many palaces and gilded domes, lying in a hollow betwixt ranges of grey, horrible hills. There was not a soul in this vast region of stone-paved streets and marble walls and columns, and the numerous statues in the public places were of strange bearded men in robes the like whereof I have never seen before or since. I was, as I said, aware of this city visually. I was in it and around it. But certainly I had no corporeal existence. I saw, it seemed, everything at once; without the limitations of direction. I did not move, but transferred my perception from point to point at will. I occupied no space and had no form. I was only a consciousness, a perceptive presence.

I recall a lively curiosity at the scene, and a tormenting struggle to recall its identity; for I felt that I had once known it well, and that if I could remember, I should be carried back to a very remote period—many thousand years, when something vaguely horrible had happened. Once I was almost on the verge of realisation, and was frantic with fear at the prospect. though I did not know what it was that I should recall. But here I awaked—in a very cramped posture and with too much bedclothing for the steadily increasing ternperature. I have related this in detail because it impressed me very vividly. (*SL* 1.62)

The context of these remarks is of the highest interest, as it seems to provide the philosophical motive for Lovecraft's subsequent writing of the tale. In this letter Lovecraft was discussing with Maurice W. Moe the "distinction between dream life and real life, between appearances and actualities" (*SL* 1.63). Moe, apparently influenced by the Pragmatism of William James, was trying to defend the usefulness of religious belief regardless of its metaphysical truth or falsity. James himself felt that there was no positive evidence either for or against religion, hence felt that the "will to believe"—a decision to believe one of two contrary propositions as true depending upon its usefulness—was applicable in this case. In spite of the severe logical fallacies behind this position,[3] it became very popular at the turn of the century and was used by orthodox religionists like Moe as a philosophical justification of belief. Lovecraft, however, cut the ground out from under this position by categorically asserting that "the Judaeo-Christian mythology is NOT TRUE" (*SL* 1.60). What Lovecraft, then, was trying to do in relating his dream to Moe was to show him the paradoxes that would follow if truth or falsity were not the first criterion for judging a phenomenon rather than its usefulness: "According to your pragmatism that dream was as real as my presence at this table, pen in hand! If the truth or falsity of our beliefs and impressions be immaterial, then I am, or was, actually and indisputably an unbodied spirit hovering over a very singular, very silent, and very ancient city somewhere between grey, dead hills. I thought I was at the time—so what else matters?" (*SL* 1.62–63). This remark is ironically echoed in the tale itself:

At first content to view the scene as an all-observant uncorporeal presence, I now desired to define my relation to it, and to speak my mind amongst the grave men who conversed each day in the public squares. I said to myself, "This is no dream, for by what means can I prove the greater reality of that other life in the house of stone and brick south of

---

3. See Bertrand Russell's devastating criticisms, "Pragmatism" and "William James' Conception of Truth," in his *Philosophical Essays* (1910).

the sinister swamp and the cemetery on the low hillock, where the Pole Star peers into my north window each night?" (*D* 21)

What conclusions can we now draw about "Polaris"? Its immediate origin was the dream of May 1918 (and it was probably written up shortly after this letter to Moe), and its philosophical source was the "distinction between dream life and real life" about which Moe and Lovecraft were arguing; its partial literary source was perhaps Poe's prose-poems, which made a great impression upon Lovecraft's early fiction; and its apparent resemblance to Dunsany's work may derive precisely from the possibility that Dunsany and Lovecraft shared a common influence in the work of Poe. We may then be justified in doubting whether Lovecraft would in fact have gone on to write his other "Dunsanian" tales had he never read Dunsany. It is a question, of course, that we can never answer and which it is probably idle to ask at all; for there can be no doubt of the importance of Dunsany's work in the development of Lovecraft's own fictional technique, as Lovecraft was fully aware: "As for [Dunsany's] influence on me—of course I had the same general cosmic attitude before, for that is why his discovery was such an event for me. But I couldn't even begin to formulate my attitude in artistic prose till I had him to follow as a model."[4]

Works Cited

Dunsany, Lord. *Patches of Sunlight*. London: William Heinemann, 1938.
Mosig, Dirk W. "'The White Ship': A Psychological Odyssey." In S. T. Joshi, ed., *H. P. Lovecraft: Four Decades of Criticism*. Athens: Ohio University Press, 1980.

---

4. Lovecraft to Elizabeth Toldridge, 14 August 1929 (ms., JHL).

What Happens in "Arthur Jermyn"

I have always admired Lovecraft's "Facts Concerning the Late Arthur Jermyn and His Family" (1920; *D* 73–82) for its compactness and relatively sober narrative style, as opposed to the floridity (effective in its own way) of other such early tales as "The Doom That Came to Sarnath" (1919) or "Celephaïs" (1920). It has been considered a precursor to some of Lovecraft's greatest tales: its opening rumination on the potentially disastrous psychological effects of knowledge brings "The Call of Cthulhu" (1926) to mind, while its account of loathsome miscegenation foreshadows "The Shadow over Innsmouth" (1931). But "Arthur Jermyn" has been deprecated for a certain narrowness of focus: unlike the spectacular miscegenation affecting an entire clan or city (and potentially all civilisation) that we find in "The Lurking Fear" (1922) or "The Shadow over Innsmouth," we appear here to be concerned only with the corruption of a single family. As such, the tale has been seen as a bridge between those of Lovecraft's tales where horror envelops a single individual ("The Tomb," "Dagon") and those where all mankind is involved. If read carefully, however, "Arthur Jermyn" may show that this schema, while on the whole accurate, may be somewhat problematical.

Let us consider the celebrated opening utterance:

> Life is a hideous thing, and from the background behind what we know of it peer daemoniacal hints of truth which make it sometimes a thousandfold more hideous. Science, already oppressive with its shocking revelations, will perhaps be the ultimate exterminator of our human species—if separate species we be—for its reserve of unguessed horrors could never be borne by mortal brains if loosed upon the world.

This passage is so well-known that critics have apparently not taken the trouble to note some anomalous details, especially if read with the whole of the tale in mind. In particular, what we have here is a *generalised* statement concerning the possibility that human beings may not be entirely "human" ("if separate species we be"); such a notion is not logically deducible from a *single* case of miscegenation, as we appear to have here. Was Lovecraft simply inept in feeling that all humanity (or at least some broad segment of humanity) is implicated in the corruption of the Jermyn line, or are there in fact broader conceptions at work here?

The crux of the tale is what Arthur Jermyn's great-great-great-grandfather, Sir Wade Jermyn, actually found in the depths of Africa. It is mentioned very early on that one of Sir Wade's "bizarre conjectures" was the existence of a "prehistoric *white* Congolese civilisation" (my emphasis). This detail seems to have passed almost entirely unnoticed by scholars: what would a white civilisation be doing in Africa? We get some description of it later on, as Sir Wade describes

> the gigantic walls and pillars of a forgotten city, crumbling and vine-grown, and . . . damp, silent, stone steps leading interminably down into the darkness of abysmal treasure-vaults and inconceivable catacombs . . . the living things that might haunt such a place [were] creatures half of the jungle and half of the impiously aged city—fabulous creatures which even a Pliny might describe with scepticism; things that might have sprung up after the great apes had overrun the dying city with the walls and the pillars, the vaults and the weird carvings.

This passage is critical, for it tells us what this city was like prior to Sir Wade's expedition there. The real implication of the story, I believe, is that this city (erected by the "white Congolese civilisation") *is the true fount of all white civilisation.* For someone of Lovecraft's well-known racialist bent, such a thing would be a horror surpassing any isolated case of miscegenation. This story is, really speaking, a mirror-image of the later "Medusa's Coil" (1930), where the true horror—intended to exceed all the other supernatural manifestations throughout the story—is that Marceline, "though in deceitfully slight proportion, . . . was a negress" (*HM* 200). The white man really comes from Africa!

Let us be clear on one point, however. The "white ape" whom Sir Wade marries is not a member of the original white civilisation, but a product of the mingling of apes with the remaining members of this civilisation: note that the "living things" Sir Wade found were "creatures half of the jungle [i.e., apes] and half of the impiously aged city [i.e., the white civilisation]." How else could the ape be "white"? The white ape is itself a result of miscegenation, and its ancestors must have migrated throughout the world to found all the known white races. By marrying this white ape, Sir Wade has, as it were, given his descendants an "extra dose" of the blood of this corrupt race, producing the physiognomic and temperamental anomalies of the Jermyn line. When the ape's mummified form is discovered by Arthur Jermyn's Belgian associate, M. Verhaeren, it is found to be "less hairy than any recorded variety [of ape], and infinitely nearer mankind— quite shockingly so." Its existence not merely reveals the source of the Jermyns' peculiar appearance, but by extension confirms the truth of all the tales of the white civilisation told by Sir Wade.

The overall implication of "Arthur Jermyn" is that all white civilisation is derived from this primal race in Africa, a race that has corrupted itself by intermingling with apes. This is the only explanation for the narrator's opening statement, "If we knew what we are, we should do as Sir Arthur Jermyn did [i.e., commit suicide]": we may not have a white ape in our immediate ancestry, but we are all the products of an ultimate miscegenation.

In *The Weird Tale* (1990) I first drew attention to the anomaly of the generalised opening of "Arthur Jermyn" and its seeming case of unique miscegenation; at that time I did not know the solution to the anomaly, and I wondered: "Does Lovecraft mean us to feel horror, by extension, at the truth of the Darwin theory? Surely even Lovecraft did not expect people to find evolution psychologically unbearable." But in fact that is exactly what is happening. Lovecraft is suggesting that the distinction between apes and human beings is a highly tenuous one—not merely in the case of the Jermyns, but of us all. In the essay "At the Root" (1918) Lovecraft wrote: "We must recognise the essential underlying savagery in the animal called man . . . civilisation is but a slight coverlet beneath which the dominant beast sleeps lightly and ever ready to awake." This could serve as the motto for "Arthur Jermyn," where the opening conjecture "if separate species we be" is ultimately to be answered in the negative.

"The Tree" and Ancient History

The Tree" (1920) is one of Lovecraft's least-regarded tales: since it was written in the midst of his initial "Dunsanian" period, it comes under general attack for being another of his wooden and lifeless imitations of Lord Dunsany; even so perceptive a critic as Donald R. Burleson dismisses the tale as "stylistically pleasing but otherwise little distinguished" (Burleson 70). And yet, "The Tree" stands out as being the only tale by Lovecraft set in the ancient world[1] (and in this fact alone it is to be distinguished from Dunsany, who rarely used historical settings for his early short stories); what is more, the tale reveals Lovecraft as a careful and profound student of ancient history, since the date when the tale's events take place can be almost exactly determined.

Lovecraft's fondness for classical civilisation needs no emphasis. His first extant poem, "The Poem of Ulysses" (second "edition," 8 November 1897), is a charming retelling of the *Odyssey* in 88 lines; and we know that he soon afterwards wrote similar verse retellings of other such epics as the *Iliad* and the *Aeneid* (both non-extant). Another non-extant juvenile work, *The Argonauts,* is presumably a retelling of the story of Jason and the Argonauts as related by Apollonius Rhodius in the *Argonautica* (mid-third century B.C.E.).

Lovecraft learnt Latin at a very early age—he may have begun at the age of eight. By the age of ten or so he produced a remarkable literal verse translation of the first 88 lines of Ovid's *Metamorphoses;* indeed, the existing manuscript of this work may be fragmentary, so that Lovecraft this time could well have translated much more of the text than we have. Lovecraft, however, never mastered Greek, although he studied it in high school. In a late letter he remarks that he "never got beyond the first six books of Xenophon" (*SL* 4.173), by which he probably refers to Xenophon's *Anabasis* (the "March Up Country"), although the *Hellenica* of Xenophon is in seven books. The *Anabasis* is still used today as a beginning Greek reader, as Xenophon employed a model Attic prose style.

When, however, Lovecraft had come to write "The Tree," he had comprehensively absorbed all branches of ancient culture—Greek philosophy (especially the Atomists and Epicurus, with such Latin thinkers as Lucretius and the Stoic Seneca), Greek and Roman history, ancient literature

---

1. Aside from his "Roman dream" of 1927, incorporated by Frank Belknap Long in *The Horror from the Hills* (1931).

from Homer to Juvenal (there is little evidence that Lovecraft read much late Latin, i.e., beyond the third century C.E.), and even ancient art and archaeology. What is remarkable about this absorption is that Lovecraft had for the most part to rely on rather inadequate school manuals and handbooks. Of the books in Greek history found in his library after his death, only a few—Mahaffy's *Survey of Greek Civilization,* Sir William Smith's *History of Greece*—are today granted any scholarly value. Lovecraft, however, clearly supplemented these manuals with extensive reading from original sources (especially, in the realm of Greek history, from Thucydides, Herodotus, Xenophon, and Diodorus Siculus) and with reference to Smith's still useful *Classical Dictionary* and *Dictionary of Greek and Roman Antiquities.*

The internal dating of the events in "The Tree" is actually a relatively simple business for anyone versed in ancient history; for Lovecraft is careful to provide unambiguous references that allow an exact pinpointing of the historical period involved. The tale concerns a contest proposed by the "Tyrant of Syracuse" (*D* 51) between the two great sculptors, Kalos and Musides, to carve a statue of Tyche for the Tyrant's city. Although the two artists are reputed to be the closest of friends, we soon find that Kalos has suddenly taken ill and eventually dies; we are clearly meant to infer that Musides has in fact poisoned Kalos so that he will not be defeated in the contest.[2] But Kalos is weirdly avenged when a strange olive tree growing out of his tomb suddenly falls upon Musides' residence, destroying both him and his statue.

Every detail in this story fits perfectly. First, the artists' names: Kalos in Greek simply means "handsome" or "fair," while Musides is a regular Greek formation meaning "son of the Muse(s)"—both apt names for artists. Moreover, the epigraph of the tale—omitted in all publications save the first, in the *Tryout* for October 1921—reads "Fata viam invenient" ("The Fates will find a way"), derived from Virgil's *Aeneid* 3.395. The mention of Fate connects directly with the contest to build a statue of Tyche, for *tyche* is nothing more than the Greek word for "chance" or "fate." Indeed, the Greek philosopher Democritus (much admired by Lovecraft for his development of the Atomic theory) equated necessity (*ananke* in Greek) or fate with chance, explaining the latter as merely those workings of fate whose precise chains of causality are not perceived by human beings (see Guthrie

---

2. Burleson's remark that "The strong indication, of course, is that Musides has poisoned Kalos . . . but this cannot be proven from the text alone," and his subsequent belief that "we have in 'The Tree' one of Lovecraft's most unreliable or dissembling narrators" is, I think, a bit perverse. Of course Lovecraft never says directly that Musides poisoned Kalos; to do so would have completely destroyed the subtlety of the story.

414f.). This seems to be the conception utilised in "The Tree": Musides was bound to perish because of his murder of Kalos, but to the human spectators his death seems to be an unexplained phenomenon of chance.

Turning to the specifically historical data, let us first consider which Tyrant of Syracuse may be in question. Syracuse, the most important Greek city in Sicily, was also one of the earliest overseas colonies of the Greeks: it was reputed to have been founded by the Corinthians in c. 734 B.C.E.[3] At this time, however, it was governed by an aristocratic group collectively called *gamoroi;* and it remained so governed for two and a half centuries. Syracuse then came under attack and was defeated by Hippocrates, the tyrant of neighbouring Gela (c. 495), but a certain Gelo espoused the cause of the *gamoroi* and became tyrant in c. 485. When Gelo died in 476, his brother Hiero succeeded to the tyranny; he ruled until his death in 467/6. It was at this time that Syracuse gained prominence as a cultural centre—many poets and philosophers (including the playwright Aeschylus) made trips there from mainland Greece.

After Hiero's death Syracuse became a democracy governed by an assembly and council, but Dionysius I re-established a tyranny in c. 406. He ruled until his death in 367, when his son Dionysius II took over, ruling in a turbulent period until 344, when he was finally overthrown and fled into exile.

Syracuse was thus under a tyranny for only two periods in its history—from 495 to 467/6 and from 406 to 344. The earlier period is, however, ruled out as the date of "The Tree," since we are told that "the Pallas of Musides surmounted a pillar in Athens, near the Parthenon." Now the Parthenon was begun only in 447, and completed in 432; hence Musides' statue can have been placed there only after these dates—perhaps a good deal later date in the fourth century B.C.E. is suggested by the very fact that the Tyrant of Syracuse suggests the building of a statue of Tyche. As we have seen, the notion of Tyche is central to the philosophical interpretation of the tale. But the worship of Tyche as a goddess in Greece cannot be dated before the late fourth century; the first known cult was established in Thebes some time after 371. Lovecraft would not have committed such an anachronism as postulating a cult in Greek society before such a cult was known to have existed; hence we are reduced to the period 371 to 344 for the dating of events in "The Tree."

---

3. Most of the historical information presented here can be found in any comprehensive history of Greece; see in particular that by J. B. Bury and Russell Meiggs (4th ed. 1975); also various articles in the *Oxford Classical Dictionary,* 2nd ed., ed. N. G. L. Hammond and H. H. Scullard (Oxford: Oxford University Press, 1970).

But a final datum can be added. When Kalos is lying terminally ill, Musides is made to remark that he would build a tomb for Kalos "more lovely than the tomb of Mausolus"; but the tomb of Mausolus (satrap of Caria), or the Mausoleum, was constructed by his widow Artemisia only in 353. We must thus conclude that "The Tree" is set in the period 353–344, perhaps toward the very end of the reign of Dionysius II. It is interesting to note that the philosopher Plato visited Syracuse three times, in 387, 367, and 358; one wonders whether we are to imagine the two great artists and the philosopher (whom, be it noted, Lovecraft despised) hobnobbing either at the court of Dionysius II or in mainland Greece.

It may be asked why Lovecraft does not specifically name Dionysius II in the story. The answer is easily forthcoming: so specific a mention (as opposed to the very allusive nature of the other historical mentions) would mar the allegorical or symbolic nature of the tale. It is not the fact that the tale is set in the middle fourth century B.C.E. in Sicily that is of importance; rather, it is an age-old theme of human baseness and divine revenge which is at the heart of this story. Some time after finishing the tale, Lovecraft remarked pointedly: "It was the result of some rather cynical reflection on the possible real motives which may underlie even the most splendid-appearing acts of mankind. With this nucleus I developed a tale based on the Greek idea of divine justice and retribution (a very pretty though sadly mythical idea!), with the added Oriental notion of the soul of a man passing into something else" (*SL* 1.121).

Although in later years Lovecraft thought little of the story, on at least one occasion he took some pains to defend it. Lovecraft had sent the tale through the Transatlantic Circulator (the Anglo-American group of *littérateurs* who criticised one another's work in manuscript) in early 1921, and replied to some adverse criticisms of it:

> Regarding "The Tree"—Mr. Brown finds the climax insufficient, but I doubt if a tale of that type could possess a more obvious denouement. The climactic effect sought, is merely an emphasis—amounting to the first direct intimation—of the fact that there is something hidden behind the simple events of the tale; that the growing suspicion of Musides' crime and recognition of Kalos' posthumous vengeance is well founded. It is to proclaim what has hitherto been doubtful—to shew that the things of Nature see behind human hypocrisy and perceive the baseness at the heart of outward virtue. All the world deems Musides a model of fraternal piety and devotion although in truth he poisoned Kalos when he saw his laurels in peril. Did not the Tegeans build to Musides a temple? But against all these illusions the trees whisper—the wise trees sacred to the gods—and reveal the truth to the midnight searcher as they chaunt knowingly over

and over again *"Oida! Oida!"* [I know! I know!] This, then, is all the climax so nebulous a legend can possess. (*MW* 156)

This has not been an attempt to resurrect "The Tree" or to claim it as one of Lovecraft's masterpieces; rather, by pointing out the obvious care Lovecraft lavished both on the conception and the historicity of the tale, I hope I have demonstrated that even one of his minor tales can reveal beauties and subtleties not to be grasped by superficial reading. In 1921 Lovecraft made a celebrated utterance: "There are probably seven persons, in all, who really like my work; and they are enough. I should write even if I were the only patient reader, for my aim is merely self-expression" (*MW* 155). Truly, Lovecraft wrote for a discerning few; the few who could approach his own intelligence and sensitivity and appreciate the philosophical, stylistic, thematic, and historical profundities that lie beneath the surface of even his slightest products.

Works Cited

Burleson, Donald R. *H. P. Lovecraft: A Critical Study*. Westport, CT: Greenwood Press, 1983.

Guthrie, W. K. C. *A History of Greek Philosophy*. Volume 2. Cambridge: Cambridge University Press, 1965.

Joshi, S. T. *Lovecraft's Library: A Catalogue*. 2nd rev. ed. New York: Hippocampus Press, 2002.

The Sources for "From Beyond"

I t is unlikely that "From Beyond" (1920) will ever be regarded as one of Lovecraft's better tales; and such a judgment is perfectly justified, since in its slipshod style, melodramatic excess, and general triteness of plot, the tale compares ill even with some of his other early tales, such as "Dagon" (1917), "The Picture in the House" (1920), and "The Outsider" (1921). But, as with everything Lovecraft wrote, the tale's poor quality does not prevent it from displaying certain features of considerable interest. In the first place, the philosophical sources of the tale can now be traced with some certainty; secondly, the story seems itself to have provided sources for several later tales.

The philosophical interest of the tale is noteworthy, for it centres upon an issue of fundamental importance in all modern philosophical speculation since Descartes—the problem of knowledge. How do we know what we know? How can we be certain that the sense-impressions we receive are accurate reflections of external reality? Is there an external reality of which they are the reflections? This problem certainly occupied some of the ancient philosophers. Parmenides and Democritus questioned the truth-value of sense-perception, and Gorgias the sophist wrote a celebrated treatise, *On Not-Being* (c. 440 B.C.E.), wherein he maintained that 1) nothing exists; 2) even if anything existed, it would be incomprehensible; 3) even if it were comprehensible, it would be incommunicable—and his whole argument was based upon the unreliability of sense-perception (see Kerford, ch. 8). Finally, the ancient Sceptics similarly believed that nothing can be known (and some were as rigorously consistent as to doubt whether even this—that nothing can be known—can be known!), and waged extended polemics against their opponents (especially the Stoics and the Epicureans) who tried to assert both the possibility of knowledge and the reliability of sense-data. After Descartes instituted his system of "Cartesian doubt," the problem of knowledge became a focus—some would say a bane—of philosophical enquiry. Lovecraft reflects this problem in "From Beyond" by conceiving of a way to "break down the barriers" (*D* 91) that our five senses impose and which prevent our catching a glimpse of reality "as it really is."

Part of the philosophical foundation of the tale is indeed derived from Descartes, although in a parodic way. Crawford Tillinghast tells the unnamed narrator how it is that we may glimpse "vistas unknown to man": "'You have heard of the pineal gland? . . . That gland is the great sense-organ of organs—*I have found out.* It is like sight in the end, and transmits visual pictures to the brain'" (*D* 93). This is a joke at Descartes' expense: when Descartes, in the *Meditations on First Philosophy,* established the distinction (one of the most pernicious ideas in the history of philosophy, rivalled perhaps only by Plato's Forms or Kant's *a priori* knowledge) between a material body and an immaterial and immortal soul, he found himself in the awkward position of being unable to explain how two such fundamentally different entities could ever interact, as they clearly do in the human being; he then (in *The Passions of the Soul*) seized upon the pineal gland as the mediator between body and soul. Lovecraft was fully aware of this celebrated venture into fatuity (see "Some Causes of Self-Immolation" [*MW* 180]), and he is having a bit of fun with it in "From Beyond."

But a more immediate and pervasive influence for the genesis of the whole tale can be found—in the form of Hugh Elliot's *Modern Science and Materialism* (1919). Lovecraft first mentions this work in a letter of June 1921 (*SL* 1.134; see also *SL* 1.158), but it is almost certain that he had read it before November 1920, the date of writing of "From Beyond" (cf. *SL* 1.121). That he found this triumphant exposition of mechanistic materialism stimulating can be seen by a few entries in his commonplace book which I have hypothesised were inspired by the volume:

> 34 Moving away from earth more swiftly than light—past gradually unfolded—horrible revelation.

> 35 Special beings with special senses from remote universes. Advent of an external universe to view.

> 36 Disintegration of all matter to electrons and finally empty space assured, just as devolution of energy to radiant heat is known. Case of *acceleration*—man passes into space. (*MW* 89)

It can be shown that each of these entries has a correlation in various passages in Elliot's book that discuss the points in question. Entry 35 is particularly interesting for our purposes, since it is precisely such an "external universe" that is brought to view in "From Beyond."

A still more concrete case for Elliot's book as inspiration for "From Beyond" can be made by collation of actual passages from the two works. In Lovecraft's tale Tillinghast boldly dilates upon the fallibility of the senses in a striking passage:

> "What do we know," he had said, "of the world and the universe about us? Our means of receiving impressions are absurdly few, and our notions of surrounding objects infinitely narrow. We see things only as we are constructed to see them, and can gain no idea of their absolute nature. With five feeble senses we pretend to comprehend the boundlessly complex cosmos, yet other beings with a wider, stronger, or different range of

senses might not only see very differently the things we see, but might see and study whole worlds of matter, energy, and life which lie close at hand yet can never be detected with the senses we have." (*D* 91)

Note a very similar passage in the introduction to Elliot's book:

Let us first ask why it is that all past efforts to solve ultimate riddles have failed, and why it is that they must continue to fail. It is, in the first place, due to the fact that all knowledge is based on sense-impressions, and cannot, therefore, go beyond what the senses can perceive. Men have five or six different senses only, and these are all founded on the one original sense of touch. Of these five or six senses, the three of most importance for the accumulation of knowledge are those of sight, hearing, and touch. By these senses we are able to detect three separate qualities of the external Universe. Now, supposing that we happened to have a thousand senses instead of five, it is clear that our conception of the Universe would be extremely different from what it now is. We cannot assume that the Universe has only five qualities because we have only five senses. We must assume, on the contrary, that the number of its qualities may be infinite, and that the more senses we had, the more we should discover about it. (Elliot 2–3)

Later in the tale the narrator is baffled by a "pale, outré colour or blend of colours which I could neither place nor describe"; Tillinghast replies: "'Do you know what that is? . . . *That is ultra-violet.'* He chuckled oddly at my surprise. 'You thought ultra-violet was invisible, and so it is—but you can see that and many other invisible things *now'"* (*D* 93). This has its exact correlate in Elliot:

Not only are our senses few, but they are extremely limited in their range. The sense of sight can detect nothing but waves in aether; all sensations of light and colour are no more than aethereal waves striking upon the retina with varying strength and frequency. And even then, it is only special aethereal undulations that give rise to the sensation of sight. The majority cannot be perceived by the retina at all; it is only when the waves follow one another within certain limits of rapidity (between four hundred billion and seven hundred billion a second) that sight ensues. If the waves are below the lower limit of rapidity, they do not give rise to the sensation of light at all, though they may give rise to a sensation of heat. If they are more rapid than the higher limit (as in the case of ultra-violet rays) they are not discernible by any sense at all. (Elliot 3)

Finally, the narrator at one point experiences great alarm when he sees, as a result of Tillinghast's machine, "huge animate things brushing past me and occasionally *walking or drifting through my supposedly solid body"* (*D* 95). Lovecraft is here merely reflecting in a vivid way the simple physical fact that solid matter is largely empty space. Elliot writes of it at length:

Let us now . . . see what matter would look like if magnified to, say, a thousand million diameters, so that the contents of a small thimble appeared to become the size of the earth. Even under this great magnification, the individual electrons would still be too small to be seen by the naked eye. Small aggregations of these invisible electrons, moving in invisible orbits round a centre, would be aggregated to form atoms, and these again to form molecules, appearing (if they could be seen) to occupy the same volume as a football. The first circumstance that strikes us is that nearly the whole structure of matter consists of the empty spaces between electrons. Matter, which appears to us so continuous in its structure, is really no more than empty space, in which at rare intervals here and there an inconceivably minute electron is travelling at high velocity upon its way. It ceases, therefore, to be remarkable that X-rays can penetrate matter and come out on the other side. How should the tiny electrons obstruct their passage? It ceases to be remarkable that an electron from radium can be shot clean through a plate of aluminium; for, from the electron's point of view, the aluminium plate is very little different from empty space. (Elliot 54)

Clearly, then, the immediate inspiration for "From Beyond" was Elliot's *Modern Science and Materialism* and the philosophical vistas it opened to Lovecraft's fertile and imaginative mind. But "From Beyond," however imperfect a product in itself, very clearly served as a springboard for certain of his later stories. It is as if Lovecraft, dissatisfied with the treatment of some themes in this early story, decided to give them fuller and better treatment elsewhere.

Firstly, the narrator of "From Beyond" remarks at the outset: "That Crawford Tillinghast should ever have studied science and philosophy was a mistake" (*D* 91). We are immediately reminded of "The Dreams in the Witch House," where it is said: "Perhaps Gilman ought not to have studied so hard. Non-Euclidean calculus and quantum physics are enough to stretch any brain" (*MM* 263). A later passage in "From Beyond" is also suggestive of Gilman's voyages into hyperspace: "I was now in a vortex of sound and motion, with confused pictures before my eyes. . . . After that the scene was almost wholly kaleidoscopic, and in the jumble of sights, sounds, and unidentified sense-impressions I felt that I was about to dissolve or in some way lose the solid form" (*D* 94–95).

We have already alluded to the "pale, outré colour or blend of colours" which the narrator of "From Beyond" sees—and we can hardly fail to recall "The Colour out of Space": "The colour . . . was almost impossible to describe; and it was only by analogy that they called it colour at all" (*DH* 59).

Finally, the central philosophical theme of "From Beyond"—the fallibility of the senses—is emphasised in several later stories. I have studied this concept elsewhere (see "'Reality' and Knowledge"), and the idea of what I have termed "supra-reality"—a reality beyond that revealed to us by the senses, or that which we experience in every-day life (what Onderdonk called the "super-normal")—is central to much of Lovecraft's fiction; finding expression particularly in "Hypnos" (1922), "The Unnamable" (1923), "The Colour out of Space" (1927), "The Dreams in the Witch House" (1932), "Through the Gates of the Silver Key" (1932–33), and others. Note also the following passage from "The Shunned House" (1924):

> To declare that we were not nervous on that rainy night of watching would be an exaggeration both gross and ridiculous. We were not, as I have said, in any sense childishly superstitious, but scientific study and reflection had taught us that the known universe of three dimensions embraces the merest fraction of the whole cosmos of substance and energy. . . . To say that we actually believed in vampires or werewolves would be a carelessly inclusive statement. Rather must it be said that we were not prepared to deny the possibility of certain unfamiliar and unclassified modifications of vital force and attenuated matter; existing very infrequently in three-dimensional space because of its more intimate connexion with other spatial units, yet close enough to the boundary of our own to furnish us occasional manifestations which we, for lack of a proper vantage-point, may never hope to understand. (*MM* 251–52)

The closeness of wording between this passage and parts of "From Beyond" suggests that the idea was one of recurrent fascination to Lovecraft—and it is an idea derived from his continuing researches into the findings of modern science and philosophy, especially such books as Elliot's *Modern Science and Materialism,* Ernst Haeckel's *The Riddle of the Universe,* and Bertrand Russell's *Our Knowledge of the External World.*

Hence "From Beyond" has in its clumsy way shown once again the unity and integration of Lovecraft's work and thought. Science and philosophy, far from being antagonistic to the creation of literature, were for Lovecraft direct stimuli for it; and his untiring delvings into the strange worlds revealed by astrophysicists, biologists, and philosophers proved to be a central—perhaps even a necessary—inspiration for some of the greatest weird tales of the twentieth century.

Works Cited

Elliott, Hugh. *Modern Science and Materialism.* London: Longmans, Green & Co., 1919.

Kerferd, G. B. *The Sophistic Movement.* Cambridge: Cambridge University Press, 1981.

Lovecraft and the Regnum Congo

> The first object of my curiosity was a book of medium size lying upon the table and presenting such an antediluvian aspect that I marvelled at beholding it outside a museum or library. It was bound in leather with metal fittings, and was in an excellent state of preservation; being altogether an unusual sort of volume to encounter in an abode so lowly. When I opened it to the title page my wonder grew even greater, for it proved to be nothing less rare than Pigafetta's account of the Congo region, written in Latin from the notes of the sailor Lopez and printed at Frankfort in 1598. I had often heard of this work, with its curious illustrations by the brothers De Bry, hence for a moment forgot my uneasiness in my desire to turn the pages before me. *(DH* 119)

This celebrated passage from "The Picture in the House" (1920) has perhaps led many to marvel at Lovecraft's recondite knowledge of Renaissance science and literature. Further descriptions of Pigafetta's *Regnum Congo* later in the story would lead us to believe that Lovecraft had not only consulted the rare volume, but had actually read it in detail. Where, then, could he have gained access to the tome? A copy exists in the John Carter Brown Library of Brown University, and Lovecraft might have seen it here; but what could have led him even to suspect the existence of this volume? The answer is now not difficult to find; and it reveals, unfortunately, that Lovecraft did not in fact consult the actual volume and that, in relying on second-hand accounts of the book, he made embarrassing mistakes concerning it.

The source for Lovecraft's knowledge of Pigafetta is nothing less than Thomas Henry Huxley's collection of essays, *Man's Place in Nature and Other Anthropological Essays* (New York: D. Appleton & Co., 1894). Lovecraft certainly knew of and read this volume, since he cites from Huxley's essay "On the Methods and Results of Ethnology" in the early essay "The Crime of the Century" (1915). In that essay Lovecraft makes use of Huxley's coined term "Xanthochroi" in reference to the yellow-haired and pale-complexioned people whom Lovecraft identified with the Aryan race. But an earlier essay in Huxley's volume—"On the Natural History of the Man-like Apes" (pp. 1–75)—provided Lovecraft all his information on the *Regnum Congo,* and he has repeated some errors and omissions that Huxley made in his own essay. The essay deals with the history of scholarship on the simian species in the 200 years before Huxley's time, and in the very opening Huxley discusses the *Regnum Congo* in some detail: "I have not met with any notice of one of these *Man-like Apes* of earlier date than that contained in Pigafetta's 'Description of the kingdom of Congo,' drawn up from the notes of a Portuguese sailor, Eduardo Lopez, and published in 1598" (pp. 1–2). In a footnote Huxley gives the Latin title:

REGNUM CONGO: hoc est VERA DESCRIPTIO REGNI AFRICANI QUOD TAM AB INCOLIS QUAM LUSITANIS CONGUS APPELLATUR, per Philippum Pigafettam, olim ex Eduardo Lopez acroamatis lingua Italica excerpta, num Latio sermone donata ab August. Cassiod. Reinio. Iconibus et imaginibus rerum memorabilium quasi vivis, opera et industria Joan. Theodori et Joan. Israelis de Bry, fratrum exornata. Francofurti, MDXCVIII. (p. 2 note)

(A translation of the above is as follows: REGNUM CONGO, i.e., a true description of the African kingdom which is called "Congo" both by its inhabitants and by Spaniards, previously rendered into Italian by Filippo Pigafetta from the verbal accounts of Eduardo Lopez, now translated into Latin by A. C. Reinius. Decorated with maps and virtually live illustrations of memorable phenomena by the toil and diligence of the brothers J. T. and J. I. De Bry. Frankfurt, 1598.)

Unfortunately, neither Huxley nor Lovecraft seemed to know that this is not the first printing of Pigafetta's account. Rather, it was first published in Italian (hence the *lingua Italica* above) in 1591. The title of this edition is as follows: *Relatione de reame di Congo et della cironvicine contrade, tratta dalli scritti & ragionamenti di Odoardo [sic] Lopez, Portoghese, per Filippo Pigafetta* (Roma: Appresso B. Grassi, 1591). What is more, there was a Dutch translation of this in 1596 (Amsterdam: Cornelis Claesz), an English translation in 1597 (London: John Wolfe), and a German translation in 1597 (Frankfurt am Mayn: Johan Saur). It was in this German edition that the De Bry plates first appeared, whence they were transferred to the Latin edition of the following year.[1] And the Latin translation is not the work of Pigafetta, as Lovecraft seems to have believed, but is by A. C. Reinius (*Latio sermone do-*

---

1. William Scott Home is therefore incorrect when he remarks ("The Lovecraft 'Books': Some Addenda and Corrigenda," *The Dark Brotherhood and Other Pieces* [Arkham House, 1966], p. 143) that "it was very likely the 1598 Frankfurt edition in which the De Bry illustrations first appeared." Indeed, Home ought to have known that this was not the case, since he reprints a plate (facing p. 134) that obviously derives from the German, and not Latin, edition, since all the accompanying text on the page is in German black-letter! It ought to be remarked that Home's essay is riddled with errors of detail and had best be used, if at all, with caution.

nata ab . . .). In addition, the real name of the "sailor Lopez" seems to have been Duarte Lopes.[2]

But what of Lovecraft's detailed descriptions of the plates by the brothers De Bry which he provides in the story? It happens that Huxley actually reprints (or, rather, has had redrawn) two plates from the *Regnum Congo,* including the important plate XII representing the butcher shop of the cannibal Anziques. Before discussing that plate, let us consider the other details in Lovecraft's account. His indication that the book "was bound in leather with metal fittings" is apparently derived from his imagination; and in any case such clasps need not have been affixed at the time of publication. (It may be worth noting that, although Lovecraft seems to imply that the book is rather large, it is in fact quite small; the Latin version is only 60 pages,[3] while a modern English translation[4] is 137 pages, and a modern French translation[5] is 147 pages.) Later in the story Lovecraft records some remarks by the preternaturally aged owner of the volume:

> "Queer haow picters kin set a body thinkin'. Take this un here near the front. Hev yew ever seed trees like thet, with big leaves a floppin' over an' daown? And them men—them can't be niggers—they dew beat all. Kinder like Injuns, I guess, even ef they be in Afriky. Some o' these here critters looks like monkeys, or half monkeys an' half men. (*DH* 122)

This is an exact description of a plate reproduced or redrawn in Huxley's volume. Huxley describes the plate as follows: "So much of the plate as contains these apes is faithfully copied in the woodcut (Fig. 1), and it will be observed that they are tail-less, long-armed, and large-eared; and about the size of Chimpanzees" (p. 3).

Lovecraft's character then continues: "'. . . but I never heerd o' nothin' like this un.' Here he pointed to a fabulous creature of the artist, which one might describe as a sort of dragon with the head of an alligator" (*DH* 122). This too derives directly from Huxley, who writes: "It may be that these apes are as much figments of the imagination of the ingenious brothers [i.e., De Bry] as the winged, two-legged, crocodile-headed dragon which

---

2. See the modern French translation of the *Regnum Congo* (*Description du Royaume de Congo et des Contrees Environnantes*) by Willy Bal (Louvain/Paris, 1965), whose introduction (esp. pp. xxif.) gives much information on early editions.

3. Cf. *Catalogue of Books Printed on the Continent of Europe 1501–1600 in Cambridge Libraries,* comp. H. M. Adams (Cambridge: Cambridge University Press, 1967), 2.79. I have not actually consulted the Latin edition.

4. *A Report of the Kingdom of Congo, and of the Surrounding Countries,* tr. Margarite Hutchinson (1881; rpt. New York: Negro Universities Press/Greenwood Press, 1969).

5. See note 2.

adorns the same plate" (p. 3). This dragon figure is not reproduced in Huxley's plate, and Lovecraft had to work merely from Huxley's verbal description.

Let us now return to Lovecraft's description of the twelfth De Bry plate:

> The engravings were indeed interesting, drawn wholly from imagination and careless descriptions, and represented negroes with white skins and Caucasian features; nor would I soon have closed the book had not an exceedingly trivial circumstance upset my tired nerves and revived my sensation of disquiet. What annoyed me was merely the persistent way in which the volume tended to fall open of itself at Plate XII, which represented in gruesome detail a butcher's shop of the cannibal Anziques. I experienced some shame at my susceptibility to so slight a thing, but the drawing nevertheless disturbed me, especially in connexion with some adjacent passages descriptive of Anzique gastronomy. (*DH* 119)

This entire description is drawn from an appendix to Huxley's essay (pp. 73–75), "African Cannibalism in the Sixteenth Century," where he recounts what Pigafetta says in chapter 5 of Book I of the *Regnum Congo*. It is here that the brothers De Bry's plate XII is reprinted—or, rather, redrawn as a woodcut by W. H. Wesley, who was presumably responsible for the redrawing of the earlier plate. Of the plate Huxley remarks: "The careful illustrators of Pigafetta have done their best to enable the reader to realize this account of the 'Anziques,' and the unexampled butcher's shop represented in Fig. 12 [i.e., of Huxley's book], is a facsimile of part of their Plate XII" (p. 75).

Lovecraft's aged character now describes the plate: "'That fellow bein' chopped up gives me a tickle every time I look at 'im—I hev ta keep lookin' at him—see whar the butcher cut off his feet? Thar's his head on thet bench, with one arm side of it, an' t' other arm's on the graound side o' the meat block'" (*DH* 122). All this again tallies with the illustration in Huxley's book. But comparison of this illustration with the actual De Bry plate from the German or Latin edition of the *Regnum Congo* (reprinted by W. S. Home in *The Dark Brotherhood*) brings to light some interesting facts. Wesley has chosen only to redraw the butcher shop at the far right of the original De Bry plate, and it seems to be he—and not the brothers De Bry—who has endowed the negroes "with white skins and Caucasian features"; the figures on the left side of the De Bry plate—left out by Wesley—are actually much more negroid in appearance.

The second-hand nature of Lovecraft's erudition in this case would be rather less culpable had he not himself accused Poe of doing similar things. In remarking on Poe's borrowing of the term "Afrasiab" in "The Premature Burial" Lovecraft notes: "[Poe] was a great boy for second-hand erudition" (*SL* 4.162); while in *Supernatural Horror in Literature* he notes that among Poe's "defects and affectations" was his "pretence to profound and obscure scholarship" (*D* 396). I am not about to assert that most of Lovecraft's knowledge was second-hand—indeed, he had a far greater and more authentic grasp of classical literature and philosophy, modern science, and many other subjects than Poe, and he integrated this knowledge into a philosophy far more profound and coherent than Poe could ever have managed—but his second-hand borrowings and attempts to assert knowledge in subjects on which he was ignorant landed him on occasion in trouble; as witness his bumbling derivation of the Greek word *Necronomicon* (although later scholars such as George Wetzel, William Scott Home, E. F. Bleiler, and others, all blithely ignorant of Greek, have been no less incompetent at the task), or the embarrassing errors of detail he made when he tried to explain the Greek-Hebrew incantation he had cribbed from the *Encyclopaedia Britannica* for "The Horror at Red Hook." Other second-hand borrowings have come to light which, while not erroneous, perhaps ought to make us cautious of attributing all-encompassing knowledge to Lovecraft: the books on cryptography, for example, cited so impressively in "The Dunwich Horror" are all derived from the article on "Cryptography" (by John Eglinton Bailey) in the 9th edition of the *Britannica*.

But these borrowings are always minor and rarely affect the success of the story in which they appear; and Lovecraft's letters testify abundantly to the real knowledge he had acquired over a lifetime's scholarship in a large number of diverse fields. We all take short-cuts when it is convenient to do so, and there is no reason to believe that Lovecraft was exempt from the habit.

Lovecraft and Dunsany's
Chronicles of Rodriguez

The influence of Lord Dunsany upon the early work of H. P. Lovecraft is no secret; but only recently have efforts been made to trace this influence beyond the so-called "Dunsanian" fantasies of 1919–21. Robert M. Price has probed some Dunsanian resonances in such works as "The Music of Erich Zann" and "The Call of Cthulhu," but few other such attempts have been made. Part of the problem is that Lovecraft confessed that he did not care much for Dunsany's later work—i.e., work subsequent to his first collections of short stories, from *The Gods of Pegāna* (1905) to *Tales of Three Hemispheres* (1919)—so that it has not occurred to readers and critics to trace influences from this body of work upon Lovecraft's fiction of the 1920s and 1930s. Lovecraft confessed that *A Dreamer's Tales* (1910) affected him "as with an electric shock" (*SL* 2.328), but of even so fine a novel as *The Curse of the Wise Woman* (1933), he merely remarks tepidly that it has a "different sort of charm" (*SL* 5.353).

It may therefore come as a surprise that Dunsany's first novel, *The Chronicles of Rodriguez* (1922; published in the U.S. as *Don Rodriguez: Chronicles of Shadow Valley*) may contain, in a single chapter, the nucleus of two of Lovecraft's stories, "He" (1925) and "The Strange High House in the Mist" (1926).

Our first order of business in establishing such an influence is determining when Lovecraft actually read *The Chronicles of Rodriguez*. After his discovery of Dunsany in 1919, Lovecraft appears to have kept abreast of Dunsany's publications, reading them shortly after publication. The American edition of *Rodriguez* came out in October 1922, and in a letter of January 1923 Lovecraft remarks: "I hope that 'Don Rodriguez' represents a return to the earlier mood" (*SL* 1.203). An unpublished letter to Samuel Loveman states clearly: "I read . . . 'Don Rodriguez' last month, & advise you to do the same." This letter, from internal evidence, must date to 1923.[1] Lovecraft, therefore, clearly read the novel well before writing either "He" or "The Strange High House in the Mist."

---

1. The letter is dated only "29 April," but it is addressed from "Old 598"; and since Lovecraft moved out of 598 Angell Street and moved to Brooklyn in March 1924, the letter must date to 1923. I am grateful to Mara Kirk Hart for providing the text of this letter. It has now been published in *Letters to Samuel Loveman and Vincent Starrett*, ed. S. T. Joshi and David E. Schultz (West Warwick, RI: Necronomicon

The Chronicles of Rodriguez is, as Lovecraft notes, a picaresque novel about Don Rodriguez, the eldest son of a nobleman who is sent by his dying father to seek his fortune in the world. Rodriguez longs to distinguish himself in battle and win a castle for himself, and to this end he traverses the byways of Spain looking for "the wars"; along the way he picks up, as a Sancho Panza-like sidekick, a lowly but eager peasant named Morano.

The third chapter of the novel, "How He Came to the House of Wonder," relates how Rodriguez and Morano approach the house of a Professor of Magic, high up on a nearly inaccessible crag of a lofty mountain. Their climb is arduous:

> Nothing invited them there in the look of that house, but they were now in such a forbidding waste that shelter had to be found; they were all among edges of rock as black as the night and hard as the material of which Cosmos was formed, at first upon Chaos' brink. . . . Then they pushed on over rocks that seemed never trodden by man, so sharp were they and slanting, all piled together: it seemed the last waste, to which all shapeless rocks had been thrown. (R 66–67)

Finally they reach the house:

> In the wall that their hands had reached there was no door, so they felt along it till they came to the corner, and beyond the corner was the front wall of the house. In it was the front door. But so nearly did this door open upon the abyss that the bats that fled from their coming, from where they hunt above the door of oak, had little more to do than fall from their crannies, slanting ever so slightly, to find themselves safe from man in the velvet darkness, that lay between cliffs so lonely they were almost strangers to Echo. (R 67)

Few readers of Lovecraft can have failed to notice the resemblance to Thomas Olney's climb up the cliff in Kingsport to see the mysterious occupant of the lofty house described in "The Strange High House in the Mist." Speaking of Olney's attempt to "find a path to the inaccessible pinnacle" (D 280), Lovecraft goes on to remark:

> As he climbed slowly east, higher and higher above the estuary on his left and nearer and nearer the sea, he found the way growing in difficulty; till he wondered how ever the dwellers in that disliked place managed to reach the world outside, and whether they came often to market in Arkham. (D 280)

Press, 1994), p. 17.

Olney finally reaches the dwelling and finds that it—like the professor's house in *Rodriguez*—has a door that is flush with the abyss over which it is perched:

> When he climbed out of the chasm a morning mist was gathering, but he clearly saw the lofty and unhallowed cottage ahead; walls as grey as the rock, and high peak standing bold against the milky white of the sea-ward vapours. And he perceived that there was no door on this landward end, but only a couple of small lattice windows with dingy bull's-eye panes leaded in seventeenth-century fashion. All around him was cloud and chaos, and he could see nothing below but the whiteness of illimitable space. He was alone in the sky with this queer and very disturbing house; and when he sidled around to the front and saw that the wall stood flush with the cliff's edge, so that the single narrow door was not to be reached save from the empty aether, he felt a distinct terror that altitude could not wholly explain. (*D* 280–81)

While the occupant of the house, who imparts a strange lore to Olney, bears some resemblance to the Professor of Magic in Dunsany's novel, an even closer resemblance can be found, oddly, in the story "He." This tale of the squalor of present-day New York would seem the furthest imaginable from Dunsany's novel of picaresque adventure, in spite of the mention of Carcassonne early in the story (*D* 266), a possible allusion to a magnificently poetic story of that name in *A Dreamer's Tales*. And yet, the actual actions of the Professor bear comparison with the visions shown to the unnamed narrator by the anomalously aged central figure in "He." Rodriguez is asked by the Professor where his interests lie; the former promptly replies, "In war." The Professor then makes a startling claim:

> He had a window, he explained, through which Rodriguez should see clearly the ancient wars, while another window beside it looked on all wars of the future except those which were planned already or were coming soon to earth, and which were either invisible or seen dim as through mist. (R 72–73)

The sight of the ancient wars through the first magic window thrills Rodriguez and Morano; the latter, in his pious simplicity, even cheers on the Christians as they battle the infidel during the Crusades. But the other window reveals something very different:

> But in the other window through that deep, beautiful blue Rodriguez saw Man make a new ally, an ally who was only cruel and strong and had no purpose but killing, who had no pretences or pose, no mask and no manner, but was only the slave of Death and had no care but for his business. He saw it grow bigger and stronger. Heart it had none, but he saw its cold

steel core scheming methodical plans and dreaming always destruction. Before it faded men and their fields and their houses. Rodriguez saw the machine. (R 81–82)

In some of the most gripping pages in all Dunsany, Rodriguez sees the horrors of World War I, which Dunsany had witnessed at first hand in the battlefields of Flanders and of which he had written poignantly in *Tales of War* (1918) and *Unhappy Far-Off Things* (1919): "Rodriguez lifted his eyes and glanced from city to city, to Albert, Bapaume, and Arras, his gaze moved over a plain with its harvest of desolation lying forlorn and ungathered, lit by the flashing clouds and the moon and peering rockets. He turned from the window and wept" (R 83).

Who cannot recall the visions of past and future New York as revealed by the aged squire in "He"? Of course, the visions are not of war, but there is an exactly analogous contrast between the past, with its closeness to Nature ("It was Greenwich, the Greenwich that used to be, with here and there a roof or row of houses as we see it now, yet with lovely green lanes and fields and bits of grassy common" [D 273]) and the cataclysmically mechanised future:

> I saw the heavens verminous with strange flying things, and beneath them a hellish black city of giant stone terraces with impious pyramids flung savagely to the moon, and devil-lights burning from unnumbered windows. And swarming loathsomely on aërial galleries I saw the yellow, squint-eyed people of that city, robed horribly in orange and red, and dancing insanely to the pounding of fevered kettle-drums, the clatter of obscene crotala, and the maniacal moaning of muted horns whose ceaseless dirges rose and fell undulantly like the waves of an unhallowed ocean of bitumen. (D 273–74)

It is, of course, unlikely that Lovecraft derived this contrast directly from Dunsany: both writers were keenly concerned about the advent of the machine age and the resultant loss of our intimate connexion with the natural rhythms of the earth. This, indeed, is really the overriding theme in all Dunsany's work, even that early otherworldly fantasy which Lovecraft mistakenly believed to have been the product of pure imagination. Nevertheless, I think that Lovecraft's idea in "He" of contrasting the past and future through apocalyptic visions might well have been derived from this arresting tableau in Dunsany's *The Chronicles of Rodriguez*.

It is not to be assumed that this one chapter in Dunsany's novel was the sole inspiration for these two very different tales by Lovecraft; indeed, attempts have been made to find a real counterpart for the clifftop house in Marblehead (the basis for Kingsport) or the surrounding area. But it is still possible that Lovecraft's reading of *The Chronicles of Rodriguez* suggested to him a means of utilising these conceptions effectively. It is not surprising that he did not develop the ideas in "He" and "The Strange High House in the Mist" until several years after his reading of Dunsany's work: he continually remarked on his difficulty in writing fiction during his stay in New York (1924–26), and "He" was one of only five stories he wrote in this period. "The Strange High House in the Mist," of course, was one of the several stories and novels—from "The Call of Cthulhu" to "The Colour out of Space," and including *The Dream-Quest of Unknown Kadath* and *The Case of Charles Dexter Ward*—that Lovecraft wrote in the first year after his return to Providence in April 1926. "The Strange High House in the Mist" is, indeed, virtually his swan-song to the Dunsanian manner, and it would be fitting if the root conception of that story were derived from the work of the writer who had given Lovecraft's fiction such a tremendous impetus in 1919.

Works Cited

Dunsany, Lord. *Don Rodriguez: Chronicles of Shadow Valley.* New York: G. P. Putnam's Sons, 1922. [Abbreviated in the text as R.]

Price, Robert M. "Dunsanian Influence on Lovecraft Outside His 'Dunsanian' Tales." *Crypt of Cthulhu* No. 76 (Hallowmass 1990): 3–5.

On "The Descendant"

We know less about "The Descendant" than about any other single story or fragment by Lovecraft. The title was supplied by R. H. Barlow; the date of 1926 was supplied by August Derleth and is, apparently, entirely conjectural. Lovecraft never mentions the fragment in any correspondence I have seen. Whereas we can guess that "Azathoth" may be an early adumbration of *The Dream-Quest of Unknown Kadath,* and "The Book" in part a rewriting of *Fungi from Yuggoth,* we have no idea what "The Descendant" is about or where it is going. It is Lovecraft's most unsatisfying yet most tantalising piece.

It is unclear how Derleth arrived at the date of the work. My own belief is that it was written in early 1927. In April of that year Lovecraft reports "making a very careful study of *London* . . . in order to get background for tales involving richer antiquities than America can furnish";[1] and "The Descendant" is the only tale of this period set in London.

The very text of the fragment is confused. Editions previous to mine (*D* 358–62) printed an introductory paragraph or fragment: "Writing on what the doctor tells me is my deathbed, my most hideous fear is that the man is wrong. I suppose I shall seem to be buried next week, but . . ." When this was printed in *Marginalia,* Derleth added the note: *"(foregoing deleted)."* It was indeed crossed out on the ms., but Derleth did not explain that when Lovecraft began "The Descendant" proper ("In London there is a man who screams . . .") he turned the paper around, so that the "deleted" passage is now at the bottom of the first page of the ms., upside down. This—along with the apparently unrelated nature of the passage—leads me to believe that it does not belong with "The Descendant" at all; I have accordingly removed it from my text. The deleted passage is in the first person, while the fragment proper is in the third; and the "I" does not seem to represent either character of the fragment, Lord Northam or "young Williams." My inclination is to regard the deleted passage as yet another, separate fragment.

This still does not allow us to make much sense of "The Descendant" as it stands. Let us see what internal evidence provides in terms of dating and content. The mention of a "Nameless City" in the "desert of Araby" at the very end of the fragment clearly points to Lovecraft's own tale of 1921. The mentions of Charles Fort and Ignatius Donnelly seem promising, but

---

1. Lovecraft to August Derleth, [15 April 1927] (ms., State Historical Society of Wisconsin).

not much can be made of them: we do not know when Lovecraft read Donnelly's *Atlantis: The Antediluvian World* (1882); as to Charles Fort, we learn that around September 1927 Lovecraft read *New Lands,* but "didn't find it as interesting as *The Book of the Damned"* (*SL* 2.174), which he must have read earlier.

More may be gleaned from the character of Lord Northam, the harried old man who has only one goal in life: "All he seeks from life is not to think." Some external features of his characterisation bring Arthur Machen and Lord Dunsany to mind, although in a superficial way. Northam lives at Gray's Inn, London; Machen lived for many years at 4 Verulam Buildings, Gray's Inn (this is what gives us the *terminus post quem* of 1923, since Lovecraft only encountered the work of Machen at this date). Northam is the "nineteenth Baron of a line whose beginnings went uncomfortably far back into the past"; Dunsany was the eighteenth Baron Dunsany in a line founded in the twelfth century.

Much of the fragment spins a peculiar tale about strange happenings in Roman Britain. Here the most interesting point is how many things Lovecraft gets wrong in his historical account. The biggest blunder is his mention of "the Third Augustan Legion then stationed at Lindum." Regrettably, Legio III Augusta was never stationed in England (it was almost always in Libya); rather, it was Legio II Augusta that was in England; and it was not, as far as I know, ever stationed in Lindum (Lincoln), but always in Isca Silurum (Caerleon-on-Usk), something Lovecraft should have known from reading Machen's *Hill of Dreams.* Lovecraft made the same mistake in "The Rats in the Walls" (1923), where he says that the legion camped at "Anchester." Here he has made three mistakes: 1) neither the second nor the third Augustan legion was ever stationed in Anchester because 2) the town never had a legionary fort, and 3) the town's name is Ancaster, not Anchester! (For the record, two other legions, IX Hispana and XX Valeria, were customarily stationed in England, at York and Chester, respectively. Other legions were transferred there as needed during revolts or to build Hadrian's Wall. Interestingly enough, IX Hispana seems to have vanished around 130 C.E., and to this day no satisfactory explanation of its disappearance has been made. Now there's a story idea for Lovecraft!) By 1933, however, when he read Arthur Weigall's *Wanderings in Roman Britain,* Lovecraft finally got the legions in Roman Britain straight (cf. *SL* 4.293).

Well, I think I have squeezed "The Descendant" dry; there does not seem anything more to be got out of it. If it was in fact written in 1926, it may have been written early in the year, when Lovecraft was still in New York: he frequently confessed to his inability to write fiction toward the end of his "New York exile." The Roman aspect is interesting in providing a link between "The Rats in the Walls" and Lovecraft's great "Roman dream" of 1927; and the scene where young Williams buys the *Necronomicon* from a "gnarled old Levite" is uncannily similar to the scene in "The Book" (1933?) where the nameless narrator buys a nameless tome from an "old man [who] leered and tittered." We would like very much to know what Lovecraft was trying to do with "The Descendant"; it embodies central themes in his work—dubious heredity, ancient horror, a Faustian quest for forbidden knowledge—but never resolves them. It is one of Lovecraft's few false starts; and yet, we can learn something even from its unsatisfying paragraphs.

Some Sources for *"The Mound" and* At the Mountains of Madness

"The Mound" was begun in December 1929 and completed in January 1930. It appears to have been written—or, rather, ghostwritten, as it was based upon the flimsiest of plot-germs supplied by Lovecraft's revision client Zealia Brown Reed—at one of several low points in Lovecraft's fiction-writing career: he had written no original work of fiction since "The Dunwich Horror" (completed in August 1928), and he would not write another original tale until he began "The Whisperer in Darkness" in February 1930. So "The Mound" appears to have provided some practice for renewed fictional composition, especially on the extended scale of a novelette or short novel. It is therefore not surprising that, in order to augment the flow of creativity, Lovecraft looked to other works of fiction for inspiration. He himself makes no secret that Clark Ashton Smith's "The Tale of Satampra Zeiros"—which he read in manuscript only in early December 1929 (*SL* 3.88)—was a key influence, as he immediately incorporated Smith's invented deity Tsathoggua into his tale; but another work of earlier vintage, found in his own library, may also have supplied suggestive hints.

A Strange Manuscript Found in a Copper Cylinder (1888) is a "lost race" novel by a Canadian popular novelist, James De Mille (1833–1880). Although apparently written in the 1860s, it was published only posthumously. Lovecraft, although owning the book, makes no mention of it in any letters I have seen; but I have little doubt that he read it prior to writing "The Mound." In this novel, the crewmen of a yacht sailing near the Canary Islands in the year 1850 come upon a copper cylinder floating in the ocean. This cylinder, when opened, contains a lengthy manuscript written on papyrus, telling the story of one Adam More, who in the year 1843 was shipwrecked in the South Pacific and managed to reach a land mass that he believes is Antarctica, although it is a land of lush and almost tropical vegetation. There he encounters a bizarre and previously unknown society of human beings, the Kosekin, whose moral and social customs are in many ways antipodal to those of the rest of the species: they hate life and are in love with death; they scorn wealth and yearn for poverty; they believe that unrequited love is the highest and most beautiful human emotion. The ending of the novel is somewhat unsatisfying; there is evidence that De Mille was uncertain how to conclude his novel, and that he worked on the ending for years, right up to the end of his life—a circumstance that probably accounts for its failure to be published in his lifetime.[1] More, who has fallen in love with a seemingly normal woman named Almah, who has been brought over from another island, becomes the Kosekin's god when he rebels at being a sacrificial victim and instead kills his captors.

The very title of *A Strange Manuscript Found in a Copper Cylinder* would appear to suggest an obvious influence on "The Mound," for of course that novelette concerns a modern-day archaeologist who, in investigating a mound in Oklahoma that appears to be haunted, finds in it a "heavy object of cylindrical shape—about a foot long and four inches in diameter" (*HM* 112), which contains the incredible narrative of Pánfilo de Zamacona in the underground civilisation of K'n-yan. More's cylinder is "about eighteen inches long and eight wide" (*S* 5). Lovecraft, of course, did not wish to have his cylinder composed of something so common as copper, so he asserts that it was "made of [some] heavy, lustrous unknown metal" (*HM* 112)—a metal found, presumably, only in the underground realm of K'n-yan. But like More's manuscript, Zamacona's account tells of a fantastic and previously unknown humanlike civilisation—Lovecraft adding somewhat implausibly that the people of K'n-yan had "come from a distant part of space where physical conditions are much like those of the earth" (*HM* 131). More struggles to learn the language of the Kosekin (which one of the crewmen on the yacht believes is related to Semitic), just as Zamacona takes months or years to master the utterly outré language of K'n-yan.

Where Lovecraft and De Mille part company is in the depiction of their respective "lost race" civilisations. De Mille's novel is evidently intended as an anti-utopia, but his satire is crude and unfocused: he never makes plausible the moral characteristics of the Kosekin, and it is not clear what message he is seeking to convey in his portrayal of this death-loving race. Lovecraft, by contrast, etches with considerable care and attention both the rise and fall of the mound civilisation, morally and intellectually, and manifestly wishes to suggest that their fate may well be our own if we do not renounce the corrupting influence of mechanisation. Whether De Mille's novel actually inspired Lovecraft in this depiction of an alien civilisation is not at all certain; but he appears to have used *A Strange Manuscript* as a suggestive framework for his own ruminations on the decline of the West.

Some features of *A Strange Manuscript Found in a Copper Cylinder* may also have found their way into another of Lovecraft's major works, *At the Mountains of Madness* (1931). The crewmen who had discovered More's

---

1 See Malcolm G. Parks's critical edition of *A Strange Manuscript Found in a Copper Cylinder* (Ottawa: Carleton University Press, 1986) for an exhaustive account of the writing of the novel. This edition will be cited in the text, under the abbreviation *S*.

manuscript conduct frequent debates as to its authenticity, one member asserting that it is a pure hoax; but another remarks, in reference to More's belief that he had reached Antarctica: "'The observations of Ross and of More show us that there is a chain of mountains of immense height, which seem to encircle the pole'" (*S* 70). This sentence would surely have piqued Lovecraft's curiosity, although possibly he already knew of that immense chain of mountains from the reports of James Clark Ross himself (recall Lovecraft's juvenile treatise, *The Voyages of Capt. Ross, R.N.* [*SL* 4.67]). A little later this same character states:

> ". . . the idea that I have gathered from his [More's] manuscript is that of a vast sea like the Mediterranean, surrounded by impassable mountains; by great and fertile countries, peopled with an immense variety of animals, with a fauna and flora quite unlike those of the rest of the world; and, above all, with great nations possessing a rare and unique civilization, and belonging to a race altogether different from any of the known races of men." (*S* 70–71)

Possibly that final sentence triggered something in Lovecraft's mind: his civilisation, however, would not be merely humanoid in appearance, but entirely and frighteningly alien—the barrel-shaped Old Ones, who themselves give way to the even more outré creature known as the shoggoth.

And yet, another work found in Lovecraft's library—W. Clark Russell's *The Frozen Pirate* (1887)—appears to have been an even more central influence on *At the Mountains of Madness*. Lovecraft's short novel, of course, is the final and triumphant product of a lifetime's interest in the Antarctic; and yet, that interest may well have been initially triggered not by his admitted fascination with the history of Antarctic exploration, but by Russell's novel itself. Here we have no need to speculate as to whether Lovecraft read the work, for he writes of it: "I read it in extreme youth—when 8 or 9—& was utterly fascinated by it . . . writing several yarns of my own under its influence."[2] Note that this reading—which, if Lovecraft's word is to be trusted, occurred in 1898 or 1899—apparently predates his interest in Antarctic exploration, which cannot be dated any earlier than 1900.[3]

W. Clark Russell (1844–1911) was, like the later William Hope Hodgson, an Englishman who used his own experiences as a sailor to become a hugely popular author of sea stories. Of the dozens of novels he wrote,

---

2. HPL to Richard F. Searight, 13 October 1934; in *Letters to Richard F. Searight*, ed. S. T. Joshi and David E. Schultz (West Warwick, RI: Necronomicon Press, 1992), p. 34.
3. See S. T. Joshi, *H. P. Lovecraft: A Life* (West Warwick, RI: Necronomicon Press, 1996), pp. 47–48.

only two—*The Frozen Pirate* and *The Death Ship* (1888), sometimes titled *The Flying Dutchman* in pirated American editions—are suggestive of the supernatural; and it is no accident that it is exactly these two novels that are found in Lovecraft's library. *The Frozen Pirate* is just the sort of work to have fascinated an imaginative youth interested in the weird and fantastic. In 1801 a shipwrecked sailor, Paul Rodney, stumbles upon an icebound pirate ship, the *Boca del Dragon,* near Antarctica and finds several of its crewmen apparently frozen to death. Rodney inadvertently resuscitates one of them, a French pirate named Jules Tassard, when he brings Tassard's body close to a fire in the ship's kitchen. He learns that Tassard has been frozen since 1754, although Tassard himself refuses to believe it. Shortly after his revival, Tassard suddenly ages half a century in a few hours, dying a hideously decrepit old man. The rest of the novel is a letdown as it merely concerns Rodney's efforts to free the ship from the ice and sail it back to England while protecting the ship's immense stolen booty from thieves or customs agents.

How can we not think of the discovery of the frozen Old Ones by Lake's sub-expedition, and the accidental revival of those entities when their bodies are warmed by the heat of the Antarctic summer sun? Lovecraft has taken the core of Russell's plot and, as it were, *cosmicised* it: he has vastly expanded its imaginative scope by depicting the revival, not merely of a rather scoundrelly human being, but of a group of fantastically bizarre extraterrestrials.

One further element in *The Frozen Pirate* may have inspired Lovecraft. As Rodney, in a lifeboat, is approaching the immense ice shelf within which the pirate ship is frozen, he sees a bizarre sight:

> . . . the sun, being low with westering, shone redly, and the range of ice stood in a kind of gold atmosphere which gave an extraordinary richness to the shadowings of its rocks and peaks, and a particular fullness of mellow whiteness to its lustrous parts, softening the dazzle into an airy tenderness of brightness, so that the whole mass shone out with the blandness visible in a glorious star. But its main beauty lay in those features which I knew it to be ice—I mean in a vast surprising variety of forms, such as steeples, towers, columns, pyramids, ruins as might be of temples, grotesque shapes as of mighty statues, left unfinished by the hands of Titans, domes as of cathedrals, castellated heights, fragments of ramparts, and the like. These features lay in groups, as if veritably the line of coast were dotted with gatherings of royal mansions and remains of

imperial magnificence, all of white marble, yet with a glassy tincture as though the material owned something of a Parian quality.[4]

Does not Dyer, when approaching the Antarctic continent, see a similar sight? "On many occasions the curious atmospheric effects enchanted me vastly; these including a strikingly vivid mirage—the first I had ever seen—in which distant bergs became the battlements of unimaginable cosmic castles" (*MM* 6). Later Dyer realises that this "mirage" was nothing less than a strange reflection of the immense city of the Old Ones that he and Danforth come upon—a city featuring buildings that "tended to be conical, pyramidal, or terraced; though there were many perfect cylinders, perfect cubes, clusters of cubes, and other rectangular forms, and a peculiar sprinkling of angled edifices whose five-pointed ground plan roughly suggested modern fortifications" (*MM* 46).

The novels of De Mille and Russell are only two of the literary works that appear to have inspired *At the Mountains of Madness*. One can hardly ignore the influence of Poe's *Narrative of Arthur Gordon Pym*, mentioned several times in the novel. David E. Schultz's conjecture that a mediocre story by Katharine Metcalf Roof, "A Million Years After," may have been the immediate trigger for the writing of *At the Mountains of Madness* remains valid: Lovecraft seems to have been so annoyed that this hackneyed tale of the hatching of a dinosaur's egg was the cover story for the November 1930 issue of *Weird Tales* that he perhaps envisioned his own "dinosaur egg" story, although of a vastly broader scope and different focus. But it seems clear that *The Frozen Pirate* provided the kernels of some central plot features in Lovecraft's novel, and that *A Strange Manuscript* may have lingered in the back of his mind as well.

There is of course no need to censure Lovecraft for borrowing key components of his tales from previous works of fiction; for, like Handel, he almost always improved upon what he borrowed. The underground civilisation of K'n-yan is incalculably more cogently and dramatically presented than that of De Mille's Kosekin; the cosmic narrative of the Old Ones makes Russell's account of the frozen pirate seem absurdly unimaginative. Nevertheless, it does appear that Lovecraft at times needed the impetus of previous literary works to fashion his own weird masterpieces—as if, perhaps half-unconsciously, he saw in these predecessors the nucleus of themes, conceptions, and images that deserved better treatment.

---

4. W. Clark Russell, *The Frozen Pirate* (Chicago: M. A. Donahue & Co., n.d.), p. 44 (chap. 6).

On "The Book"

Lovecraft's fictional fragments have not received much attention from critics, and perhaps deservedly so; for by their very incompleteness they are aesthetically unsatisfying, the more so since we have no idea how he intended to finish them. The fragments can gain value only by the possible light they may shed upon the history and progression of his writing.

R. H. Barlow, who supplied the title to the untitled fragment "The Descendant," also devised the title for "The Book" (*D* 362–64) and dated it hesitantly to 1934. Brief as it is, it offers some insights into Lovecraft's techniques of fiction-writing which make it not entirely devoid of interest.

Let us first attempt to date the fragment as precisely as possible. Barlow's date of 1934 is probably not far off, for the manuscript is written in that tiny, spidery handwriting typical of Lovecraft's late works. We can, however, perhaps be a bit more exact. Note this passage from a letter of November 2–5, 1933:

> I am at a sort of standstill in writing—disgusted at much of my older work, & uncertain as to avenues of improvement. In recent weeks I have done a tremendous amount of experimenting in different styles and perspectives, but have destroyed *most* [my emphasis] of the results. (*SL* 4.297)

Perhaps "The Book" could be referred to here. We may also note that the dream of an evil clergyman that Lovecraft wrote into a brief tale (actually an excerpt from a letter to Bernard Dwyer) dates to October 1933.[1] This period seems to have been a time of great psychological stress for Lovecraft in terms of fiction-writing: he had suffered painful rejections (*At the Mountains of Madness* by *Weird Tales;* collections of his work by Putnam's and Knopf), and appeared to have difficulty in recapturing the fluency in writing that had characterised his 1926–27 period (after his return from New York), when he produced *The Dream-Quest of Unknown Kadath* and *The Case of Charles Dex-*

---

1. See *SL* 4.289–90. Derleth's dating it to 1937 has no authority at all. Indeed, even the possibility that Lovecraft wrote up the dream at a later time seems refuted by the following letter from Dwyer to Clark Ashton Smith (n.d., but soon after Lovecraft's death): "I sent [Farnsworth] Wright [editor of *Weird Tales*] a short story of his [Lovecraft's]—a dream—never published. . . . I copied it out of an *old* [my emphasis] letter to me. A very odd little story; I call it 'The Wicked Clergyman'" (ms., Clark Ashton Smith Coll., JHL).

ter Ward, plus several shorter tales, in a period of about eleven months. Indeed, after writing "The Thing on the Doorstep" in August 1933, he would write no more original fiction save "The Shadow out of Time" (which itself went through three drafts [*SL* 5.346]) in November 1934–February 1935, and "The Haunter of the Dark" in November 1935.

"The Book" may then date to late 1933; but it is far more interesting not when considered by itself, but in connexion with one of Lovecraft's most celebrated works—the *Fungi from Yuggoth* sonnets, written in late 1929 and early 1930.

The relations between the *Fungi* and Lovecraft's prose fiction have perhaps not been fully realised. Some of the sonnets are echoes or—more interestingly—foreshadowings of themes and plots used in his fiction. "The Courtyard" (IX) perhaps contains vague references to the earlier story "He" (1925):

> As edging through the filth I saw the gate
> To the black courtyard where the man would be. (ll. 7–8)

"The Bells" (XIX) mentions the name "Innsmouth" (cited first in "Celephaïs" [1920], but set there in England), used later, of course, in "The Shadow over Innsmouth." "Night-Gaunts" (XX) of course employs the entities cited in the earlier *Dream-Quest* and stemming from Lovecraft's boyhood nightmares. "Nyarlathotep" (XXI) seems to be an exact retelling of the prose-poem of 1920, while "Azathoth" (XXII) may provide clues as to the theme of the unfinished novel of 1922. The "thing . . . [with] a silken mask" from "The Elder Pharos" (XXVII) had made a vivid appearance in the *Dream-Quest,* while "The Dweller" (XXXI) may be retelling the events of the very early "Statement of Randolph Carter" (1919). "Alienation" (XXXII) perhaps echoes the theme of "The Strange High House in the Mist" (1926). Such examples could be multiplied upon additional study.

Lovecraft made, indeed, a revealing remark soon after completing the *Fungi* sequence: "Some of the themes [expressed in the sonnets] are really more adapted to fiction—so that I shall probably make stories of them whenever I get that constantly deferred creative opportunity I am always waiting for" (*SL* 3.116–17). Is it possible that "The Book," written at a time when Lovecraft's creative urge may have been at a lull, was such an attempt to rewrite *Fungi from Yuggoth* into prose?

Only the first three of the *Fungi* sonnets are openly linked, although R. Boerem has attempted to find continuity in the whole sequence. Comparison between "The Book" and the first three sonnets reveals a striking similarity of theme, plot, and even language, such that we can hardly fail to conclude that the fragment bears a distinct relation to the sonnets.

The plot of both the prose tale and the poems is that of a man's discovery of a forbidden book (presumably, though not necessarily, the *Necronomicon*) and its effect upon him as he reads it. The setting of "The Book" tallies with that of the first sonnet "The Book" (I): in the former we read of a "dimly lighted place near the black, oily river where the mists always swirl." In the sonnet we read of "old alleys near the quays" (l. 2) and "queer curls of fog" (l. 4). The old bookshop is, in the fragment, "very old" (recall the "old alleys") and "[had] ceiling-high shelves full of rotting volumes." In the sonnet we find "the books, in piles like twisted trees, / Rotting from floor to roof" (ll. 6–7). In the fragment the narrator finds the book amidst "great formless heaps of books on the floor and in crude bins"; in the sonnet the narrator "from a cobwebbed heap / Took up the nearest tome and thumbed it through" (ll. 9–10).

At this point Lovecraft in the fragment makes a glancing reference to the third sonnet of the *Fungi* sequence, "The Key": "it was a key—a guide—to certain gateways and transitions. . . ." Quickly, however, he appears to return to the first and second sonnets, and retells them in order. "I remember how the old man leered and tittered," says the narrator in the fragment. In the sonnet "The Book" we read

> Then, looking for some seller old in craft,
> I could find nothing but a voice that laughed. (ll. 13–14)

The narrator of the fragment then "hurried home through those narrow, winding, mist-choked waterfront streets." In "Pursuit" (II) the narrator is seen "Hurrying through the ancient harbour lanes / With often-turning head and nervous face" (ll. 3–4). In the fragment "I had a frightful impression of being stealthily followed by soft padding feet." At this point the verbal correspondence becomes almost exact, for in the sonnet "far behind me, unseen feet were padding" (l. 14). The narrator of the fragment speaks of "the centuried, tottering houses . . . with fishy, eye-like, diamond-paned windows that leered." In the sonnet "Dull, furtive windows in old tottering brick / Peered at me oddly as I hastened by" (11. 5–6).

In the fragment Lovecraft now begins to describe the events as recorded in the third *Fungi* sonnet, "The Key." In the fragment the narrator "locked [himself] in the attic room. . . . Then came the first scratching and fumbling at the dormer window." Note the last line of the sonnet: "The attic window shook with a faint fumbling."

Here, in the last two paragraphs of the fragment, the correspondence with the *Fungi* becomes blurred, and may indicate Lovecraft's perplexity as to how to continue the tale, since the rest of the thirty-three sonnets of the *Fungi* are not, as previously noted, ostensibly linked, at least in terms of plot.

Only a few parallels can be drawn. In the fragment the narrator confesses: "Nor could I ever after see the world as I had known it." We are reminded of "Alienation" (XXXII): "He waked that morning as an older man, / And nothing since has looked the same to him" (ll. 9–10). The narrator of the fragment continues: "Every once-familiar object loomed alien in the new perspective brought by my widened sight." In "Alienation" we read:

> Objects around float nebulous and dim—
> False, fleeting trifles of some vaster plan.
> His folk and friends are now an alien throng
> To which he struggles vainly to belong. (ll. 11–14)

Later, the narrator of "The Book" recalls: "I was swept by a black wind through gulfs of fathomless grey with the needle-like pinnacles of unknown mountains miles below me. After a while there was utter blackness, and then the light of myriad stars forming strange, alien constellations." This is vaguely reminiscent of "Azathoth" (XXII):

> Out of the mindless void the daemon bore me,
> Past the bright clusters of dimensioned space,
> Till neither time nor matter stretched before me,
> But only Chaos, without form or place. (ll. 1–4)

But the resemblance is vague, tenuous, and hardly exact, and the fragment soon ends. Whether Lovecraft simply tired of the attempt to rewrite the *Fungi* into prose (we may perhaps be thankful that he never fully did so) or whether he found it difficult to string all or even some of the sonnets together into a coherent story, we may never know. Boerem's thesis of a "continuity" in the *Fungi* sonnets is neither confirmed nor refuted by the above correspondences; for if we accept the theory that "The Book" is an attempt to write out the *Fungi* in prose, then we must equally accept the possibility that Lovecraft could have written all or some into a tale, or at least conceived the possibility of so doing.

As it is, the fundamental theme of both the fragment and the *Fungi* sonnets as a whole is that of time—a central concept in Lovecraft's writing. Throughout the fragment the narrator hints of the new conceptions of time gained from reading the book he has discovered: "At times I feel appalling vistas of years stretching behind me, while at other times it seems as if the present moment were an isolated point in a grey formless infinity. . . . That night I passed the gateway to a vortex of twisted time and vision. . . . Mingled with the present scene was always a little of the past and a little of the future. . . ." All this is expressed—if oftentimes with less a feeling of horror than of exhiliration or "adventurous expectancy"—in the sonnets:

> At last the key was mine to those vague visions
> Of sunset spires and twilight woods that brood
> Dim in the gulfs beyond this earth's precisions,
> Lurking as memories of infinitude. (III.9–12)

> The winter sunset . . .
> Opens great gates to some forgotten year. . . .
> It is a land where beauty's meaning flowers;
> Where every unplaced memory has a source;
> Where the great river Time begins its course
> Down the vast void in starlit streams of hours. (XIII.1, 2, 9–12)

> I do not know what land it is—or dare
> Ask when or why I was, or will be, there. (XXIII.13–14)

> In that strange light I feel I am not far
> From the fixt mass whose sides the ages are. (XXXVI.13–14)

"The Book," then, while not of great intrinsic interest, typifies Lovecraft's despair at his own ability to write fiction during his later years. Certainly his powers were not failing—rather, the reverse seems to be the case, if we take "The Shadow out of Time" into consideration. But Lovecraft felt increasingly that "I'm farther from doing what I want to do than I was 20 years ago" (*SL* 5.224); the result was a series of experiments dating as early as "The Shadow over Innsmouth,"[2] of which "The Book" may represent another example. In his later years Lovecraft confessed that his "right medium" might perhaps be "the cheapened and hackneyed term 'prose-poem'" (*SL* 5.230); and perhaps "The Book," its basis drawn from some of his best poetry, is a step in that direction.

Works Cited

Boerem, R. "The Continuity of the *Fungi from Yuggoth.*" In S. T. Joshi, ed., *H. P. Lovecraft: Four Decades of Criticism.* Athens: Ohio University Press, 1980.

---

2. Cf. *SL* 3.435: "I am using the new [story] idea as a basis for what might be called laboratory experimentation—writing it out in different manners, one after the other, in an effort to determine the mood & tempo best suited to the theme."

Lovecraft's Fantastic Poetry

The judgment on Lovecraft's poetry has been severe. Winfield Townley Scott, although himself only a minor poet—perhaps more minor than Lovecraft—declared, in tones of magisterial doom, that the bulk of Lovecraft's verse is "eighteenth-century rubbish" (Scott 214). If this verdict cannot be overturned, then we must add that most of Lovecraft's early fantastic poetry is "Poesque rubbish." What this means is that Lovecraft, while developing the knack of imitating Poe's metre and rhythm-patterns ably enough, found nothing of his own to say in most of this body of work. And yet, as with so much of Lovecraft's inferior work—and it is perhaps this that distinguishes him from most other writers—it is possible to find things to note and even enjoy in nearly all his fantasy verse.

It is interesting that the first two examples of Lovecraft's fantastic poetry are, at least in part, parodies. "Unda; or, The Bride of the Sea" (1915) is subtitled "A Dull, Dark, Drear, Dactylic Delirium in Sixteen Silly, Senseless, Sickly Stanzas," and tells the histrionic tale of a romantic young swain who falls in love with a sea-nymph (or whatever Unda is supposed to be), loses her when she returns to her native deep, and then himself drowns so that he is now "safe with my Unda, the Bride of the Sea." Lovecraft utters the ostensible moral of the poem in a witty "Epilogue" of tripping heroic couplets:

> Brothers, attend! if cares too sharply vex,
> Gain rest by shunning the destructive sex!

But in fact, it appears that what is really being parodied is the late Romantic ballad with its florid imagery and sexual undercurrent. It is as if Alexander Pope were satirising a poem of Thomas Moore.

Much more may be said of "The Poe-et's Nightmare" (1916), Lovecraft's most significant work of fantastic poetry aside from *Fungi from Yuggoth*. R. Boerem has already written a thoughtful and detailed study of this poem (Boerem, "Nightmare"), and I shall add only a few notes. In the first place, the structure of the poem parallels "Unda," although here we have both a lengthy introductory section and a concluding section in heroic couplets, with a long central portion in pentameter blank verse. I am not sure that this structure is very efficacious; for the comic outer portions tend to subvert the point of the cosmic centrepiece, and yet we know that Lovecraft's real views are embedded in this middle section. By attributing the "nightmare" of Lucullus Languish merely to overeating and excessive reading of Poe, especially in such lines as

> He feels his aching limbs, whose woeful pain
> Informs his soul his body lives again,
> And thanks his stars—or cosmoses—or such—
> That he survives the noxious nightmare's clutch.

the cosmic vistas revealed in the nightmare are made the butt of jest. This is probably why, when in 1936 R. H. Barlow wished to include "The Poe-et's Nightmare" in a proposed collection of Lovecraft's fantastic verse, Lovecraft advised dropping the comic framework.[1] This is in fact what was done when *Weird Tales* published the poem posthumously (July 1952) under the subtitle of the central portion, *Aletheia Phrikodes* (The Frightful Truth).

What I find most interesting about "The Poe-et's Nightmare" is its mere existence. This is really the first instance of Lovecraft's artistic expression of cosmicism, written a year before his resumption of fiction-writing with "Dagon" (itself only marginally cosmic) and a full decade or more before his crystallisation of cosmicism in "The Call of Cthulhu" (1926), *At the Mountains of Madness* (1931), and "The Shadow out of Time" (1934–35). And yet, it would be difficult to find a more concentrated dose of cosmicism than in "The Poe-et's Nightmare":

> Alone in space, I view'd a feeble fleck
> Of silvern light, marking the narrow ken
> Which mortals call the boundless universe.
> On ev'ry side, each as a tiny star,
> Shone more creations, vaster than our own,
> And teeming with unnumber'd forms of life;
> Tho' we as life would recognise it not,
> Being bound to earthy thoughts of human mould.

More important, we learn that this cosmicism is derived not from literature but from philosophy. Such lines as

> . . . whirling ether bore in eddying streams
> The hot, unfinish'd stuff of nascent worlds

make clear the dominant influence on this central section—Lucretius. And although Lucretius, unlike Lovecraft, finds not terror but only awe and wonder and majesty in the contemplation of infinite space, both see in the vastness of the cosmos a refutation of human self-importance. In this

---

1. Lovecraft to R. H. Barlow, 13 June 1936 (ms., JHL).

sense "The Poe-et's Nightmare" is a clue to the development of Love-craft's whole cosmic philosophy. Although he later remarked that he derived much of that philosophy (at least as far as fictional technique is concerned) from Dunsany,[2] the fact that this poem precedes Lovecraft's reading of Dunsany by three years points to the conclusion that his cosmicism was not literarily influenced but taken from his early readings in the atomic philosophy of Democritus, Epicurus, and Lucretius, tempered by nineteenth-century advances in biology, chemistry, and astrophysics. Poe's imagination is—Lovecraft's effusive comments to the contrary notwithstanding—only sporadically cosmic, in such vignettes as "The Conversation of Eiros and Charmion" or the philosophical prose-poem *Eureka;* and in the end Lovecraft found even Dunsany's cosmicism wanting.[3] Lovecraft's cosmicism rested upon a sturdier foundation.

The linkage of horror and philosophy that we find in "The Poe-et's Nightmare" informs many of Lovecraft's other fantastic poems. The Latin motto of the central section of that poem—*Omnia risus et omnia pulvis et omnia nihil* ("All is laughter, all is dust, all is nothing")[4]—underscores the bleak nihilism of the work, while the meaningful subtitle "Aletheia Phrikodes" could serve as the motto for a whole string of Lovecraft's poems of the 1916–19 period. Lucullus Languish finds the truth about the ultimate secrets of the cosmos too hard to bear:

> He bade me brave th' unutterable Thing,
> The final truth of moving entity.
>   . . . but my soul,
> Clinging to life, fled without aim or knowledge,
> Shrieking in silence thro' the gibbering deeps.

Similarly, in "The Rutted Road" (1917) the narrator, wondering what he will encounter at the end of his journey, concludes:

---

2. It was Dunsany "from whom I got the idea of the artificial pantheon and myth-background represented by 'Cthulhu', 'Yog-Sothoth', 'Yuggoth', etc." "Some Notes on a Nonentity" (1933; *MW* 561).

3. "What I miss in Machen, James, Dunsany, de la Mare, Shiel, and even Blackwood and Poe, is a sense of the cosmic" (*SL* 5.341).

4. Translated into Greek, it served as the epigraph to Lovecraft's hilarious parody "Waste Paper." The motto is Lovecraft's own coinage and is not derived from Juvenal, as Barton Levi St Armand and John H. Stanley believe ("H. P. Lovecraft's *Waste Paper:* A Facsimile and Transcript of the Original Draft," *Books at Brown* 26 [1978]: 41). St Armand and Stanley also assert, without cause, that Lovecraft's Greek translation is "faulty." It is not.

> What lies ahead, my weary soul to greet?
> *Why is it that I do not wish to know?*

But this poem is merely a contrived shudder, for we are not led to believe
that the forthcoming vision is of any philosophic relevance. This poem,
like many of Lovecraft's, including even the famous "Nemesis" (1917), is
deserving of Winfield Townley Scott's censure: "To scare is a slim purpose
in poetry" (Scott 215). Merely to send shudders up one's spine is an inadequate motive for writing a poem (or, for that matter, a prose tale); those
shudders must have some broader significance. Happily this is the case
with several Lovecraft poems, in particular "The Eidolon" (1918). Here
the narrator, "at a nameless hour of night," fancies he looks upon a beauteous landscape:

> Fair beyond words the mountain stood,
> Its base encircled by a wood;
> Adown its side a brooklet bright
> Ran dancing in the spectral light,
> Each city that adorn'd its crest
> Seem'd anxious to outvie the rest,
> For carven columns, domes, and fanes
> Gleam'd rich and lovely o'er the plains.

But the daylight shows a grimmer scene:

> The East is hideous with the flare
> Of blood-hued light—a garish glare—
> While ghastly grey the mountain stands,
> The terror of the neighb'ring lands.

Lovecraft is careful to indicate that the horror is more than a spook or a
haunted wood:

> Aloft the light of *knowledge* crawls,
> Staining the crumbling city walls
> Thro' which in troops ungainly squirm
> The foetid lizard and the worm.

Repelled by the sight, the narrator asks to see "the living glory—Man!" But
an even more loathsome sight greets his eyes:

> Now on the streets the houses spew
> A loathsome pestilence, a crew
> Of things I cannot, dare not name,
> So vile their form, so black their shame.

In its way "The Eidolon" is as nihilistic as "The Poe-et's Nightmare," although lacking its cosmic scope. What is more interesting is the notion that knowledge (here symbolised by the light of day) is in itself a source of horror and tragedy. This same conception is found not only in another fine poem, "Revelation" (1919), but in the celebrated opening of "The Call of Cthulhu," where again the metaphors of light (knowledge) and darkness (ignorance) are at play:

> The most merciful thing in the world, I think, is the inability of the human mind to correlate all its contents. We live on a placid island of ignorance in the midst of *black* seas of infinity, and it was not meant that we should voyage far. ... some day the piecing together of dissociated knowledge will open up such terrifying vistas of reality, and of our frightful position therein, that we shall either go mad from the revelation or flee the deadly *light* into the peace and safety of a new *dark* age. (*DH* 125)

The question of why Lovecraft found certain types of knowledge frightful is too large a question to be dealt with here; but it informs his whole aesthetic of horror.

Lovecraft's fantastic poetry virtually comes to an end by 1919; from the period between 1920 and 1928 we find almost no examples, just as we find few works of poetry generally. There are several causes for this: first, it is clear that by 1919 fiction has become his principal aesthetic outlet; second, I believe that Lovecraft's reading of the poetry of Clark Ashton Smith in the summer of 1922 did much to stifle his own poetic output. Here was a poet who, although inspired by Swinburne and George Sterling, was writing fresh, vigorous fantastic poetry of a quality that Lovecraft could never achieve. "Nero," "The Star-Treader," and *The Hashish-Eater* may have done much to show Lovecraft how wooden and mechanical were such of his poems as "Despair" and "The House." It is significant that Lovecraft, the inveterate mimic in poetry, never produced a "Clark Ashton Smith imitation"—he could never have done so. As it is, Poe remained the dominant influence on his early fantastic verse, and it may be amusing to see the lengths to which Lovecraft went to ape Poe, especially in metre.

To take the simplest metre—iambic tetrameter couplets, used by Lovecraft in "The Eidolon," "The Nightmare Lake," "A Cycle of Verse," and "To Zara"—the prototypical example is Poe's early poem "Alone":

> From childhood's hour I have not been
> As others were—I have not seen
> As others saw—I could not bring
> My passions from a common spring—

Compare Lovecraft's "The Eidolon":

> 'Twas at a nameless hour of night
> When fancies in delirious flight
> About the silent sleeper reel
> And thro' his mindless visions steal . . .

The metre used by Lovecraft in "Astrophobos"—

> In the midnight heavens burning
> > Thro' ethereal deeps afar,
> Once I watch'd with restless yearning
> > An alluring, aureate star;
> Ev'ry eye aloft returning,
> > Gleaming nigh the Arctic car.

—and, with modifications, in "Revelation" and "Hallowe'en in a Suburb" (1926) is derived roughly from Poe's "The Haunted Palace":

> In the greenest of our valleys
> > By good angels tenanted,
> Once a fair and stately palace—
> > Radiant palace—reared its head.
> In the monarch Thought's dominion—
> > It stood there!
> Never seraph spread a pinion
> > Over fabric half so fair!

Typically, however, Lovecraft irons out the metrical irregularity in line 6, producing monotony.

Curiously, the metre that strikes us as the most "Poesque" in Lovecraft's work, that used in "Nemesis"—

> Thro' the ghoul-guarded gateways of slumber,
> > Past the wan-moon'd abysses of night,
> I have liv'd o'er my lives without number,
> > I have sounded all things with my sight;
> And I struggle and shriek ere the daybreak, being driven to madness with fright.

and, with modifications, in "The City," "The House," and "Festival" (more commonly known as "Yule Horror"), is, as Lovecraft himself states, "a cross betwixt that of Poe's 'Ulalume' & Swinburne's 'Hertha'" (*SL* 1.52), although owing much more to the latter than the former; consider that celebrated poem's first stanza:

> I am that which began;
>> Out of me the years roll;
> Out of me God and man;
>> I am equal and Whole;
> God changes, and man, and the form of them bodily; I am the soul.

But it is possible that Swinburne himself adapted this metre from Poe's
"Dream-Land":

> By a route obscure and lonely,
> Haunted by ill angels only,
> Where an Eidolon, named Night,
> On a black throne reigns upright,
> I have reached these lands but newly
> From an ultimate dim Thule—
> From a wild weird clime that lieth, sublime,
>> Out of Space—out of Time.

Amusingly, Lovecraft parodied himself in a Christmas greeting, "A Bru-
malian Wish," in which the debt to "Ulalume" is more evident:

> From the damnable shadows of madness,
>> From the corpse-rotten hollow of Weir,
> Comes a horrible message of gladness,
>> And a ghost-guided poem of cheer—
> And a gloom-spouting pupil of Poe sends the pleasantest wish of the year!

Similarly, "Nathicana"—

> And here in the swirl of the vapours
> I saw the divine Nathicana;
> The garlanded, white Nathicana;
> The slender, black-hair'd Nathicana;
> The sloe-eyed, red-lipp'd Nathicana;
> The silver-voic'd, sweet Nathicana;
> The pale-rob'd, belov'd Nathicana.

is a pungent parody of the ponderous repetition of words and phrases in
"Ulalume"—

> The skies they were ashen and sober;
> The leaves they were crisped and sere—
> The leaves they were withering and sere:
> It was night in the lonesome October

> Of my most immemorial year:
> It was hard by the dim lake of Auber,
> In the misty mid region of Weir:—
> It was down by the dank tarn of Auber,
> In the ghoul-haunted woodland of Weir.

"Despair" approximately imitates this metre—

> Thus the living, lone and sobbing,
> In the throes of anguish throbbing,
> With the loathsome Furies robbing
>   Night and noon of peace and rest.
> But beyond the groans and grating
> Of abhorrent Life, is waiting
> Sweet Oblivion, culminating
>   All the years of fruitless quest.

while deriving its message from "For Annie":

> The sickness—the nausea—
> The pitiless pain—
> Have ceased, with the fever
> That maddened my brain—
> With the fever called "Living"
> That burned in my brain.

The slight variations in metre and rhythm in Lovecraft's poems cannot conceal their obvious debt to Poe in mood and word-choice. It is clear that Lovecraft read Poe's better-known horrific poems with care, although he fortunately avoided imitating—metrically or otherwise—such of Poe's highly original poems as "The Raven" or "Bells."

The one other detectable influence in Lovecraft's early fantastic poetry is, apparently, Sir Walter Scott, evidently the model for the entirely undistinguished horror-ballad or "tale in rhyme," "Psychopompos" (1918), although there does not seem to be any poem of exactly this type in Scott's poetical works. For much of his life Lovecraft refused to consider "Psychopompos" a poem at all, inserting it in a list of his prose tales.[5]

The remarkable outburst of poetry, most of it fantastic, in late 1929 is a phenomenon parallel to Lovecraft's tremendous surge of fiction-writing in late 1926 and early 1927. But while the cause for the latter—his euphoric re-

---

5. See the list in *Lovecraft at Last* (Arlington, VA: Carrollton-Clark, 1975; rpt. New York: Cooper Square Press, 2002), p. 224.

turn to Providence after two traumatic years in New York—is easy to detect, the cause for the former is more difficult to ascertain. Now that the supposed influence of Edwin Arlington Robinson, suggested independently by Winfield Townley Scott and Edmund Wilson, has been exploded, the matter does not seem attributable to merely literary influences. David E. Schultz has put forward Lovecraft's extensive work on Maurice W. Moe's never-published handbook, *Doorways to Poetry,* but I think this motive must be taken in conjunction with an anomalous hiatus in his fiction-writing. Between the completion of "The Dunwich Horror" in the fall of 1928 and the commencement of "The Whisperer in Darkness" in February 1930, Lovecraft wrote no fiction—except the (admittedly significant) ghost-written novelette "The Mound" (late 1929–early 1930). Even here we note that by the fall of 1929 it had been a full year since Lovecraft had written any fiction at all; perhaps he felt that horrific poetry would help to revive his fictional powers. It was also an appropriate time for him to implement some new theories on poetry-writing: gone was the desire to imitate the eighteenth-century poets, Lovecraft urging instead—both to himself and to his correspondents—a modern idiom shorn of hackneyed inversions and poeticisms. The results are such works as "The Ancient Track," "The Messenger," and *Fungi from Yuggoth.* With the exception of the last, however, the poetry of this period lacks any sort of philosophical underpinning. Although "The Messenger" is as flawless a horrific sonnet as was ever written by Clark Ashton Smith or Donald Wandrei (whose *Sonnets of the Midnight Hours* Lovecraft had read in 1927 [*SL* 2.186]), it does nothing but very artistically provide a shudder. The same is true of "The Wood"—Donald R. Burleson is fond of citing its imperishable line, "Forests may fall, but not the dusk they shield"—or, less competently, the windy and meaningless "The Outpost."

Even many of the *Fungi from Yuggoth* sonnets have no other intention but to horrify. That they do so very skilfully is a secondary matter. Much has been written about this sonnet cycle, but I wonder how many have noticed that its dominant feature is utter randomness of tone, mood, and import. Unlike Wandrei's *Sonnets of the Midnight Hours,* unified by the fact that they are all derived from Wandrei's dreams and by their narration in the first person, in Lovecraft's sonnet series we have miniature horror stories ("The Well") cheek by jowl with autobiographical vignettes ("Expectancy," "Background"), pensive philosophy ("Continuity"), apocalyptic cosmicism ("Nyarlathotep"), and versified nightmares ("Night-Gaunts"). I assuredly cannot see any "continuity" or "story" in this cycle, as R. Boerem and Ralph E. Vaughan purport to do. The mere idea of continuity seems demolished by Lovecraft's claim that he might "grind out a dozen or so more before I consider the sequence finished" (*SL* 3.116)—this after having written 33 (or 34) of the 36 sonnets. Recent claims by Dan Clore and

Robert H. Waugh that the cycle exhibits some kind of "thematic" unity do not signify much: almost any composite work of this kind can be made to yield some kind of thematic unity, as can Lovecraft's work as a whole. I have already pointed out that, around 1933, Lovecraft attempted to rewrite the *Fungi* into prose, in the fragment called "The Book"; he seems to have got as far as the first three sonnets (which are indeed a continuous narrative), but beyond this his inspiration appears, not surprisingly, to have flagged. Even if we assume that the first three sonnets are a sort of framing device and that the other 33 are vignettes derived from the book the narrator has discovered (it need not be the *Necronomicon,* either here or in the fragment "The Book"), it is difficult to conceive the cycle as an unified whole. It seems more likely that Lovecraft looked upon *Fungi from Yuggoth* as an opportune means of crystallising various conceptions, types of imagery, and fragments of dreams that would otherwise not have found creative expression—an imaginative housecleaning, as it were. The degree to which he embodied items from his commonplace book in the sonnets supports this conclusion; in effect, *Fungi from Yuggoth* could be read as a sort of versified commonplace book.

Of course, the *Fungi* not only resurrect ideas used in previous tales (the sonnet "Nyarlathotep" is very close in conception to the prose-poem of 1920) but also anticipate those used in later tales. Yuggoth is mentioned for the first time here, prior to its extensive use in "The Whisperer in Darkness"; shoggoths are introduced in "Night-Gaunts," although it is not clear whether they are the same entities that appear, a year and a half later, in *At the Mountains of Madness:*

> . . . that foul lake
> Where the puffed shoggoths splash in doubtful sleep.

Still more significantly, Innsmouth (first cited in "Celephaïs" [1920], and evidently set in England) is transferred to New England and made a component of Lovecraft's fictional topography:

> Ten miles from Arkham I had struck the trail
> That rides the cliff-edge over Boynton Beach,
> And hoped that just at sunset I could reach
> The crest that looks on Innsmouth in the vale.

But if the value of *Fungi from Yuggoth* as an adjunct to Lovecraft's fiction is clear, its independent value as poetry is no less so. Even if individual poems are, as Lovecraft himself admitted and as David E. Schultz has proven, "pseudo-sonnets" in the sense that they do not—or, at least, do not consistently—follow the metrical norms of either the Italian or the Shakespearean sonnet form (even with all its possible variants), they are nevertheless Lovecraft's finest poems from the standpoints of metre, word-choice, imagery, and texture. I do not know if there is a more satisfactory example of his poetry than "Continuity":

> There is in certain ancient things a trace
> Of some dim essence—more than form or weight;
> A tenuous aether, indeterminate,
> Yet linked with all the laws of time and space.
> A faint, veiled sign of continuities
> That outward eyes can never quite descry;
> Of locked dimensions harbouring years gone by,
> And out of reach except for hidden keys.
>
> It moves me most when slanting sunbeams glow
> On old farm buildings set against a hill,
> And paint with life the shapes which linger still
> From centuries less a dream than this we know.
> In that strange light I feel I am not far
> From the fixt mass whose sides the ages are.

Much of the power of this sonnet rests upon its reflection of Lovecraft's personal philosophy: we know from the bulk of his other writings how he cherished "old farm buildings set against a hill"—but, far from a harmless antiquarianism, this sentiment becomes a symbol for his aesthetic and spiritual allegiance to "centuries less a dream than this we know." This single line is worth all the "eighteenth-century rubbish" Lovecraft ever wrote, for it shows how he has finally learned to make aesthetic use of his sense of alienation from his time—not by mechanically donning the ill-fitting dress of an archaic poetic idiom, but by skilfully manipulating the language of his own day. In the final line, the faintly archaic "fixt"—emphatically placed after the metrical irregularity of the preceding word—gives the whole sonnet a sense of timeless cosmicism. It is a fitting conclusion to *Fungi from Yuggoth*, that heterogeneous repository of so many of Lovecraft's dreams and fancies.

We need take little notice of Lovecraft's later fantastic verse: "Bouts Rimés" (1934) is a harmless bit of fun, where R. H. Barlow provided the end-rhymes and Lovecraft worte the rest of the verse to match them; the acrostic to Edgar Allan Poe (1936) and the sonnets to Clark Ashton Smith and Virgil Finlay, perhaps his last creative utterances, written very late in 1936, are pleasing and competent but no more. The entirety of Lovecraft's fantastic poetry can certainly take its place next to that of his friends Frank Belknap Long and Donald Wandrei, although it is cast into the shade not only by that of Clark Ashton Smith but also of the unjustly neglected Samuel Loveman.

In the final analysis, Lovecraft's weird poetry gains its greatest value for the light it sheds on his fiction. More could perhaps be done with the early work, since so much of it was written before Lovecraft's fiction-writing really got underway; and the *Fungi* are inexhaustible sources for details and conceptions found in tales early and late. It is, however, fortunate that Lovecraft ultimately came to the conclusion that he was principally a *"prose realist" (SL* 3.96); for if he had written nothing but poetry he would not be much remembered today, nor deserve to be. This is because he never really found a distinctive voice as a poet. It is true that his early fiction bears—sometimes too strongly—the marks of his reading of Poe, Dunsany, Machen, Blackwood, and others; but in the end Lovecraft's fiction became uniquely his own. This his poetry never did, save fleetingly toward the end. And yet, his poetry refuses to fade away, and commands our attention if only for its skill, precision, and occasionally an unforgettable line, conception, or image.

Works Cited

Boerem, R. "A Lovecraftian Nightmare." In S. T. Joshi, ed. *H. P. Lovecraft: Four Decades of Criticism*. Athens: Ohio University Press, 1980, pp. 217–21.

———. "The Continuity of the *Fungi from Yuggoth*." In Joshi, *Four Decades*, pp. 222–25.

Clore, Dan. "Metonyms of Alterity: A Semiotic Interpretation of *Fungi from Yuggoth*." *Lovecraft Studies* No. 30 (Spring 1994): 21–32.

Schultz, David E. "The Lack of Continuity in *Fungi from Yuggoth*." *Crypt of Cthulhu* No. 20 (Eastertide 1984): 12–16.

Scott, Winfield Townley. "A Parenthesis on Lovecraft as Poet" (1945). In Joshi, *Four Decades*, pp. 211–16.

Vaughan, Ralph E. "The Story in *Fungi from Yuggoth*." *Crypt of Cthulhu* No. 20 (Eastertide 1984): 9–11.

Waugh, Robert H. "The Structural and Thematic Unity of *Fungi from Yuggoth*." *Lovecraft Studies* No. 26 (Spring 1992): 2–14.

BOOKS BY S. T. JOSHI

Books Written

An Index to the Selected Letters of H. P. Lovecraft (1980)

Lovecraft's Library: A Catalogue (1980; rev. 2002)

H. P. Lovecraft and Lovecraft Criticism: An Annotated Bibliography (1981)

H. P. Lovecraft (Starmont Reader's Guide 13) (1982)

Selected Papers on Lovecraft (1989)

The Weird Tale (1990)

John Dickson Carr: A Critical Study (1990)

H. P. Lovecraft: The Decline of the West (1990)

An Index to the Fiction and Poetry of H. P. Lovecraft (1992)

Lord Dunsany: A Bibliography (with Darrell Schweitzer) (1993)

The Core of Ramsey Campbell: A Bibliography & Reader's Guide (with Ramsey Campbell and Stefan Dziemianowicz) (1995)

Lord Dunsany: Master of the Anglo-Irish Imagination (1995)

H. P. Lovecraft: A Life (1996)

A Subtler Magick: The Writings and Philosophy of H. P. Lovecraft (1996)

Sixty Years of Arkham House (1999)

Ambrose Bierce: An Annotated Bibliography of Primary Sources (with David E. Schultz) (1999)

The Modern Weird Tale (2001)

A Dreamer and a Visionary: H. P. Lovecraft in His Time (2001)

Ramsey Campbell and Modern Horror Fiction (2001)

An H. P. Lovecraft Encyclopedia (with David E. Schultz) (2001)

God's Defenders: What They Believe and Why They Are Wrong (2003)

Primal Sources: Essays on H. P. Lovecraft (2003)

Editions of Works by H. P. Lovecraft

Uncollected Prose and Poetry (with Marc A. Michaud) (1978–82; 3 vols.)

Science vs. Charlatanry: Essays on Astrology (with Scott Connors) (1979)

Saturnalia and Other Poems (1984)

The Dunwich Horror and Others (1984)

Juvenilia: 1897–1905 (1984)

In Defence of Dagon (1985)

At the Mountains of Madness and Other Novels (1985)

Medusa and Other Poems (1986)

Dagon and Other Macabre Tales (1986)

Uncollected Letters (1986)

The Horror in the Museum and Other Revisions (1989)

The Conservative (1990)

The Fantastic Poetry (1990)

Letters to Henry Kuttner (with David E. Schultz) (1990)

Letters to Richard F. Searight (with David E. Schultz and Franklyn Searight) (1992)

Autobiographical Writings (1992)

Letters to Robert Bloch (with David E. Schultz) (1993)

The H. P. Lovecraft Dream Book (with David E. Schultz and Will Murray) (1994)

The Shadow over Innsmouth (with David E. Schultz) (1994)

Letters to Samuel Loveman and Vincent Starrett (with David E. Schultz) (1994)

Miscellaneous Writings (1995)

The Annotated H. P. Lovecraft (1997)

More Annotated H. P. Lovecraft (with Peter Cannon) (1999)

The Call of Cthulhu and Other Weird Stories (1999)

Lord of a Visible World: An Autobiography in Letters (with David E. Schultz) (2000)

The Annotated Supernatural Horror in Literature (2000)

The Shadow out of Time: The Corrected Text (with David E. Schultz) (2001)

The Ancient Track: Complete Poetical Works (2001)

The Thing on the Doorstep and Other Weird Stories (2001)

Mysteries of Time and Spirit: The Letters of H. P. Lovecraft and Donald Wandrei (with David E. Schultz) (2002)

From the Pest Zone: The New York Stories (with David E. Schultz) (2003)

Letters to Alfred Galpin (with David E. Schultz) (2003)

Letters from New York (with David E. Schultz) (2004)

Collected Essays (2004f.; 5 vols.)

Books Edited

H. P. Lovecraft in "The Eyrie" (with Marc A. Michaud) (1979)

H. P. Lovecraft: Four Decades of Criticism (1980)

Sonia H. Davis, The Private Life of H. P. Lovecraft (1985)

Donald Wandrei, Collected Poems (1988)

The H. P. Lovecraft Centennial Conference: Proceedings (1991)

An Epicure in the Terrible: A Centennial Anthology of Essays in Honor of H. P. Lovecraft (with David E. Schultz) (1991)

The Count of Thirty: A Tribute to Ramsey Campbell (1993)

H. P. Lovecraft in the Argosy (1994)

Caverns Measureless to Man: 18 Memoirs of Lovecraft (1996)

Bram Stoker, Best Ghost Stories (with Richard Dalby and Stefan Dziemianowicz) (1997)

Henry Ferris, A Night with Mephistopheles (1997)

Algernon Blackwood, The Complete John Silence Stories (1998)

Ambrose Bierce, A Sole Survivor: Bits of Autobiography (with David E. Schultz) (1998)

Documents of American Prejudice (1999)

Great Weird Tales (1999)

Ambrose Bierce, Collected Fables (2000)

Civil War Memories (2000)

Sir Arthur Quiller-Couch, The Horror on the Stair and Other Weird Tales (2000)

W. C. Morrow, The Monster Maker and Other Stories (with Stefan Dziemianowicz) (2000)

Ambrose Bierce, The Unabridged Devil's Dictionary (with David E. Schultz) (2000)

Robert W. Chambers, The Yellow Sign and Other Stories (2000)

Atheism: A Reader (2000)

Ambrose Bierce, The Fall of the Republic and Other Political Satires (with David E. Schultz) (2000)

Rudyard Kipling, The Mark of the Beast and Other Horror Tales (2000)

From Baltimore to Bohemia: The Letters of H. L. Mencken and George Sterling (2001)

Arthur Machen, The Three Impostors and Other Stories (2001)

Robert Hichens, The Return of the Soul and Other Stories (2001)

Clark Ashton Smith, The Black Diamonds (2002)

Great Tales of Terror (2002)

H. L. Mencken, H. L. Mencken on American Literature (2002)

Algernon Blackwood, Ancient Sorceries and Other Weird Stories (2002)

H. L. Mencken, H. L. Mencken on Religion (2002)

R. H. Barlow, Eyes of the God (with Douglas A. Anderson and David E. Schultz) (2002)

Ramsey Campbell, Ramsey Campbell, Probably (2002)

Herbert Gorman, The Place Called Dagon, (2003)

Ambrose Bierce, A Much Misunderstood Man: Selected Letters (with David E. Schultz) (2003)

George Sterling, The Thirst of Satan: Poems of Fantasy and Terror (2003)

Lord Dunsany, The Pleasures of a Futuroscope (2003)

Arthur Machen, The White People and Other Stories (2003)

H. L. Mencken, Mencken's America (2004)

Lord Dunsany, The Complete Jorkens (2004; 3 vols.)

Lord Dunsany, In the Land of Time and Other Fantasy Tales (2004)

Encyclopedia of Supernatural Literature (with Stefan Dziemianowicz) (forthcoming)

Ambrose Bierce, Collected Short Fiction (with Lawrence I. Berkove and David E. Schultz) (forthcoming)

Books Translated

Maurice Lévy, Lovecraft: A Study in the Fantastic (1988)